Visible and Invisible Whiteness

Alice Mikal Craven

Visible and Invisible Whiteness

American White Supremacy through the Cinematic Lens

Alice Mikal Craven
Department of Comparative Literature
American University of Paris
Paris, France

Department of Film Studies
American University of Paris
Paris, France

ISBN 978-3-319-76776-5   ISBN 978-3-319-76777-2   (eBook)
https://doi.org/10.1007/978-3-319-76777-2

Library of Congress Control Number: 2018935695

Cover illustration: Courtesy of the Library of Congress, LC-DIG-ppmsca-12888
Cover design by Ran Shauli

Printed on acid-free paper

This Palgrave Macmillan imprint is published by the registered company Springer International Publishing AG part of Springer Nature.
The registered company address is: Gewerbestrasse 11, 6330 Cham, Switzerland

Dedicated to Olivier and Zoe
and to Henriette Kasaruhanda

PREFACE

The seeds for this book were planted a long time ago, and though I may have invented some of the details as I have grown older, the memories still persist. They may ultimately be myths that I invented for myself, but they have certainly marked me. My grandmother ran a florist service from home in the small town of Elliott, South Carolina, population one hundred or so. There were three gas stations and three churches: There was the Baptist church, the Methodist church, and the black church. Apparently, my grandmother was the only white woman who ever entered the black church, since she was in charge of the floral arrangements. When I was six years old, she took me there and explained to me that this was a church only for black people. It was a revelation to me that there could be such a thing as a church only for black people.

When I was eight or nine, my elementary school in Durham, North Carolina, became "integrated." This entailed having one black child enter my class. He was the only black who came to my school that year and his name was John Wise. As I recall, I was one of the few people who ever talked to him. Plenty of the other children seemed to be talking *at* him. Only much later did I realize just how miserable he must have been in that alienating situation. Samuel Fuller recounts a similar instance in his film *Shock Corridor* (1963), a film which I have unfortunately not been able to treat in detail in this book. I have thought about John Wise and the obstacles facing him in being an American social experiment ever since I met him and was reminded of this episode in my childhood when I first watched Fuller's film.

When I was a bit older, maybe twelve, the pastor of the Baptist church where my parents were members invited a young, upper-middle-class black couple to join our congregation. During the Sunday service when he welcomed the couple, white members of the congregation stood up one by one and called for the pastor's resignation. I told my mother I would never set foot in that church again.

This book began to take shape in my head while I was working on the Richard Wright Centennial Conference at the American University of Paris in 2008. Later, when attending the James Baldwin Conference in New York in 2011, the direction such a book might take was still vague but felt more and more compelling. I was teaching a course on James Baldwin at Eugene Lang College in New York in 2012 when Trayvon Martin was killed. I learned of his death while doing research at the Schomburg Center in Harlem. At the Schomburg, I was not quite sure where my research was going to lead me, but there was a sense of urgency about getting there. This book was in its home stretch when Heather Heyer was killed in Charlottesville in 2017.

The world I grew up in was no uglier than the world in which I live today, though my perspective has evolved and I look at it from across the Atlantic and have done so for the past twenty-four years or so. I have spent years reading and at times teaching the works of authors such as Maya Angelou, James Baldwin, Chester Himes, and Richard Wright. I have also written and taught about film directors who found themselves in new and alienating environments. Adding to that twenty-four years of expatriation, it seemed appropriate to me to look more closely at the world of the white supremacist mythologies that grounded my childhood through the lens of my profession. This is an academic book, but I would never have written it if I were not haunted by my past and fearful about the world in which I live today.

Paris, France   Alice Mikal Craven

ACKNOWLEDGMENTS

I would like to thank the American University of Paris for a sabbatical research period that allowed me to complete research on this book. I am also grateful for an opportunity to teach and research in New York thanks to a visiting professorship funded by Mellon and granted by the American University of Paris. I am indebted to my past chair, Jula Wildberger, who helped secure my sabbatical and to my current chair, Geoffrey Gilbert, for his support in the final phases of the manuscript. My collaborations with William E. Dow and Yoko Nakamura have been an invaluable source of inspiration for thinking through this project. In particular, William made some insightful suggestions at the inception of this project that enabled me in shaping the book. Yoko has been extremely helpful in many of my projects. I owe great thanks to them both and hope to continue working with them in the years to come.

At Palgrave, I have had the privilege of working with Shaun Vigil and Glenn Ramirez, who have been gracefully patient with me in seeing this project through to the end. I was also happy to get advice in the initial planning stages from Palgrave editor Brigitte Shull. Her perspectives contributed a great deal to the final shape of the project.

An earlier version of the first chapter of the book, "The Gangster in *The Devil Finds Work* as a Template for Reading the Parisian *Banlieues*," appeared in Rich Blint and Douglas Field, eds., *African American Review* 46, no. 4 (Winter 2013): 573–586. Though the current chapter is altered from the original article, I was grateful for my opportunity to work with these editors. Our continued communication up to and throughout the

International James Baldwin conference, which I cohosted in May 2016, has been a positive influence on my work.

I have had much support and encouragement from many of the participants of this and other conferences, and some of them, such as Rashida K. Braggs, James Campbell, Anna Everett, and Douglas Field, have shared their work with me. My colleagues, university librarians, and many others at the American University of Paris have been supportive in many ways. Ann Borel was helpful with the final submissions of the manuscript. Isabelle Dupuy, Ann Mott, Sally Murray, and others aided me in locating hard-to-find materials or walked me through important details of the manuscript process. Mark Rostollan cheered me on when I got bogged down in details, and Ursula Darien was always an encouraging presence.

Many colleagues and friends were supportive, and, in particular, Susan Fox and Gail Hamilton never became impatient with my frustrations along the way. Deborah Magocsi and Jason Boyd made suggestions on certain portions of the manuscript when I was unsure if the tone was correct. My family in the United States kept tabs on my progress and cheered me along as well. My daughter Zoe was always solicitous, and I thank her for her support. My biggest debt of thanks is to my husband, Olivier, who during the final stages of writing had to listen every day to every single detail of my thoughts and decisions concerning the manuscript. I guess he will thank me for submitting it.

Finally, I take the words of Ossie Davis seriously when he claims that "the social consequences of a book do not always act out the good intentions of the author," a remark he made in his 1968 exchange with James Baldwin and William Styron concerning the publication of Styron's novel *The Confessions of Nat Turner*. Despite my well-intentioned efforts, I take responsibility for any mistakes or negative consequences that might be occasioned by this book.

CONTENTS

List of Figures

CHAPTER 1

Visible and Invisible Whiteness: An Introduction

American white supremacy has profoundly shaped the evolution of the classical Hollywood narrative, ensuring its place at the heart of American cinema's critical apparatus as well as in Hollywood studios.[1] *Visible and Invisible Whiteness: American White Supremacy through the Cinematic Lens* offers perspectives on this shaping and also considers the fascination with supremacist themes on the part of *émigré* filmmakers or European filmmakers who have at times turned their attention to narratives rooted in American culture. The book reframes the debates on D. W. Griffith's *Birth of a Nation* (1915), arguably the most controversial white supremacist film ever made, through its focus on reviews of that film by James Agee and James Baldwin. In this way, the book sets up the poles of visible and invisible whiteness as roughly approximated by Agee's and Baldwin's respective approaches to the criticism of racially inflected films.[2] Close examination of the two writers and their assessments of Griffith's film suggest that despite their ultimate perspectives, their appreciations of the film show more commonalities than differences.

Two theoretical dichotomies are juxtaposed throughout: (1) the dichotomy between classical Hollywood narrative and art cinema and (2) the work of film critics and filmmakers who rely, either consciously or unconsciously, on notions of visible and invisible whiteness, following Richard Dyer's work on whiteness studies.[3] The goal is to explore how these two sets of critical categories are affected by each other in terms of the supremacist assumptions of much of Hollywood cinema and the

© The Author(s) 2018
A. M. Craven, *Visible and Invisible Whiteness*,
https://doi.org/10.1007/978-3-319-76777-2_1

institutionalization of narrative and generic techniques used by filmmakers, critics, and theorists in distinguishing Hollywood cinema from art cinema in both form and ideological content.

The critical parameters of this book are determined by the perspectives of these two notable authors, Agee and Baldwin, and there is therefore an exclusive focus on American white supremacy with respect to African Americanism and whiteness. Both Baldwin and Agee are ultimately concerned with the controversy of whiteness as well as the questions stemming from America's treatment of its slave and post-slavery populations as depicted in Griffth's film. Though the privileging of whiteness is a trope that has been explored by many authors in relation to Native American, Asian, Latino, and other ethnic populations, this volume remains focused on representations of African Americans, in keeping with the major concerns treated by Baldwin and Agee in their analyses of Griffith's *Birth of a Nation*.[4]

Recent developments in the study of the "transnational turn" in literary and cinema studies can be seen as pertinent to the chapters that follow, though the term "transnational" is rarely evoked. Notable studies in the transnational turn, such as Paul L. Jay's seminal work highlight the importance of the transnational concept, which increasingly affects contemporary analyses of literary works crossing national boundaries. Austin Fisher and Iain Robert Smith's formation of a scholarly interest group devoted to "transnational cinemas" prepares the groundwork for advancing transnational cinema studies and for defining more precisely what is meant by the "transnational" in relation to film studies.[5]

The wide range of films analyzed in *Visible and Invisible Whiteness* does not allow for in-depth engagement with the transnational turn in cinema, as the book's ultimate goals are more deeply rooted in looking at the intersectional relationship between theories on narrative and genres explored by David Bordwell's and Richard Dyer's seminal work on whiteness in cinema. Tim Bergfelder nonetheless suggests that "the term [transnational] works best when it has a concrete case study at hand."[6] In keeping with that premise, *Visible and Invisible Whiteness* is arranged according to case studies rather than chronologically. Films that many readers might expect to see in a chronological treatment of American white supremacy, such as *The Jazz Singer* (1927) or *To Kill a Mockingbird* (1962), are notably absent.

Case studies of individual films dealing with American white supremacy are highlighted in the chapters of this volume in order to follow some of the recent tenets of transnational cinema studies. Namely, as

Robert Burgoyne suggests, privileging critical perspective over traditional methodologies inherited from the study of national cinemas is key. Studies within the fields of national cinemas are often dependent upon chronologies, and my focus on case studies is intended to capitalize on Burgoyne's position.[7] Given the necessary attention to the source materials used for each of the films under examination, transnational theory remains an essential prop in this respect for certain chapters.

A crucial premise for this book is the claim that cinema can function as a "transparent window" onto racial realities, as noted by Anna Everett. The racial reality upon which cinema gazes is nonetheless strange, often frightening, and, according to the dichotomous readings offered by Agee and Baldwin, subject to much interpretation. Cinema's "received acceptance as transparency" on the part of many audience compounds spectator confusion when viewing racially inflected films. In other words, *American* white supremacy has shaped not only classical Hollywood narrative but also its spectators, critics, and other national cinema traditions as well. As Steve McQueen, British-born director of *12 Slaves* (2012), pointed out in a recent review, "I could never make American movies—they like happy endings. I made *Shame* in America, but it's not a Hollywood movie. I'm about challenging people. Like, properly challenging them and their assumptions. Audiences make their minds up about people they see on screen, just like they do in real life."[8] Audiences and their receptions are part and parcel of the dichotomies to be discussed here in addition to the more institutionalized language of film criticism and theory.

Filmmakers, spectators, and critics emerging from European traditions have long been fascinated by the evolution of classical Hollywood aesthetic traditions, which are indeed rich despite having been plagued by America's long-standing and troublesome racial mythologies.[9] This is true for filmmakers, such as Fritz Lang, Jean Renoir, and Douglas Sirk, as well as for filmmakers who are drawn to question supremacist myths and themes in America, such as R. W. Fassbinder and Rachid Bouchareb. Indeed, current trends in European cinemas concerned with visible whiteness, represented here in Chap. 9 on Bouchareb's films, suggest that concepts such as the postracial imaginary, discussion of which is usually limited to the fields of American and African American studies, may be made relevant to European contexts.

As mentioned, the book is structured as a set of case studies on films that are directly or indirectly identified as hybrid productions with respect to David Bordwell's critical categories. Though Bordwell's article, "The Art Cinema as a Mode of Film Practice," is considered seminal and still relevant, the critical evolution of his categories and debates surrounding the lack of precision associated with the term "art cinema" are traced through the works of David Andrews, Steve Neale, Jeffrey Sconce, and others.[10] It is crucial to note that while "classical Hollywood narrative" as a critical term remains fairly stable, "art cinema" as a critical term has always been somewhat nebulous due to the fact that it was historically defined in large part as a defense against the stability of the former category. A closer look at Thomas Elsaesser's *European Cinema: Face to Face with Hollywood* reveals that the more recent trends in reexamination of Europe's supposed "hostility to Hollywood" and the links of said hostility to the dichotomous relations around which this book is structured are crucial for understanding future directions in cinema studies.[11] The films chosen for analysis speak to particular tenets and pivot points of that debate.

The goal of analysis in each case study is to build an argument examining why and to what extent American white supremacy has been so instrumental in shaping Hollywood filmmaking from *Birth* onward and how this has in turn shaped criticism of films that touch on themes concerned with visible and invisible whiteness. By using examples that exhibit an intersectional relationship between terms designed to comment on form (Bordwell) and terms designed to comment on thematic content (Dyer here being used as a point of departure), I provide deeper perspectives on the tenacity of supremacist myths of Hollywood cinema. The voluminous material available on the debate about *Birth* (upon which my arguments rely) has therefore led to the reframing and repositioning of that debate through a comparative analysis of Agee's and Baldwin's reviews of the film in this text.

Agee's film criticism belongs to the world of what, following Dyer's initiatives in *White: Essays on Race and Culture,* can be referred to as invisible whiteness or, alternatively, a concept of whiteness as an assumed and unquestioned privilege for its bearers/makers. Agee's other writings indicate his discomfort with racial issues during his lifetime, but his film criticism is for the most part veiled with respect to these sensibilities. In his article "Racial Violence, Receding Bodies," James A. Crank refers to the attitudes toward America's racial problems in many of Agee's writings as an "anatomy of guilt." That anatomy is traced in Agee's critique of *Birth*.[12] In contrast, Baldwin succinctly frames visible whiteness as a signal of American dysfunction and articulates a mythology of that dysfunction that can be profitably applied to the study of the classical Hollywood narrative. Taken together, the perspectives of Agee and Baldwin reveal intellectually rich but nonetheless contrasting analyses of whiteness in American cinema culture.

By using the distinction between classical Hollywood narrative and art cinema as a critical base, the chapters of this book argue progressively that some whiteness is visible because it functions as an ideological obstacle for the critic or filmmaker.[13] This is more likely to be the case for some émigré directors when approaching supremacy from within an American context. Other whiteness is invisible because it is assumed as a cultural given for filmmakers, notably Griffith, or critics raised in a segregated America. This premise addresses Dyer's contention that to be white entails certain visible traits as well as invisible or symbolic traits. As Dyer states, "[W]hites are not of a certain race, they're just the human race." Most important, his contention is that whiteness as power "is maintained by being unseen."[14] Dyer's exploration of whiteness is rooted in representation, and *Visible and Invisible Whiteness* is similarly concerned with cinematic representation and its critique. Dyer's concepts are reflected in Agee's and Baldwin's film criticism in various ways.

The definition of whiteness is dependent not only on the dichotomous perspectives offered by Agee and Baldwin but also on the works of Dyer, Daniel Bernardi, and others. As Bernardi specifies, "[T]hough present since the founding of the Republic, the discourse of whiteness is nonetheless historical: a shifting, reforming system of meanings that, while consistently privileging physiognomic and cultural difference moves people up and down the racial privilege ladder." Bernardi's stress on the historical is in keeping with Baldwin's desire to uncover and articulate a mythology that bears traces of American manipulation of ideologies to create its own racially slanted history. Other debates concerning *Birth of a Nation* are influenced by Everett's work, *Returning the Gaze*, cited earlier, as well as the work of Melvyn Stokes's.

The hybrid nature of the films examined in these case studies can be caused by circumstances linked to geographical location, time, and social contexts, though these case studies have not been geographically or chronologically arranged. For example, though American made by a Hollywood insider, Samuel Fuller's *White Dog* (1982) was shelved precisely because it could not be considered as a classical Hollywood narrative, and only once it was marketed as an art cinema film did it find a place in distribution networks. The hybrid nature of the film was directly influenced by Fuller's desire to question rather than replicate the supremacist structure normally imposed by Hollywood while scripting his source material, Romain Gary's *Chien Blanc* (*White Dog*, 1970). The films under examination enjoy a certain status due to their explicit focus on racial themes, for example, John M. Stahl's *Imitation of Life*. They are featured here either for those reasons or because they have been largely misinterpreted due to a conflict between their thematic content and the form or genre used by the filmmaker to express this content, as is the case in Fuller's *White Dog*.

Extending these debates through studies of cinematic hybrids helps to: (1) articulate the specificity of American white supremacy and how it has shaped Hollywood cinema aesthetically; (2) consider the impact of American supremacist myths on selected directors who have influenced or have been influenced by art cinema; and (3) gauge how precisely exploration of Hollywood representation of racial themes can raise questions about the racism and white supremacy of other national contexts. What happens when the most deeply rooted ideologies of a particular national culture are scrutinized and used to reflect on the ideologies of another culture? This is the focus of Chap. 9 on Bouchareb, Chap. 6 on Fassbinder, and Chap. 7 on Renoir.[15]

Birth of a Nation is central for this project but to dwell on it purely and simply would not push the argument into new territory. The key debates on *Birth* can be extended into the examination of other films, both major and minor ones, in order to consider the concept of cinema as a presumed transparency from alternative perspectives. Indeed, Stokes meticulously maps out the genesis of the film *Birth* and its creators' belief that it reflected a transparent history of the Civil War and Reconstruction period in the South. Chapter 8 traces Stokes's development of his indispensable study of the history and reception of the film.[16] Equally, W. E. B. Du Bois's concept of living "within the veil" or looking through a glass darkly as applied to the lives of spectators shows just how murky the idea of transparency can be, if it is already rooted in dominant ideologies, such as white supremacy.

Viewing and critiquing films through the unquestioned assumption that American whites are a superior race is yet another version of living "within the veil."[17] Thus the spectator, both as viewer of films and reader of film reviews, is equally at the root of the perpetuation of this dominant ideology. With respect to these aspects of my work, I am dependent on the research of Susan Courtney, Manthia Diawara, Ryan Friedman, and Jacqueline Stewart.[18]

Each of these critics contributes to the debates on methods for examining black spectatorship and reveal the extent to which Agee and Baldwin's film criticism anticipate contemporary ethnic reception theory. Chapters 2 and 3 on Agee and Baldwin, which are focussed on *Birth of a Nation* also consider other films, such as *In the Heat of the Night* (1967, critiqued by Baldwin) or producer David O. Selznick's *Since You Went Away* (1944, critiqued by Agee) in this light.[19] American white supremacy is ever present both in form and content for many of the films discussed by Agee and Baldwin but in sharply distinguished ways for each of these authors. While Agee speculates that Selznick's style will no doubt dominate Hollywood for years to come, he ends his review by stating that this style operates according to the law of a "dream life for which, I am afraid, neither Selznick or anyone else can be blamed."[20] Agee's seeming desire to separate *form* from *content* in many of his reviews, notably that of *Birth*, is a symptom of most American film criticism and filmmaking in the mid-twentieth century and is in need of dissection. Nonetheless, viewing Agee as a critic purely in line with the idea of a separation of form from content is misleading, as his other writings reveal that his relationship to America's race problems is much more complex, and this complexity needs to be put into context with his film criticism, particularly in the case of Griffith.

In contrast, the Bordwell distinction anchors analysis since the films to be closely read function through the different aesthetic foundations that he established for film theory, despite the evolution of his terms since 1979. That aesthetic does ultimately rely on an awareness of the boundaries between form and ideological content. Some are classical Hollywood narratives, others are art cinema, and some must be regarded as being hybrids of the two aesthetic traditions.[21] The classical Hollywood narrative is defined by its seamless or continuity editing, among other attributes to be explored, but one given is that the point-of-view shots in most of these films are controlled by the positioning of the American white male subject. Much has been written on this crucial dimension of American cinema from both racial and gender perspectives, and I am here dependent on the work of Mary Ann Doane, Laura Mulvey, and Kaja Silverman among others.[22] It is through the agreement between narrative structure and the white male gaze of classical Hollywood narrative that grounds for looking at intersections between Bordwell's theory and a reexamination of racial themes in the films chosen for analysis can be established.

Limiting discussion of *Birth* to a comparative analysis of the film criticism of Agee and Baldwin is useful in order to better contextualize the films analyzed in subsequent chapters. Though Agee and Baldwin are important authors in many other ways, this particular pairing has not been explored in depth. By putting their reviews side by side, new perspectives on the two authors as critics and, indeed, as Americans can be discovered. By extending perspectives on selected émigrés and foreign directors who focus on American racial themes or American-style genres and narratives, the book's critical reach with respect to racially inflected films is broadened.

The place of the white Southern intellectual is also introduced as an important theme through the in-depth examination of Agee's film criticism in the "age of the Negro"[23] and through William Faulkner's contribution to Renoir's American-produced film, *The Southerner* (1945). As Bernardi points out in his review of Anthony Slide's *American Racist: The Life and Films of Thomas Dixon*, both Griffith and Thomas Dixon were Southerners before they were Americans, and their claims to fame and intellectual fortune were fed by their respective assertions of ideological positions *as* Southerners.[24] Self-identification as a Southerner is often, though not always, linked to Agee's reviews of films with explicit racial content, a form of self-identification also evident in his recently rediscovered article "America, Look at your Shame."[25]

In Chap. 2, the focus is on *The Devil Finds Work* (1976), where Baldwin theorizes American white supremacy as a visible mythic structure[26] and insists on the fact that *Birth* is a film from which assumptions of white supremacy cannot be separated. While acknowledging the aesthetic value of the film, Baldwin nonetheless states, "*Birth of a Nation* is really an elaborate justification for mass murder. The film cannot possibly admit this, which is why we are immediately placed at the mercy of a plot labyrinthine and preposterous."[27] The narrative structure guides the film, which recounts the superiority and privilege of the white man in America. This master narrative influences the subsequent evolution of American cinema and restricts it by default. Baldwin strengthens this argument through a comparison of *Birth* with Norman Jewison's *Heat* (1967), a film that Baldwin claims shares the racial sentiments of Griffith's film, even though it was made 50 years later.[28]

The narrative structure created by Griffith is built on his foundations and innovations, and the shadows of that structure can be seen everywhere, not only in subsequent American-made films but also in many of the assumptions of film criticism and film theory.

Baldwin's analyses are forms of "resisting ideology by questioning cinema," as Martin Fradley suggests is the goal of Bernardi's collection, *The Persistence of Whiteness.*[29] Nonetheless, Baldwin was certainly not the only critic to have taken this route. Everett has already written the definitive text on the subject of black film criticism from 1909 to 1949, cited earlier. Her work serves as a crucial backdrop in contextualizing Baldwin's film criticism, though a conscious questioning of the relation of form to content is not always a focus in the work of the critics she chronicles. Nonetheless, as she rightly reminds the reader, black film criticism had a long and rich history prior to Baldwin, and his work must be put in place with respect to that genealogy. More important, it must be placed alongside the criticism of Agee, whose film criticism was only secondarily concerned with the views of black film critics, given his roots in a primarily segregated and therefore by default, white America. Agee and Baldwin were film critics who are rarely mentioned in the same breath since they belong to opposing poles as spokespersons respectively for the mainstream (invisible) and marginal (visible) approaches to films concerned with race in America and beyond.[30]

By contrast, Chap. 3 focuses on Agee as a way of underscoring the strength and appeal of what Baldwin accomplishes in *Devil*. Agee's analysis of most American films that treat racial issues (and by consequence can be shown to assume the truth or privilege of invisible whiteness) is of crucial importance. Questioning supremacy as an obstacle to racially balanced filmmaking is not explicit in Agee's work because he could skirt around the ideological complications posed by white supremacist assumptions, given his role as a Southern white intellectual writing in "the age of the Negro." For Agee, the supremacy of the American white is tacitly assumed in the aesthetic function of the American cinema, no matter what his ultimate views on America and race were. It would appear that Agee did not deem appropriate a discussion of race issues in a film review, though some of the reviews analyzed in Chap. 3 do make passing commentary on race in America.

Nonetheless, even when reviewing films produced in Europe, Agee is acutely aware of how the American "Negro" is represented. For example, in his review of Luigi Zampa's *To Live in Peace* (1947), which he describes as "the wisest and most deeply human film of its time," Agee critiques the depiction of one American "Negro" character in the film.[31] In this review, he derides another critic for belittling the behavior of the troublesome Negro by saying "he [the critic Archer Winsten] wrote that it was impossibly inconsiderate and ungrateful of the solider (the Negro) to behave as he did in the [situation depicted in the narrative]. No doubt it was. But there is no evidence that the Negro, the peasants, or even the people who made the film looked at it in that light. To them, it was unfortunately, the most natural thing in the world."[32] Despite many telling examples such as this one with respect to Agee's appreciation of "Negro" characterizations, Agee remains fundamentally supportive of Griffith's *Birth, though with* certain telling disclaimers, which are further explored in Chap. 3. Baldwin is broadly dismissive of racial concerns in Griffith's film despite his admission that aesthetically the film is valuable. Agee seems less able to voice his views on Griffith's stance on American white supremacy.

Nonetheless, comparing Agee's film criticism to his other writings, notably *Let Us Now Praise Famous Men* (1941) or his letters to Father Flye (1962), shows that Agee was not oblivious to the painful ambiguities of racial relations in the United States during his lifetime, but his *film* criticism avoids those difficulties because he ostensibly benefits from the division between form and content, something Bernardi suggests is a misconception when analyzing the intents and purposes of *Birth of a Nation*. As Agee suggests throughout the text *Let Us Now Praise Famous Men*, his trip to the South to chronicle the lives of poor tenant farmers was punctuated by incidents of observing the unquestioned treatment of Negroes as inferior. As a witness to such imbalance, he notes that he could only "in a play of self-torture, play his part through."[33] Chapter 3 seeks to bring balance to the hyperbolic review of Griffith's film offered by Agee and his other writings, which are far more cautionary when it comes to understanding the problems both of filmic representation of the "Negro" and the actual social complexities of America's struggle with racial imbalance.[34] Of particular interest is the recent discovery and publication of Agee's essay "America, Look at Your Shame," which provides deeper insight into his most private views on racial issues in America.[35]

John M. Stahl's *Imitation of Life* (1934) is classic Hollywood narrative produced according to traditional studio methods, and Chap. 4 contrasts it to its 1959 "remake" of the same title by German filmmaker Douglas Sirk.[36] Stahl's film is one where whiteness is invisible, and its narrative conforms with classic Hollywood norms. Sirk relies on the same aesthetic structure to retell this story of biracial friendship and a young black girl's attempts to pass for white. In the original film, all racial tensions are ultimately resolved due to the strength and selflessness of the white businesswoman played by Claudine Colbert.

A closer look at the actual structure of the film reveals that its generic specificity has to be transformed in order for this resolution to make sense under studio narrative conditions. The film begins as a melodrama and is resolved as a romantic comedy, thus relegating the visible whiteness with which the film is opened to a safe and marginal subplot. Chapter 4 explores the relation between form and content and the strategies of racial resolution in Stahl's and Sirk's films from a *generic* perspective. As Andrews has pointed out, one of the debates concerning Bordwell's categories is whether they are uniquely tied to narrative structure as opposed to also affecting or being affected by questions of genre.[37]

Sirk's film can be viewed as a classic Hollywood melodrama, but closer analysis of the striking differences in the way Sirk films the narrative reveals (1) his love-hate relationship with American culture and (2) his subtle but nonetheless insistent questioning of American whiteness as invisible. Sirk counterpoints certain aspects of the earlier film through his use of cinematic excess, thereby creating a visual resistance to the supremacist ideologies implicit in the classical Hollywood narrative represented and legitimated by Stahl's Universal Studios production.

Close analysis of the structural distinctions between the two films reveals an instance of intersectionality with respect to Bordwell's categories and visible and invisible whiteness. Sirk's deconstructive strategies with respect to the classical Hollywood narrative attracted the attention and praise of the New Wave critics, and Chap. 4 equally incorporates discussion of their appreciation of Sirk's films in their critiques of Sirk's *Imitation of Life*. As is argued by most who engage in the classical Hollywood versus art cinema debates, the French New Wave was instrumental as a trigger for deepening the debate, a subject that we return to in Chap. 8 on the subject of film noir and Hollywood.[38]

Ironically, Sam Fuller chooses an odd protagonist for his film *White Dog*, which is the main focus of Chap. 5. For the film, Fuller "casts" a white dog, who is white both in terms of his actual color and in the fact that he was trained to violence and cruelty against blacks by his owner. The dog is thus a hybrid character in a narrative that was rejected by Hollywood due to Fuller's choice of protagonist for the film. As an insider to the Hollywood studio system, Fuller was hired to make a classical Hollywood film on the basis of Romain Gary's novel *Chien Blanc*. In other words, the film was commissioned by Hollywood and intended as a classic Hollywood entertainment about a young white girl and her dog, modeled loosely on the structure of the earlier and highly successful 1975 film *Jaws* directed by Steven Spielberg.

The then-popular child actress Kristy McNichol is here cast in one of her first adult roles. The wholesome girl and her dog ultimately triumph over the evils of racism brought about by the trailer-trash white man who had raised the dog to attack people with black skin, but at a cost unbefitting of a happy Hollywood ending. The film was shelved before ever being shown in Hollywood and was misinterpreted by the National Association of the Advancement of Colored People (NAACP) for reasons that are explored in Chap. 5. What Fuller essentially did was to suppress the narrative structure of this story of American white supremacy and replace it with a film about the psychological makeup of a dog trained to "embrace" the supremacy of white America through its ability to distinguish between black and white *skin*. The ambiguity of the film's structure led to questions about its racial intent. In this case as well, a film that was planned to be consistent with the evolution and structure of Hollywood cinema was ostracized because it raised key questions about the assumptions of that structure.

In essence, the film rendered whiteness visible. For the most part, audience sympathy is with the dog. Fuller intended that the audience identify with the dog rather than view him as a parallel to the vehicle of senseless violence depicted by the sharks in *Jaws*. In transforming the material in this way, Fuller essentially made an art cinema film (in defiance of the narrative demands of Hollywood entertainment) simply by highlighting the close ties between classic narrative and the perversion of the privileging of the white gaze. Indeed, much of the film is narrated through the subjective position of the "supremacist" dog. Fuller made those ties between classic narration and the white gaze more visible than was acceptable in Hollywood with its need for a marketable, entertaining American film.

As in Chap. 4 on *Imitation of Life*, where Fanny Hurst's novel must be analyzed in relations to the two versions of the films based upon it, a close comparison of Fuller's film to its source material is crucial. Gary's novel *Chien Blanc* is a critique of racial issues in America and, notably, in the Hollywood milieu. The novel is very liberally adapted by Fuller to create a film that ultimately questions the value of American white supremacy as an ideological base for making films in Hollywood. During Gary's extended stay in the United States as Consul General in Los Angeles, he was constantly reminded that he could not understand and therefore could not comment on American white supremacy because he was not

American. His complaints on this count are often frustrated. As he says, "I wish some Americans black and white would get over once and for all the idea that they possess a kind of privileged, secret, esoteric and exclusive knowledge of themselves."[39]

Gary's novel is nonetheless one of the most targeted commentaries on the subject by an "outsider" (nationally and culturally), and since it becomes the source material for one of the least understood Hollywood films by an insider, Fuller, it highlights the intersectional relationship between the two theoretical dichotomies under examination here. Though Fuller does not adapt his source material from a narrative perspective for the most part, his film finds new structural ways of highlighting the main message in Gary's novel.

Fuller's protagonist, is a white dog in both senses of the term, literally and as a dog trained to attack blacks. As a protagonist, he is strange in many ways that are echoed in Fassbinder's protagonist Whity in his film of the same title. Though the principal structures of the film engage with American supremacist themes, Fassbinder was primarily a spectator of Hollywood's dazzling dream machine in contrast to Sirk, who spent a fair amount of real working time in Hollywood. Though Sirk worked directly in the studio system, Fassbinder was influenced from afar, and Hollywood structures and mechanisms affected many of his films. In *Whity* (1971), which is the focus for Chap. 6, Fassbinder instructs his spectator on the level of genre *as structure*. He deconstructs the Western genre by using a quasi–art cinema approach. Chapter 6 explores how this generic structure can be shown to be a natural outgrowth of the epic *Birth of a Nation*. As Dyer suggests, "[A] side from being one of the founding myths of the USA," the Western also "continues to leave its mark on the international imagination." The Western was one of the most controlling genres with respect to European fascination with American cinematic culture.[40]

Through *Whity*, Fassbinder allows one to see the Western as a logical extension of the supremacist doctrines of *Birth of a Nation*. In effect, Fassbinder's film asserts that the American white supremacy that becomes blatantly visible as a theme of *Whity* is born out of its necessity as part of the structure of the Western and Southern Plantation genres. If we accept the structure of the genre as necessary, the supremacy remains invisible. If the structure itself questions that necessity, supremacy becomes visible and therefore ideologically questionable.

This chapter further comments on one of the original differences between classical Hollywood narrative and art cinema as defined by Bordwell when he first wrote his article on art cinema. The psychological makeup of Whity's character severely undermines the seamless narrative structure, a narrative that assumes the supremacy of the American white male gaze. As Bordwell states, "[T]he art cinema is classical in its reliance upon psychological causation; characters and their effects on one another remain central. The Hollywood protagonist speeds directly towards the target; lacking a goal, the art-film character slides passively from one situation to another."[41]

In each chapter of this book, modifications and specifications characterize how the films under examination partake in art cinema or classical Hollywood techniques. Particularly in Chap. 6, the vast divide between how protagonists of the Western function according to highly determined goals versus the almost accidental violent actions of the character Whity at the end of the film attest to its hybrid nature. The character Whity is indeed no more than a servant to a cruel and sadistic family though he is equally a member of that family since he is the son of the master of the home. He is the offspring of the master's abuse of one of his female slaves. Whity's psychological makeup is already a commentary on the cruelty of his father/owner. In similar ways, one can see that Fuller's emphasis on his dog protagonist's psychological makeup has parallels to the psychological makeup of Fassbinder's protagonist Whity.

Whether directors looked at Hollywood from within or without, as was the case with Sirk and Fassbinder, respectively, the influences of Hollywood on their films was not their only challenge. The uniqueness of American white supremacist mythologies was also a force to be contended with for the films under consideration in Chaps. 4 and 6. Jean Renoir found himself equally stymied by the mystery of American whiteness during his Hollywood career, where he was hired by Hollywood studios to make stereotypical films about France for American audiences. His early demand to make films using American themes was met with resistance, and he prevailed in being allowed to choose explicitly American settings for his films as opposed to being restricted to making films in America *about* French topics. Though his entire Hollywood career was originally rejected as inferior, later scholarship has revalorized his American work, which is in accordance with the goals of Chap. 7. Chapter 7 explores just how valuable Renoir's desire to plumb the depths of American invisible whiteness has been for understanding the dichotomies under examination in this book.

Renoir's collaboration with William Faulkner on the screenplay for his American-made film *The Southerner* (1945) is one example of a European director experimenting with representations of American invisible whiteness. As Dudley Andrews, André Bazin, and others have established in their writings on Renoir's career and filmmaking techniques, Renoir plays a fundamental role in the evolution of European cinema. This book introduces *The Southerner* as an example of a film made in the "age of the Negro" by a non-American filmmaker fascinated by Southern white culture. Though it has been plausibly argued that some of Renoir's American-themed films might be read as racial allegories rather than straightforward narratives about racial conflicts, it is clear that to reflect on Southern white culture necessarily implies speculation about race relations in the South, a point noted by Charles Burnett, the African American independent filmmaker, in his assessment of Renoir's film.[42]

Opening shots of cotton pickers in the South play on the stereotypical Hollywood pans of slaves picking cotton, but in Renoir's film, the race of those in the fields is not distinguishable. As is the case in Agee's film criticism and Gary's novel, Renoir does seem to realize his limitations in representing the life of African Americans. Nonetheless, his presentation of the main white protagonists in the film evidences his reflections as an outsider on the pride associated with southern American whiteness and equally represents its triumphs as an ideology. As Dyer points out, "[A] white complexion is a kind of promise to the bearer that he or she may have access to privilege."[43]

Indeed, though white, the Devers family, enemies of protagonist Sam Tucker and his family in the film, are more shadowed and darkened than the main characters, thus approximating degrees of whiteness that can be traced in an allegorical reading of the film. Dyer traces these shades of whiteness in many of his examples in his book *White*, and they are of constant importance in the analysis of many of the films targeted in this book. Renoir looks at poor white Americans in a way that affirms the supremacy of whiteness while equally creating a counterargument on how the film *The Southerner* implicitly comments on the dysfunction of those supremacist assumptions with respect to racial difference in America.

Renoir is inevitably also influenced by Faulkner's positions on poverty and race in the southern United States through the men's collaborative work on the dialogue of the screenplay. Though Renoir relied on luminaries such as Faulkner in his bid for authenticity, and though the film is American-made, it nonetheless carries distinctive traits of Renoir's style and thus functions as a hybrid between the narratives about class emerging from Hollywood at the time of its making and the European art aesthetic that he was instrumental in shaping. Another hybrid relation is afforded by a close study of Renoir's film in that it was independently produced by Loew and Hakim, and thus Renoir was allowed greater liberty to experiment with filmmaking techniques and the source material. Hollywood productions at this time were primarily studio-prodcued. By working with independent producers, Renoir's free hand in directing decisions revealed much about the tensions between Hollywood methods and the methods he had developed in Europe.

Agee's review of *The Southerner* serves as a framing device, as do Baldwin's writings on Faulkner and desegregation from his collection of essays *Nobody Knows My Name: More Notes of a Native Son*.[44] Indeed, Agee considered *The Southerner* one of the best American-made films he had ever seen, though he does suggest that Renoir has not completely understood the life of the Southerner in a fully authentic way. Chapter 7 contextualizes Renoir's Hollywood career through works by scholars such as Dudley Andrew, André Bazin, and others. Of central importance is William Gilcher's unpublished dissertation, "The Hollywood Films of Jean Renoir, 1942–1948," and Elizabeth Vitanza's recent work on Renoir's Hollywood career.[45]

Renoir was admittedly a formidable force in the canon of French cinema, but he was not unique in his fascination with American racial issues. Indeed, there was a general fascination with American culture in postwar France, particularly with America's music and cinema. Most criticisms of Boris Vian's novel *I Shall Spit on Your Grave* (1946) begin with this fundamental turn toward an obsession with American culture in postwar France. Vian wrote his novel under the pseudonym Vernon Sullivan, ostensibly an obscure Negro American writer whose work was refused publication in the United States. Vian's tactic in writing the novel highlights the oppression of the creative expression of the American Negro at the time.

As emphatically pointed out by Baldwin in *Devil*, Michel Gast's 1959 film adaptation of *I Shall Spit on Your Grave* was not at all faithful to Vian's intentions, particularly because it was limited structurally to the narrative of the novel itself and could not reproduce the metanarrative construct provided by Vian's creation of a fictional Negro author. Vian's protest against Gast's adaptation was devastating, as it resulted (or so the dramatization of the controversy goes) in the death of the novelist during the première of the film in a Parisian cinema. Chapter 8 explores Gast's foray into American-style filmmaking and offers arguments for why the film was so badly received. My own studied review of the film concludes that it has been too easily dismissed and needs to be reexamined in light of the hybrid forms of film language in rapid development in France in 1959. Renewed examination of Hollywood techniques and their impact on French filmmaking in the late 1950s is of central concern in Chap. 8.

Since Gast's filming techniques incorporate aspects of classical Hollywood narrative, there is a necessary repression of Vian's deconstruction of the multiple layers of gratuitous supremacy and invisible whiteness in the structure of his novel. Even though Vian's novel is also parading as an American product, the author is able to retain the multiple layers that the film is unable to capture. Both the film and the novel are examinations of visible and invisible whiteness by non-Americans. But the sharp distinctions between Vian's and Gast's sensibilities again show how untranslatable this distinction could prove to be in the American context. In Chap. 8, I evoke Baldwin's review of this film from *Devil* in order to tie together issues raise earlier in the book.

As a last example of a more contemporary perspective on transnational filmmaking, Chap. 9 of the book looks at Franco-Algerian film director Rachid Bouchareb as an example of a filmmaker who aims to render an authentic representation of American white supremacy, despite having been raised and educated in Europe. In *Two Men in Town* (2012), Bouchareb conscientiously uses his characters as a connotative source for considering visible and invisible whiteness in comparison with themes of supremacy in his own country of origin, France.

In other films, Bouchareb relies on generic structures often linked to Hollywood narrative, particularly in *Hors-la-loi* (*The Outlaws*, 2010). In this film, he makes use of the gangster genre in order to examine the racial violence of the Franco-Algerian controversy. Just as Griffith's *Birth* is a "history" of the Civil War and Reconstruction period told from the point of view of a Southerner, *The Outlaws* is a history of the Franco-Algerian conflict told from the Algerian perspective. It therefore not only makes use of a popular American genre, it also plays on some of the myths generated about the causes of the Civil War in America as incorporated by Griffith into his film.[46] Though ultimately relying on different national mythologies, the two films share a subjective narration positioning from the point of view of the underdog. *Hors-la-loi* was controversial in France and therefore received similar though not as pronounced critical attention as did *Birth*.

The film *Two Men in Town* takes up specific American-centered themes and is a Franco-American production by a European director. Like Renoir, Bouchareb brings a European perspective and European filmmaking techniques into play, though his setting is thoroughly American. Film reviews for Bouchareb's *Two Men in Town* were for the most part unflattering in America and more generous in Europe largely due to the hybrid nature of the film's structure in relation to its plotline. As part of Bouchareb's American trilogy, the film is an explicit exploration of a popular Hollywood genre filmed through more traditional European techniques. Bouchareb's ultimate goal is to use generic structures in order to create cultural transpositions. He creates a self-reflexive mirror for the Franco-Algerian controversy while taking risks on the popular reception of his films. His mirror is framed through a hybridization of the aesthetic tradition of Hollywood from a generic perspective and his own ideological positions as a Franco-Algerian director.

In Chap. 9, intersectionality plays a role in ways that depart from its more common usage in feminist theory to consider how theories of intersectionality might be applied to cultural difference in Bouchareb's films.[47] Concerns about visible whiteness inform Bouchareb's evolution as a filmmaker and are strongly anticipated in his film *Little Senegal* (2001). This film, most ostensibly about the African diaspora, also comments through its visual and dialogic cinematic excess on the specificity of invisible whiteness in America and its role in creating fissures among African, American, and European black lives.

A brief conclusion relates the primary issues configured by this book to the contemporary debates about Hollywood whitewashing and contextualizes that those debates with respect to specific films, notably Nate Parker's *Birth of a Nation* (2016). Baldwin argues that nothing has changed in terms of racial representation in the fifty years separating the filming of Griffith's *Birth* and Jewison's *Heat* (1967). In like manner, contemporary Hollywood, in order to be fully understood, needs to be seen in light of deeper contexts as well as cultural reception of cinematic narratives, genres, and images. This can be accomplished by studying films that have been marginalized but are nonetheless revealing when it comes to Hollywood film language.

There is a need to better understand the critical categories and aesthetic rules that are used in film theory, criticism, and filmmaking. Though some might consider contemporary films as progressive in terms of dialogues and critiques about race and cinema, their defenders and even their detractors need to be more sensitive to the fact that they perhaps inadvertently replicate certain aspects of classical Hollywood narrative. They therefore cannot definitively be said to have freed themselves from the invisible whiteness that informs that language. A comparative study of the films and their reception show how a reexamination of aesthetic categories, such as Bordwell's (classical Hollywood n versus art cinema) and Dyer's (visible and invisible whiteness) are still relevant to the current debates about racial issues in both European and American cinemas.

NOTES

1. The seminal text is David Bordwell, Janet Staiger, and Kristin Thompson, *Classical Hollywood Narrative: Style and Mode of Production to 1960* (New York: Columbia University Press, 1985). The article "The Art Cinema as a Form of Film Practice" written by Bordwell in 1979 is the one most often quoted in later articles that take up analysis of his categories. The article is reprinted in many places, notably in Leo Braudy and Marshall Cohen, eds., *Film Theory and Criticism*, 7th ed. (New York: Oxford University Press, 2009), 649–657.
2. For extensive review of the debate over *Birth of a Nation* please cf., Melvyn Stokes's *D. W. Griffith's The Birth of a Nation: A History of the Most Controversial Film of All Time* (Oxford: Oxford University Press, 2008).
3. Richard Dyer's text *White: Essays on Race and Culture* (London: Routledge, 1997, 2002). As Dyer specifies, "[W]hiteness as race resides in invisible properties and whiteness as power is maintained by being unseen" (45). As he equally emphasizes, any analysis of visual culture requires giving close attention to what is visible.
4. Notable examples include Angela Aleiss, *Making the White Man's Indian: Native Americans and Hollywood Movies* (Westport, CT: Praeger, 2009); Michael J. Shapiro, *Cinematic Political Thought: Narrating Race and Gender* (New York: New York University Press, 1999); Daniel Bernardi, ed., *Classic Hollywood, Classic Whiteness* (Minneapolis: University of Minnesota Press, 2001) or *The Persistence of Whiteness: Race and Contemporary Hollywood Cinema* (New York: Routledge, 2007); and Jason A. Smith and Bhoomi K. Thakore, eds., *Race and Contention in 21st Century Media* (New York: Routledge, 2016), to name only a few.
5. Paul L. Jay, *Global Matters: The Transnational Turn in Literary Studies* (Ithaca, NY: Cornell University Press, 2010. Austin Fisher and Iain Robert Smith, "Transnational Cinemas: A Critical Roundtable," *Frames Cinema Journal.* http://framescinemajournal.com/article/transnational-cinemas-a-critical-roundtable/.
6. Tim Bergfelder, in "Transnational Cinemas," 3.
7. Robert Burgoyne, in "Transnational Cinemas," 5.
8. "Steve McQueen: 'I could never make American Movies—They like happy endings,'" *The Guardian*, January 8, 2012. https://www.theguardian.

com/theobserver/2012/jan/08/steve-mcqueen-shame-sex-addiction-interview.

9. In this instance, I evoke the concept of "mythology" derived from the works of Roland Barthes in his seminal text *Mythologies*, though the ultimate purpose of the second chapter is to lay out the similarities between Barthes's notion of mythic structure and that of Baldwin. Barthes, *Mythologies* (Paris: Editions de Seuil, 1970).

10. Steve Neale's "Art Cinema as Institution" (1980) is also considered to be a seminal text on this subject, reprinted in C. Fowler, ed., *The European Cinema Reader* (London: Routledge, 2002), 103–120; of interest as well is David Andrews, "Art Cinema as Institution Redux: Art Houses, Film Festivals and Film Studies," *Scope: An Online Journal of Film and Television*, October 18, 2010. Jeffrey Sconce, "Irony, Nihilism and the new American 'Smart' Film," *Screen* 43, no. 4 (2002): 349–369. Other scholars will also be referenced in due course.

11. Thomas Elsaesser, *European Cinema: Face to Face with Hollywood* (Amsterdam: Amsterdam University Press, 2005).

12. In Michael Lofaro, ed., *Agee at 100: Centennial Essays on the Works of James Agee* (Knoxville: University of Tennessee Press, 2012).

13. The seminal text is Bordwell, Staiger, and Thompson, *Classical Hollywood Narrative*.

14. Dyer, *White: Essays on Race and Culture*, 3, 45.

15. A useful reference in film theory is Jean-Luc Comolli and Jean Narboni, "Cinema/Ideology/Criticism," *Cahiers du cinéma* 216 (October 1969), translated by Susan Bennett in *The Politics of Representation*, ed. Nick Browne (London: Routledge, 1990), 58–67. The hybrid films I wish to examine are most closely associated with Comolli and Narboni's category C films, which operate "against the grain" of dominant ideologies. Comolli and Narboni claim that these types of movies would be the main subject of criticism for the *Cahiers du cinéma*, but I would also claim that this category is particularly useful for considering films of directors who are working across cultural boundaries and therefore challenging dominant ideologies that are assumed by the culture featured in their narratives but *not* taken for granted in their own cultures.

16. Melvyn Stokes, *D. W. Griffith's The Birth of a Nation: A History of the Most Controversial Motion Picture of All Time*.

17. Du Bois's concepts are summarized in *The Souls of Black Folks*, (Chicago: A.C. McClurg & Co.) 1903. As he states on the first page of his foreword, "I have stepped within the veil, raising it that you may view faintly its deeper recesses."

18. Susan Courtney, *Hollywood Fantasies of Miscegenation: Spectacular Narratives of Gender and Race, 1903–1967* (Princeton, NJ: Princeton

University Press, 2005). Manthia Diawara, "Black Spectatorship: Problems of Identification and Resistance," in Braudy and Cohen, eds., *Film Theory and Criticism*, 767–776. Ryan Jay Friedman, "Enough Force to Shatter the Tale to Fragments: Ethics and Textual Analysis in James Baldwin's Film Theory," *ELH: Journal of English Literary History* 77, no. 2 (2010): 385–412. Jacqueline Stewart, "Negroes Laughing at Themselves?: Black Spectatorship and the Performance of Urban Modernity," *Critical Inquiry* 29, no. 4 (2003): 650–677.

19. Agee addresses most directly issues of Selznick's contribution in film history through Selznick's work on *Gone with the Wind* (1939) in his comments on *Since You Went Away*, but it is important to establish the connection. *Since You Went Away* is riding on the success of *Gone with the Wind* but does not address explicit racial themes. It nonetheless assumes a restoration of order under the guise of white supremacy, as I will argue and as Agee intimates.

20. *Agee on Film, Volume I, Essays and Reviews by James Agee*, (New York: Perigree, 1958), 107–108.

21. In the course of researching and planning this book, I have considered many different films that might be useful for my purposes, though the ones I finally selected are intended as exemplary for building the argument I wish to pursue.

22. Representative articles by each of these critics may be found in the text *Film Theory and Criticism*, 5th ed., ed. Leo Braudy and Marshall Cohen (New York: Oxford University Press, 1998).

23. The expression "the age of the Negro" derives from the title of the first chapter of Anna Everett's *Returning the Gaze: A Genealogy of Black Film Criticism 1909–1949* (Durham, NC: Duke University Press, 2001). It will remain in quotation marks throughout this volume as a reminder that criticism of racially inflected films is markedly different prior to the advent of the Civil Rights period in the United States and thereafter.

24. Daniel Bernardi, Review of Anthony Slide's "*American Racist: The Life and Films of Thomas Dixon*," *Journal of American History* 92, no. 2 (September 2005): 644.

25. Agee's article "America, Look at Your Shame!" published in *The Oxford American*, no. 43 (January/February 2003) is of particular value. Though written much earlier in the 1940's, Agee's article was lost in his files and has only recently been published.

26. Much of mainstream film theory is formed by structuralist- or poststructuralist-trained scholars and so concepts from Barthes, Benjamin, and others are assumed and will be documented throughout. The phrase in the title "through a glass darkly" alludes to W. E. B. Du Bois's *The Souls of Black Folk* and his discussions of what it means to be "living within the

veil," which is to say, subject to the assumptions of American White supremacy.

27. James Baldwin, *The Devil Finds Work*. (New York: Laurel, 1976). 54–55.
28. A useful critique with respect to this issue is Jean Michel Frodon, *La projection nationale: nation et cinéma* (Paris: Editions Odile Jacob, 1998). Frodon explores how Hollywood has controlled the imagination of filmmakers from other national cinemas as well as how Hollywood production styles and modes of production have affected filmmaking practices outside the United States.
29. Martin Fradley, "Review: *The Persistence of Whiteness: Race and Contemporary Hollywood Cinema*, ed. Daniel Bernardi," *Film Quarterly Review* 63, no. 3 (Spring 2010): 71–73, 71.
30. James A. Crank's "Racial Violence, Receding Bodies: James Agee's Anatomy of Guilt" in Lofaro, ed., *James Agee at 100*, 53–74, is an insightful article on Agee's film criticism in relation to his other writings. It would be unfair to say that Agee was not thoughtful about race relations in America, but close analysis of his work indicates that he did not feel compelled to take a strong public stand on racial issues in his film reviews.
31. *Agee on Film*, 283.
32. *Agee on Film*, 283.
33. It is clear that unequal treatment of African americans was by no means restricted to the South, but in order to understand Agee's position with respect to racial issues, one is largely dependent on the penetrating treatment of class issues in the United States that one finds in *Let Us Now Praise Famous Men* and its ability to allow us glimpses into the racial imbalance which played a role in class distinctions in the American South. This quote is from Walker Evans and James Agee, *Let Us Now Praise Famous Men: Three Tenant Families* (Boston: Mariner, 1939/2001), 28.
34. Crank's "Racial Violence, Receding Bodies" also gives an insightful perspective on this issue.
35. Agee, "America, Look at Your Shame," www.oxfordamerican.org.
36. According to Daniel Itzkovitz's introduction to the reissue of Fanny Hurst's novel *Imitation of Life* (Durham, NC: Duke University Press, 1933/2004), xxxiii, Douglas Sirk was introduced to the novel, which served as the source material for both Stahl's film and Sirk's. (by producer Ross Hunter).
37. In "Art Cinema as Institution Redux," Andrews he specifies that one distinction between Bordwell's and Neale's treatment of art cinema concerns whether it should be considered as strictly linked to narrative or also to genre. The choice of films for this book allows for consideration of both sides of this debate.

38. My argument in Chap. 8 takes into consideration Douglas Field's article "Even Better than the Real Thing: Boris Vian, Vernon Sullivan and Film Noir," *African American Review* 45, no. 1/2 (Spring/Summer 2012): 157–166, concerning Gast's film's partial use of film noir aesthetics. In this context, James Naremore's *More than Night: Film Noir in Its Contexts* (Berkeley: University of California Press, expanded version 2008), is crucial in setting reasonable timelines for the phenomenon and the dissemination of its American manifestations in France.

39. Romain Gary, *White Dog* (Chicago: University of Chicago Press, 1970), 50.

40. Dyer, *White: Essays on Race and Culture*, 1997. 32.

41. Bordwell, "The Art Cinema as a Mode of Film Practice," 651.

42. As several articles on Renoir's work in America argue, confrontation with American racial issues was effected through racial allegories rather than actual black-white confrontational plotlines, due to Renoir's lack of comfort in treating such controversial relations as a non-American. Cf. Ben Dooley's "Swamp Water: Renoir's American Outsider Film," September 24, 2007, https://ayearinthedark.wordpress.com/2007/09/24/swamp-water-renoirs-american-outsider-film/.

43. Dyer, *White: Essays on Race and Culture*, 52.

44. James Baldwin, *Nobody Knows My Name: More Notes of a Native Son* (London: Penguin, 1954, 1991), 101–107.

45. Elizabeth Vitanza, "Interconnected Sites of Struggle: Resituating Renoir's Career in Hollywood," in Alastair Phillips and Ginette Vincendeau, eds., *Wiley Companion to Jean Renoir* (London: Blackwell, 2013), Chap. 29. William Harry Gilcher, Jean Renoir in America: A Critical Analysis of his films from Swamp Water to The River, Thesis (Ph.D.), University of Iowa, 1979.

46. Given the controversy surrounding the film *The Outlaws*, I will be using multiple references to that debate. It must be noted that Melvyn Stokes spends quite some time breaking down the mythic structures one finds in *Birth of a Nation*. Therefore, I will be linking his observations to my own observations about the mythic structures that inform *The Outlaws*.

47. An interesting article to consider in terms of this realignment is Sirma Bilge, "Intersectionality Undone: Saving Intersectionality from Feminist Intersectionality Studies," *Du Bois Review: Social Science Research on Race* 10, no. 2 (Fall 2013): 405–424.

CHAPTER 2

Looking at American White Supremacy "Through a Glass Darkly": James Baldwin on *Birth of a Nation*

The law in this country, just like in most countries, is for the privileged
and if you are White in America, you are privileged. We hope for the
law to protect us, but it doesn't.
—*John A. Williams,* The Man Who Cried I Am

A black man, in any case, had best not believe everything he sees
in the movies.
—*James Baldwin*

James Baldwin's early initiation into moviegoing had a profound impact on his worldview throughout his lifetime as is attested to in his essay *The Devil Finds Work* (1976). Defeating the world's intentions for him and his own became a matter for conscious calculation upon his entrance into the "cinema" of his mind. When speaking of "his own," Baldwin points to a literal need on his part, as the eldest in his family, to protect his younger siblings from being wrongly influenced by the movies they watched. Baldwin's essay recounts the fears and desires of a spectator under specific social and political circumstances, which Baldwin claimed offered a metaphor for "the ordeal of black-white relations in America, an ordeal ... which has brought us [blacks and whites] closer together than we know."[1]

Nowhere is this more evident than in Baldwin's critique of the 1915 D. W. Griffith film *Birth of a Nation*, which serves a focal point for his essay. Just as Susan Courtney traces how the film served to create the

© The Author(s) 2018
A. M. Craven, *Visible and Invisible Whiteness*,
https://doi.org/10.1007/978-3-319-76777-2_2

"Great White Spectator" in America, Baldwin intimates that it also played a major role in constructing the black American spectator, albeit over a longer period of time.[2] By contrast, Siegfried Kracauer, in his 1947 *From Caligari to Hitler: A Psychological History of German Film,* located his own spectator under the shadow of Hitler's rise to power. Kracauer creates an apologetics for Germany's move toward an acceptance of Nazism. He posits that "the films of a nation reflect its mentality in a more direct way than any other media" because they are never the product of a single individual and because they appeal to the "anonymous multitude."[3]

Kracauer's methods can be seen as indirectly applicable to the study of reception theory in Hollywood. The works of Courtney, Anna Everett, Jacqueline Stewart, and others trace the links between the making of *Birth of a Nation* and the evolution of black and white American spectators. Baldwin's condemnation of the film and its manipulative relationship to the American collective memory are anticipations of the more formal theoretical work on reception theory about filmic representations of American race relations. Most scholars of reception theory believe that Griffith's monumental film caused irreparable damage in terms of spectatorship and identity politics in America.

For Stewart, a distinctive characteristic of Baldwin's contribution to studies of black audience reception research is his ability "to embrace the contradictions that characterize black spectatorship and couch them in terms of a collective, urban experience." Stewart's comprehensive study focuses primarily on black spectatorship in an American context, though she rightly suggests that "much historical and theoretical work remains to be done on black spectatorship in its many historical and geographical contexts (beyond the urban North)."[4]

Due to *Devil*'s testimonial nature, any engagement with it as an approach to film reception theory must take into account its emotional edges as well as Baldwin's deeper engagement with relations among history, memory, and dream. The essay is a vital part of the broader social critique of American society so crucial to Baldwin's corpus. Against the backdrop of a racially troubled America, the essay focuses on the evolution of Baldwin's memories and his cinematic imagination as he matures.[5] Ryan Friedman notes that Baldwin established a balance of theoretical perspectives from which to read films as texts with ethical dimensions in *Devil*, a technique that merits greater appreciation than it has received to date.[6]

According to Friedman, Baldwin creates an "oblique analytical perspective, from which he can read a film text's internal contradictions." Friedman argues that *Devil* can be viewed as part of Baldwin's "larger project in his mid-career nonfiction writing, that of deconstructing the 'mythic' consciousness that sustains America's racial categories and hierarchies." With reference to notable film theorists, such as the *Cahiers du cinéma* critics Jean-Louis Comolli and Jean Narboni, Friedman concludes that the "cinema" of Baldwin's mind is rooted in the ability to discern the internal contradictions of Hollywood film language.[7]

Baldwin's critique of classical Hollywood narrative indirectly informs *Devil* since the essay focuses not only on spectator response but also on Baldwin's interest in deconstructing cinematic ideologies. Though Baldwin was not directly engaged with the French New Wave movement, his strategies in *The Devil Finds Work* are similar to the ones employed by French New Wave critics. Beginning in 1958 and extending through the 1960's and beyond, the French New Wave helped to accelerate the evolution of internationally institutionalized film theory. The resultant film theories offered more sophisticated analytical methods than the straightforward film reviews that dominated journalistic writing about film in America in the early to mid-twentieth century.

Another perspective from which to understand Baldwin's approach is that of cinematic excess, as articulated by Kristen Thompson in her article "The Concept of Cinematic Excess". Thompson suggests that the meaning of any given film can extend beyond the meaning of its controlling narrative through its cinematic excess. The spectator's reading of the excess (which has been either consciously or unconsciously inserted into the screen space by the director) allows the spectator to construct multiple and even contradictory meanings. The spectator's newly constructed meanings work "against the grain" of other unifying elements, most notably the narrative or diegetic spaces of the film. As Thompson states, "Each film dictates the way it wants to be viewed by drawing upon certain conventions and ignoring or flouting others. But if the viewer recognizes these conventions and refuses to be bound by them, he/she may strive to avoid having limitations imposed on his/her viewing without an awareness of that imposition."[8]

Both deconstruction of cinematic ideologies and attention to cinematic excess are crucial in Baldwin's film analysis. The study of cinematic language in formal theory equally relies on an awareness of the ideological underpinnings of a film and on how that language enables and enhances the fim's narrative structure. The two main dichotomies structuring my argument thus become intertwined in that Dyer's studies on whiteness are largely linked to cinematic ideologies. By contrast, Bordwell's studies on classical Hollywood cinema are focussed on the structures of cinematic language. To understand the cinematic representation of *Birth of a Nation* requires looking at its contribution to classical Hollywood narrative and it equally requires recognizing the creation of ideological foundations of invisible whiteness, which is part and parcel of the plot of the film.

In his reading of *Birth of a Nation*, Baldwin becomes what Stewart has referred to as a spectator with "reconstructive strategies" who reads the film in more complex ways than as simply "assimilationist identity or as primitive externality or dis-identification."[9] One of the most curious aspects of Baldwin's treatment of Griffith's film is its placement in his essay. The film is not specifically addressed until the second subsection of the essay titled "Who Saw Him Die? I, Said the Fly." After a long discussion of Michel Gast's *I Shall Spit on Your Graves* (1959) and just before an extended analysis of Norman Jewison's *In the Heat of the Night* (1967), Baldwin inserts his analysis of *Birth of a Nation*. An analysis of Gast's film is the subject of Chap. 8 of this book. Baldwin reads Gast's film as a representation both of revenge as a human dream and as Europe's dream of America.[10]

Through the juxtaposition of these three films, Baldwin indirectly suggests that *Birth of a Nation*, an American narrative of human revenge has had its impact not only on Gast's European perspectives on America but also on Jewison's depiction of 1960's US racial conflict. Baldwin ends his analysis of *Birth of a Nation* by turning to the film *In the Heat of the Night*. In claiming that there has been little progress in America's racist history, he asserts that Jewison's 1967 film is a sad justification for Griffith's film and a deceptive representation of the claim that there has been progress in America's fight against racism. In Baldwin's view, the Jewison film is like the descendant of a crime. Baldwin's placement of his review of Griffith's film is crucial in understanding the stakes of his judgment of Griffith. He creates a view of cinematic history through these juxtapositions which suggests that the Hollywood film industry is not at all interested in representing historical progress but is rather more interested in reinforcing white supremacist mythologies. Baldwin's reading of Gast's America-style French film rests on similar assumptions.

Baldwin begins his review of *Birth of a Nation* by referring directly to its source material, Thomas Dixon's *The Clansman* (1905), which he claims he will never read. After mentioning Stuart Heisler's 1952 film *Storm Warning*, which is also about the Ku Klux Klan but is pro-Union rather than pro-Confederacy, Baldwin states that *Storm Warning* is a negligible film in the history of cinema. He equally affirms that Griffith's

Birth of a Nation "is known as one of the great classics of the American cinema; and indeed it is."[11] His implication is nonetheless clear. *Storm Warning* is a film that speaks to the injustice of American white supremacy in a way that *Birth of a Nation* never can.

Like Heisler's film *The Negro Soldier* (1949), *Storm Warning* succeeds as a pre–Civil Rights period film representing America's white supremacist tendencies in all of their intimacies and horror. In the film, Marsha (Ginger Rogers) goes to visit her sister Lucy (Doris Day) and, upon arrival in the small all-American town, witnesses a murder committed by members of the Ku Klux Klan (KKK) (Fig. 2.1). She is able to identify two of the murderers when they remove their hoods (Fig. 2.2). After telling her sister what she has witnessed, she is introduced to her sister's husband Hank (Steve Cochran), whom she recognizes as one of the murderers (Fig. 2.3). In the interest of protecting her sister and having believed Hank's claim that he was simply pulled into something over which he had no control, she remains silent and thus complicit in the murder.

Fig. 2.1 *Storm Warning*, Stuart Heisler, Warner Brothers. Witnessing the Crime 7:33

Fig. 2.2 *Storm Warning*, Stuart Heisler, Warner Brothers. Unmasked and Guilty 8:14

Fig. 2.3 *Storm Warning*, Stuart Heisler, Warner Brothers. The KKK Culprit = the Husband. White Supremacy in the Home 21:23

Through various machinations by the town's district attorney, Burt Rainey (Ronald Reagan), the proof against Hank and other members of the KKK is established but not without Hank's attempted rape of Marsha and the eventual death of Lucy, suggesting that the violence of white supremacy enjoys its own form of revenge against the silent majority afraid to speak up against it. Without belaboring the plot, chaos ensues yet justice is restored. The film explores the extent to which white supremacy is at the heart of small-town America rather than an external force of evil. It is no doubt for this reason that Baldwin differentiates it from *Birth of a Nation*.

It is worth dwelling on the form and content of this film, which is only briefly alluded to by Baldwin prior to his analysis of *Birth of a Nation*. Unlike Griffith's film, Heisler's film "fails" in terms of its place in cinema history because it sacrifices form to content. It offers a brutal appraisal of how American white supremacy functioned in these small-town contexts. Baldwin's claim just after referencing this film is that *Birth of a Nation* succeeds where *Storm Warning* fails due to the Griffith film's innovative creation of a form that both promotes and also protects and reinforces supremacist mythologies.

Baldwin's claim is somewhat buried in the deeper pain most likely to be felt by a black spectator of *Birth of a Nation* in that it clearly separates form from content and does not denigrate the form of the film despite its objectionable content. Baldwin equally remarks that the power of Griffith's film is to be found in its images. He states that the film "has the Niagara force of an obsession."[12] Baldwin therefore cannot be held accountable for rejecting the film on the basis of its ideological content, which is an affront to himself as a black spectator.

Just as with Baldwin's insistence on juxtaposing *Birth of a Nation* with *I Shall Spit on Your Graves* and *In the Heat of the Night*, his passing reference to *Storm Warning* is crucial. Baldwin's next move in the analysis of Griffith's film is to distinguish between the story and the plot. He specifies that a story has a necessity to *reveal* whereas a story has nothing to hide. Any responsibility for the resolution of a story lies with the spectator. The resolution of the story depends on how the spectator contends with the questions the story has evoked. By contrast, Baldwin asserts that a plot must seek resolution and must prove a point. Before speaking directly to *Birth of a Nation* and its participation in either story or plot, Baldwin contrasts *In the Heat of a Night*, a film that requires a plot, with *The Defiant Ones* (1958), which he claims "attempts to tell a story."[13]

The division between story and plot is crucial for understanding Baldwin's analysis of Griffith's film, as are the specific comparative examples he provides. Other examples in these distinctions are the *story* of Job and the *plot* of the biblical account of Joseph and his many brothers. Baldwin claims that the account of Joseph is an elaborate plot of revenge skillfully hidden behind the details involving Joseph's coat. These details cloak that revenge through an emphasis on Joseph's kind treatment of his brothers after they have attempted to leave him for dead. Baldwin suggests that none of them, neither Joseph nor the brothers, will ever forget their attempt to kill him, and thus the chances of this episode being repeated are high. The episode cannot be forgotten, and it cannot be forgiven, no matter how much the plot seems to suggest that it can be.

By using this specific contrast, Baldwin suggests that plots can be used in the distortion of histories, and his follow-up to his analysis of *Birth of a Nation* precisely suggests that even though *In the Heat of the Night* is a film made fifty years after Griffith's film, it contains a plot that repeats the ideological pain and ugliness of the 1915 film. What Baldwin suggests is hidden behind the plot of Griffith's film is an "elaborate justification for mass murder."[14] Through a very incomplete and sardonic summary of the plot, Baldwin suggests that the "film is concerned with the Reconstruction, and how the birth of the Ku Klux Klan overcame that dismal and mistaken chapter in our-American-history."[15]

The dismal chapter to which Baldwin refers is the Civil War, and though he is somewhat tongue-in-cheek in his description of how the war plays itself out, he does specify that the apologetics of the film is rooted in trying to assert the myth of the Lost Cause and the victimization of Southern whites. What is more important in this observation is that Baldwin reminds readers that this is not a plot about the Southern whites' history; it is rather a story about *our American* history. He concludes his assessment of the film by suggesting that the plot of the film is ultimately dependent on the damage caused not by the n***er but rather by the mulatto.

According to Baldwin, the mulattoes are driven by their lust for whites. Due to the hysterical hatred of these mulattoes by whites, the film presents us with "the spectacle of a noble planet brought to such a pass that even their loyal slaves are subverted."[16] In order to save these defeated slaves, the violated social order must be restored, a need echoed by one of the main tenets of the myth of the Lost Cause, which asserts that slave owners were benevolent and protective of their slaves.

A question that Baldwin claims the film cannot concern itself with, given its dependence on a labyrinthine plot that cannot allow for much questioning, is one about the origins of the mulatto. He suggests through an etymology of the word that "mulatto" is linked to the concept of the mule, which he specifies is defined as a sterile animal. He further asserts that possible reasons for the absolute hatred of the mulattoes by whites in *Birth of a Nation* has ultimately to do with America and its shame about its mulatto children who were "proof of abandonment to savage, heathen passion."[17] Baldwin concludes by suggesting that America's history of self-destruction is linked to this shame. His observations about such self-destruction are tied not to the white forefathers but rather to *our* fathers.

Baldwin shifts his analysis from *Birth of a Nation* to *In the Heat of the Night* at this point in order *directly* to suggest that many films about race in America after Griffith's film are intended to show us the "essential decency" of its plot. *In the Heat of the Night*, he ironically suggests, is a film intended as a sign of progress. It is a proof that the maintenance of the social order dependent on the privileging of American white supremacy is crucial to our sense of identity. Baldwin insists that he cannot lay the blame for this unfortunate reinforcement of the message of Griffith's film on the makers of *In the Heat of the Night*; he can only state that the film is proof that Americans are a people trapped in a legend. That legend is one born and bred in Hollywood, according to his critique. By so carefully distinguishing between story and plot throughout his critiques of both films, Baldwin also reinforces the idea that Griffith's contribution to cinematic narrative has not been challenged by Jewison's film.

One last point made by Baldwin in the closing sections of his review of Jewison's film is truly chilling. Again by focusing on the need for plot, Baldwin points out that it is the widow of the rich businessman who has been murdered in this small Southern town who insists that Virgil Tibbs, the black Northern policeman, be put in charge of the investigation. Tibbs was originally gratuitously accused of the murder since he was a strange black man visiting a small Southern town when the murder occurred, and therefore he was the most likely suspect. The racial injustice or profiling against him, according to Baldwin's logic, masks the fact that the wealthy widow is obeyed only because she is wealthy and white. Because the town stands to profit from her promise to invest in the town's industries, following in the footsteps of her deceased husband, her wishes are granted. Baldwin asks the seriously dangerous question that reveals the fragility of black-white relations undergirding the film: What if she had asked that this man be accused and sentenced for this murder instead of having a full investigation of the crime carried out?

When Baldwin raises this question about the wishes of the widow he underscores the film's similarity to its 1915 counterpart, which is that blacks are still at the mercy of the whims of powerful whites. Fortunately in *In the Heat of the Night*, the wife's wishes work in Virgil Tibbs' favor but it could just as well have been otherwise. But Baldwin intimates that the film cannot ask this question and the spectator seeking progress in American racial relations wants to avoid considering the flip side of the widow's power. Because she is white and wealthy, she can condemn or save the black man. He equally suggests that her power and her identity are rooted in her visible whiteness. Baldwin notes that "the question of identity is a question involving the most profound panic—a terror as primary as the nightmare of the mortal fall" and suggests that "[a]n identity is questioned only when it is menaced, as when the mighty begin to fall or when the wretched begin to rise."[18] Baldwin echoes Stewart's accounts of black spectatorship, where characters such as Bigger Thomas in *Native Son* and Pauline in *The Bluest Eye* confront their own terrors on the screen.[19] Stewart asserts that identity formation for these characters is intricately tied up with their viewing experiences just as Baldwin's identity is shown to be shaped by the films he watched.

Baldwin's essay also traces what Kaja Silverman refers to as the lack of suture afforded to a black American when viewing films portraying characters with whom he was not invited to identify.[20] At a time when Hollywood was producing only white heroes or loathsome representations of blacks, none of whom was heroic, a preadolescent black boy had very few characters on the silver screen with whom he could connect in terms of racial identity. His reality and the reality of the movies were not only worlds apart; they were on a collision course that always ended in a confirmation of the myth of white supremacy. When viewing *In the Heat of the Night*, Baldwin concludes that the film shows that it is a terrible thing to "be trapped in one's history" and that it most decidedly proves that "white Americans have been encouraged to keep dreaming, and black Americans have been enticed to wake up."[21]

Devil chronicles Baldwin's mastery over the disjunction between his viewing experience and the expectations that were targeted by narratives in the films to which he was taken as a child. It does so in prescient ways that allow Baldwin to speak about the human condition and its past, present, and future dangers. His later adult viewing experiences were no doubt informed by these early childhood excursions. As he observes, "The people of *In the Heat of the Night* can be considered moving and pathetic only if one has the luxury of an assurance that no one will ever be at their mercy. And that *no one in the world has the luxury of this assurance is beginning to be clear: all over the world.*"[22] By looking *in* to the cinema of his mind, he is able to speak powerfully about the world and its controlling ideologies. As he states, "[I]t is claimed that the camera cannot lie, but rarely do we allow it to do anything else, since the camera sees what you point it at: the camera sees what you want it to see. The language of the cinema is the language of our dreams."[23]

Just as James Agee refers to the images in *Birth of a Nation* as capturing a collective dream, Baldwin pointedly remarks that the collective dream cannot be shared by all Americans due to the racial tensions the film evokes. Collective dreams, as understood by Agee, appear increasingly linked to Baldwin's discussions of mythologies, which work to exclude the black man from America's histories and, by extension, from its cinematic language. In essence, Baldwin insists that the narrative of the films he analyzes, insofar as they are controlled by the ideologies of white supremacy, can *claim* to present racial progress in their narratives. But the *visual* image as experienced by someone like himself for whom those ideologies are unacceptable can always give truth to the lie. He notes that "[t]his observation [i.e., that blacks must say "I cannot believe what you say because I see what you do"] ... denies, simply, the validity of the legend which is responsible for these films; films which exist for the sole purpose of perpetuating the legend."[24]

According to Baldwin, authentic depictions of racial progress were indeed rare in the films he viewed and that he reviewed in *The Devil Finds Work*. His disparagement deeply informs his reading of *Birth of a Nation*. He does however suggest that Fritz Lang's film *You Only Live Once* (1937) is one that spoke to him. In a sense, he intimates that a German-born filmmaker from outside Hollywood circles might have a chance at breaking through the strongholds of supremacist mythologies on Hollywood filmmaking technique. Though his argument about Lang's filmmaking does not suggest that Lang will blatantly betray Hollywood methods, Baldwin does assert that Lang's European methods allow for a certain visibility of whiteness not found in mainstream films made by American filmmakers. This is primarily due, according to the logic of his argument, to the fact that Lang himself is a stranger to *American* white supremacy but also recognizes how it mirrors the supremacist values of his native country.

Baldwin asserts that *You Only Live Once* is the epitome of Lang's Hollywood filmmaking career because in this film Lang begins to figure out his American audience. *You Only Live Once* is devoid of any direct commentary on *racial* relations in America, but it rang true to Baldwin concerning obstacles facing the black man in twentieth-century America. "The premise of *You Only Live Once* is that Eddie Taylor (Henry Fonda) is an ex-convict who wants to go 'straight' but this apparently banal situation is thrust upon us with so heavy a hand that one is forced—as I was, even so long ago—to wonder if one is resisting the film or resisting the truth".[25] More important, the film intimates that the only honest way for European directors to contribute to a discussion of race in America was through the creation of racial allegories. The same argument might be made about Jean Renoir's use of American material, to which I turn in Chap. 7.

Baldwin intuits the racial allegory when watching *You Only Live Once*. It was Baldwin who made the leap from gangster to "n***er," whether Lang intended that connection to be made or not.[26] Baldwin's exposure to Lang's use of the gangster to approximate the life of the "n***er" was an identification that influenced him greatly. Baldwin claims to have appreciated Lang's faithful application of the gangster genre while still creating an interface of meanings with which he himself could identify.

Baldwin's positive response to the film must be weighed against his rejection of Jewison's film *Heat* as a purportedly progressive critique of American racism. Baldwin implies that the direct treatment of racial issues, as represented in Jewison's film, was nowhere near as precise as Lang's treatment of violence and injustice in *You Only Live Once* when he claims that viewing Jewison's film "demands one's complicity in a lie: which state of affairs, having gone beyond progress, is sometimes called brotherhood, the achievement of which state of grace is exactly what *In the Heat of the Night* imagines itself to be about."[27]

Despite the fact that *In the Heat of the Night* is an overt depiction of racial tensions in the late 1960s, Baldwin's argument is that it portrays the dream of the self-satisfied white viewing population rather than that of the liberated black viewer. Baldwin's position is that the intended effect of *Heat* is to "increase and not lessen white confusion and complacency, and black rage and despair." The film "helplessly conveys—without confronting—the anguish of people trapped in a legend."[28]

In his article on Richard Wright's fascination with the criminal image and black manhood, a fascination shared by other public intellectuals in the 1940s, Maurice Wallace suggests as well that "[t]he picture is always subject to reproducing ideational blinds spots."[29] Capturing the essence of the criminal in the photographic or cinematographic shot of the black man would, according to Wallace's paraphrase of Heidegger, be necessarily read differently by the white and the black viewer. Baldwin suggests that such is the case with the film *Heat*. In the final moments of the film, the white Southern sheriff and the black Northern policeman say good-bye in a way that "speaks of reconciliation, of all things now becoming possible"— a moment Baldwin reads as inauthentic and unreal.[30] Despite their many differences, certain points of agreement between the writings of Baldwin and Agee can be discerned in this observation in that both black Harlemite and white Southern intellectual knew that progress in racial affairs in America faced insurmountable obstacles.

Though attempts by Wright and others to showcase a study of the hegemonic vision controlling relations between the criminal and black manhood did not come to fruition, according to Wallace, the *failure* of the project is consistent with Baldwin's judgment of *Heat*. Baldwin's analysis of the ending of the film implies that the white viewer's understanding of the triumph of Virgil Tibb (Sidney Poitier) would not accord with the viewing perspective of a black spectator. As a result of deeply entrenched ideational blind spots on both sides of the viewing population, Poitier's "friendship" with the small town police chief (Rod Steiger) could only be seen as falsely hopeful. Baldwin rightly names it as a stereotypical fade-out kiss for the standard Hollywood buddy film.

That Baldwin identified more with Lang's depiction of the white gangster subjected to social injustice than he did with a Hollywood narrative of a forced "friendship" between a black policeman and a white one shows his resistance to some intentions of the filmmakers and his acceptance of others according to his "knowledge and cultural tradition" both about race and about generic conventions.[31] Baldwin's memoir is thus a record of the resistances and recognitions of cinematic codes and their intentions. He articulates tensions between narrative structure and screen space in the context of social and racial injustice. His analysis of *Birth of a Nation* lacks any discussion of identification, and despite his pronouncement that the film is indeed valuable for American cinematic history, there is no even approximate way, if we follow his analysis, that the black spectator can identify with any of the characters on the screen.

Studying the internal contradictions of a Hollywood film is facilitated by recourse to genre analysis where camera codes and unifying functions of the film are strongly indicated. In Baldwin's imagination, Lang was able to pinpoint the undeniable obstacles to progress for the "n***ger" though his structural application of the gangster genre. As previously mentioned, though *You Only Live Once* does not take up racial injustice as a specific theme, Baldwin asserts that in the film Lang reveals painful truths about *American* injustice. Baldwin equally claims that Lang's representations of American injustice resonated with his own feelings about racial injustice from which he suffered in his everyday life. Speaking of some of the real people in his life who had suffered from racial injustice just as he had, he claimed that they were "now being murdered by my fellow Americans ... my countrymen were my enemy, and I had already begun to hate them from the bottom of my heart."[32]

Lang began his career in the United States with an urgent need to work through his own demons—those imposed by his precipitate exit from Germany at the end of the Weimar Republic and at the beginning of the Third Reich. As Baldwin notes, Lang's alienation, both from Germany in the early 1930s and from America upon his arrival in Hollywood in 1934, began with his study of mob violence in the film *Fury* (1936). Baldwin criticizes this film for its inability to say anything about America since he considers that Lang has not yet been able to extract himself from the *connotative* issues of Nazi Germany even though his *denotative* narrative is placed in middle America. "Lang's is the fury of the film, but his grasp of the texture of American life is still weak: he has not really left Germany."[33] The mob depicted by Lang in the film is accurately conveyed, according to Baldwin, but Lang's hatred of the members of the mob remains unreal.

Based on his viewing of Lang's later film *You Only Live Once*, Baldwin concludes that "we were all n***ers in the thirties [in America]" and "Lang's indictment of the small faceless people ... who are society" articulates American guilt and suffering with precision and communicates its resonance for victims of American racism. Unlike *In the Heat of the Night*, despite the absence of actual black characters, there is room for the black spectator to identify with Eddie Taylor, according to Baldwin's interpretation of what is happening on the screen. Of Eddie's question about why should *he* not try to kill *them* before *they* try to kill *him*, Baldwin says, "I understood that: it was a real question. I was living with that question."[34] For if there was one truth for the 1930s black man, it was that the American dream was unattainable, and happiness as an implicit outcome to attaining the American dream was a key component for the gangster genre.

If one adheres to the premise of Robert Warshow in his article "The Gangster as Tragic Hero" (1948), the American gangster aspires to the happiness of the American dream. The gangster is able to accept the impossibility of such happiness only once he tragically realizes that he can never overcome the dictates of his role *within the context of the American dream*. Warshow's thesis is that the gangster is the cinematic code for a man who knows that the American dream is his *only* if he transgresses the boundaries that have been set for him and in so doing paradoxically forfeits his right to happiness.[35] Though Lang wisely did not consider himself capable of making a film about race from the authentic perspective of the American black man, he did grasp the rules of the gangster genre and, according to Baldwin, Lang followed them in order to represent the dubious chance at happiness offered to American blacks. Lang represented this hard truth in ways that struck Baldwin's imagination dramatically. As previously discussed, opportunities for happiness offered to the black man in *Birth of a Nation* lies in the plot's claim that a necessary social order which privileges white supremacy has been restored by the end of the film. The film righteously claims to restore a sense of place for the Negro who has been victimized throughout the film by the ravages of mulattoes. Unfortunately, this is a bleak notion of happiness, and it echoes Baldwin's perspective in his poem "Imagination," which is that "imagination creates the situation and then the situation creates the imagination."[36]

Though *Birth of a Nation* predates the Motion Picture Production Code, which was instituted in 1930, it met with plenty of resistance and with calls for censorship from viewers. The production code (popularly known as the Hays Code after William H. Hays who was fundamental in its establishment) essentially formalized questions of spectatorship and the moral purpose of the cinema that are implicit in Baldwin's film critiques. According to Koepnick, the US production codes explicitly signaled film as *the* art form that could "speak to the cultivated and to the uneducated."[37] The Code's rules and regulations imply that the motion picture industry had an obligation to self-censorship when speaking to uneducated and thus potentially vulnerable spectators. Baldwin indeed suggests in *Devil* that he was perhaps vulnerable in his early viewing experiences. Unfortunately, according to Melvyn Stokes, the NAACP did indeed begin to appeal to Will Hays as early as 1921 to speak out against Griffith's film when Hays was chairman of the Motion Picture Producers and Distributors of America. As Stokes points out, the NAACP's appeal did not go too far since Hays was himself an admirer of Griffith's film.[38]

For Baldwin, watching films at such an early age gave his imagination access to moral perspectives on cinematic genres and on the American society as viewed by Hollywood as well as by émigré filmmakers such as Lang. Baldwin suggests throughout his commentary on Lang's work that the moral weight of Lang's films did not escape his attention. Baldwin's analysis of *You Only Live Once* in turn forms part of the moral project that Friedman suggests is a crucial aspect of *Devil*. In his analysis of *Birth of a Nation* as well, Baldwin's comments on the moral dimensions of the film precede any comments he makes on the form of the film. Despite his distaste for the moral content of Griffith's film, Baldwin is well aware of the ways in which the director was able to wed form with content and thereby create a fusion of American white supremacy mythologies with cinematic language in Hollywood. This set a precedent for film history that was partially formalized in the production code.

The moral dimensions of the code play a role in determining the relations between the myth and the reality depicted in film. As Friedman points out, "[For] Baldwin the medium of film is crucial insofar as it can dramatize the tensions between mythic and real consciousness."[39] Baldwin ends *Devil* by expressing his concerns about the audience: "When I saw the film again [*The Exorcist*, 1973] I was most concerned with the audience. I wondered what they were seeing and what it meant to them."[40] His life of filmgoing and conscious calculation about his responsibility to defeat the world's intentions for black spectators had come full circle.

The interplay of myth and history is indeed one of the central moral tensions for Griffith's film which Stokes analyses extensively in his history of the film. Griffith's claim that his film was grounded in historic realities rather than in the myths of supremacy he was developing in it was questionable. Griffith's desire to contribute to a controlling narrative over Americans' memory of the Civil War went relatively uncontested in 1915.[41] Had the Hays Code been in effect, Griffith might indeed have been faulted for making a film that actively encouraged whites to join the KKK.

As it turned out, the film allowed white spectators to play out fantasies of revenge against blacks and reinforced white supremacist views. Spectators felt enabled based on their viewing of a purportedly realistic representation of the history leading up to the Civil War and its aftermath. One of the general principles of the Hays Code was that "the sympathy of the audience should never be thrown to the side of crime, wrongdoing, evil or sin."[42] Baldwin faults Griffith not for consciously flouting this code but for creating a trap of history by having his audience identify with the

Ku Klux Klan. Griffith's celebration of the Klan reinforces the ideological beliefs in white privilege created by the Lost Cause myth that still holds sway today.[43] Since for Baldwin the Klan is necessarily seen as an evil and misguided group, the implication is that to incite sympathy for them is equally misguided and goes against the dictates of the Code.

Baldwin intimates throughout his analysis of *You Only Live Once* that Lang avoids the trap of history. He equally implies that *Birth of a Nation* constructs one of the many traps of American cinematic history, as is attested to in his observation that *In the Heat of the Night* cannot free itself from this particular snare. For Baldwin, reading the cinema of his mind hinges on not being trapped into reductive readings of Hollywood films or of reproducing Hollywood films that are there to victimize the spectator. As he puts it, "[T]he film cannot accept—because it cannot use—this simplicity. The victim who is able to articulate the situation of the victim has ceased to be a victim: he, or she, has become a threat."[44] The film viewer *can* make a difference. Baldwin's rejection of Griffith's *Birth* and Jewison's *Heat* is not simply a rejection of their messages but a rejection of their senses of history as well.

According to Baldwin, if *Heat* is a revisitation of the racist film *Birth of a Nation*, it proves that not much had changed for native-born white Americans in the fifty-two years that passed between the two films. The fact that *Heat* film escapes scrutiny from the Hays Code is partly due to the fact that the code was disbanded in 1968 but also, and more important, because the similarity of its message to that of the 1915 film remains masked to a certain extent under a cloak of progress or invisible whiteness.

While Baldwin dismisses the idea that the creators are acting out of base motives—"I do not wish to be guilty of the gratuitous injustice of seeming to impute base motives to the people responsible for its [the film's] existence"—he does assert that they, unlike Lang, failed to understand the implications of their own historical moment: "The history which produces such a film cannot, after all, be swiftly understood, nor can the effects of this history be easily resolved. Nor can this history be blamed on any single individual; but at the same time, no one can be let off the hook."[45]

Baldwin wrote *Devil* because he felt he had the responsibility to defeat the world's expectations for black spectators, and thus his book-essay anticipates an increasing attention to the invisibility of privileged whiteness in the Hollywood industry. In writing, he comes to terms with his own historical moment and with his moral obligations, as Friedman suggests. As Friedman states, "If what Baldwin fears comes to pass, then the society as a whole will become trapped in despair and myth: it will be without hope and unable to use its past."[46] In other words, Baldwin's filmgoing serves a moral purpose, and just as perhaps only Lang could have made the film *You Only Live Once* as a way of exorcising his engagement with Nazism, only Baldwin could have provided the perspective one discovers in *Devil*.

In *The Devil Finds Work*, Baldwin stated that one of the most important ways in which he could defeat the terrible and crushing blow of America's whitewashed sense of history was something he began to discover by going to the movies on that first Saturday afternoon, an event that he soon realized was an entrance into the cinema of his mind. Like Kracauer's study of a Germany that gives way to the Nazi regime, Baldwin's essay illuminates how the mythologies of America came to control classical Hollywood narrative language. Baldwin also provides a key to reading Hollywood cinematic language from outside the boundaries of privileged whiteness and of Hollywood studio production. The remaining chapters in this book explore that potential from varying strategic perspectives. Baldwin's prescient perspective is indeed relevant and potentially applicable to a broader global context, as subsequent chapters explore.

NOTES

1. James Baldwin, *The Devil Finds Work* (New York: Dial, 1976), 78.
2. Susan B. Courtney, *Hollywood Fantasies of Miscegenation: Spectacular Narratives of Gender and Race, 1903–1967* (Princeton, NJ: Princeton University Press, 2005), 50–99.
3. Siegfried Kracauer, *From Caligari to Hitler: A Psychological History of the German Film* (Princeton, NJ: Princeton University Press, 1947), 5.
4. Jacqueline Stewart, "Negroes Laughing at Themselves?: Black Spectatorship and the Performance of Urban Modernity," *Critical Inquiry* 29, no. 4 (2003): 650–677. 677.
5. In some cases, Baldwin insists on a very jarring use of the present tense: "I am about seven. I am with my mother or my aunt" (3). In other cases, there is as much description given to the *conditions* in which he was viewing a film as there is to the analysis of the film itself. Of his viewing experiences during the McCarthy era, he states, "I wandered, then, in my confusion and isolation—for almost all the friends I had were in trouble, and therefore, in one way or another, *incommunicado*—into a movie, called *My Son John*. And I will never forget it" (104).
6. Ryan Jay Friedman, "'Enough Force to Shatter the Tale to Fragments': Ethics and Textual Analysis in James Baldwin's Film Theory," *ELH: Journal of English Literary History* 77, no. 2 (2010): 385–412.

7. Friedman, "'Enough Force to Shatter the Tale to Fragments,'" 391.
8. Kristen Thompson, "The Concept of Cinematic Excess," in Leo Braudy and Marshall Cohen, eds., *Film Theory and Criticism*, 5th ed. (Oxford: Oxford University Press, 1999), 487–498.
9. Stewart, "Negroes Laughing at Themselves?," 673.
10. Baldwin, *The Devil Finds Work*, 53.
11. Baldwin, *The Devil Finds Work*, 53.
12. Baldwin, *The Devil Finds Work*, 53.
13. Baldwin, *The Devil Finds Work*, 53.
14. Baldwin, *The Devil Finds Work*, 54.
15. Baldwin, *The Devil Finds Work,* 56.
16. Baldwin, *The Devil Finds Work*, 59.
17. Baldwin, *The Devil Finds Work*, 60.
18. Baldwin, *The Devil Finds Work*, 93.
19. Stewart. "Negroes Laughing at Themselves?," 677.
20. Kaja Silverman, "On Suture," in Braudy and Cohen, eds., *Film Theory and Criticism*, 5th ed., 137–147.
21. Baldwin, *The Devil Finds Work*, 69.
22. Baldwin, *The Devil Finds Work*, 69; emphasis added.
23. Baldwin, *The Devil Finds Work*, 41.
24. Baldwin, *The Devil Finds Work*, 71.
25. Baldwin, *The Devil Finds Work*, 28.
26. Baldwin, *The Devil Finds Work*, 28.
27. Baldwin, *The Devil Finds Work*, 62.
28. For a more complete discussion of Norman Jewison's intentions in making the film and how it reflects on the representation of the "Negro problem," see Alice Mikal Craven, "*In the Heat of the Night*: Teaching the American Nightmare to the World," *Tamkang Review* 35 (2005): 3–4. In this article, I argue that the film can be read as a critique of the economic conditions controlling the reconstruction of the South in relation to the soft drink industry and that such an argument requires looking at how the filmmakers adapted John Ball's original novel *In the Heat of the Night* in order to focus explicitly on that industry. Baldwin was no doubt unaware of the novel or does not suggest that he has read it in *The Devil Finds Work*. The quotations cited here from *The Devil Finds Work* are from pages 65–67.
29. Maurice Wallace, "I'm Not Entirely What I Look Like: Richard Wright, James Baldwin, and the Hegemony of Vision; or, Jimmy's FBEye Blues," in Dwight A. McBride, ed., *James Baldwin Now* (New York: New York University Press, 1999), 289–306. 290.
30. Baldwin, *The Devil Finds Work*, 67.
31. Thompson, "The Concept of Cinematic Excess," 490.
32. Baldwin, *The Devil Finds Work*, 22.

33. Baldwin, *The Devil Finds Work*, 27.
34. Baldwin, *The Devil Finds Work*, 27–30.
35. Robert Warshow, "The Gangster as Tragic Hero," in Leo Braudy and Marshall Cohen, eds., *Film Theory and Criticism*, 7th ed. (Oxford: Oxford University Press, 2009), 576–579.
36. *Jimmy's Blues: Selected Poems by James Baldwin* (London: Michael Joseph, 1983).
37. Lutz Koepnick, *The Dark Mirror: German Cinema Between Hitler and Hollywood* (Berkeley: University of California Press, 2002), 138.
38. Melvyn Stokes, *D. W. Griffith's The Birth of a Nation: A History of "the Most Controversial Motion Picture of All Time"* (Oxford: Oxford University Press, 2007), 239.
39. Friedman. "'Enough Force to Shatter the Tale to Fragments,'" 386.
40. Baldwin, *The Devil Finds Work*, 142.
41. It must be noted that though there was plenty of protest about the film, as is chronicled by Everett, it nonetheless is still recognized as one of the landmarks of cinema history.
42. A transcript of the Hays Code can be found on the website of Arts Reformation. www.artsreformation.com.
43. At the time of this writing, the debate concerning the need to destroy or preserve Confederate monuments is an active source of violent racial clashes across the American landscape. The most dramatic clash thus far occurred during the Charlottesville protests, which resulted in the death of Heather Heyer.
44. Baldwin, *The Devil Finds Work*, 134.
45. Baldwin, *The Devil Finds Work*, 67–68.
46. Friedman, "'Enough Force to Shatter the Tale to Fragments,'" 403.

CHAPTER 3

"A Monstrous Wrong": James Agee and the Miraculous *Birth of a Nation*

The South seems to be the myth that both most consciously asserts whiteness and most devastatingly undermines it.
—*Richard Dyer*

Anything that comes out of the South is going to be called grotesque by the Northern reader, unless it is grotesque, in which case it is going to be called realistic.
—*Flannery O'Connor*

James Agee's high praise of D. W. Griffith's film *Birth of a Nation* masks his enduring guilt about his inability to speak effectively to America's racial discord.[1] Many commentators base their critique of *Birth* on several fundamental positions that are keys to appreciating Agee's review of the film. One common critical position is that the film is more concerned with the reunion of Southern and Northern Whites in the face of the sexual and violent aggression of the "Negro" and, more particularly, the mulatto, which is a vital aspect of Baldwin's critique of the film, as discussed in Chap. 2.

The film is therefore a reassertion of the privilege of whiteness and the need to establish this privilege through the unprecedented cinematic storytelling techniques initiated by Griffith. These techniques have indelibly marked American film history. Michael Rogin traces the techniques to be found in earlier Griffith films and their contributions to

© The Author(s) 2018
A. M. Craven, *Visible and Invisible Whiteness*,
https://doi.org/10.1007/978-3-319-76777-2_3

Griffith's "racist epic" from which American cinema is born.[2] The only way to appreciate the film is to separate its form from its admittedly offensive racial content, though this approach is precisely at the root of the controversies concerning the film's reception history.

Daniel Bernardi suggests that to separate form and content is the mistake that ultimately grounds *Birth* as a building block for Hollywood filmmaking technique. Melvyn Stokes's overview of this trend in *Birth* criticism is thus crucial in showing how this early impulse in analyzing the film became definitive for cinema history.[3] The trend toward regarding the film as a technical classic stems from as early as 1935, when members of the NAACP became alarmed at various nontheatrical venues that were regularly offering showings of *Birth* as part of cultural events scheduling. Examples include the Young Men's Hebrew Association or, even more threatening, the decision by Dean Ned H. Dearborn of New York University to allow *Birth* to be included in a series of films to be shown in an adult film class in 1938. Though there was some back and forth on this issue, the professor of the course, Robert R. Gessner, finally informed the NAACP that the film would be shown, but only for its technical and historical importance.[4] Gessner assured the NAACP that he would stress the film's objectionable racial content before it was shown.

Moves toward displaying *Birth* on the basis of its technical merit alone became increasingly standard with instances such as the Stone Film Library in New York which enabled local schools wishing to show "this film classic of the Civil War" in 1938.[5] This separation of form from content continued to be standardized with the institutionalization of film studies programs in universities. *Birth* is common fare in many introductory film courses in U.S. universities today. With respect to technical innovation and the evolution of cinematic narrative techniques, a brief survey of critiques of the film from filmmakers such as René Clair and Charlie Chaplin suggests that the film was definitive in shaping cinematic language and the classical Hollywood narrative, despite its racist themes. Both of these directors are cited in Agee's critique of the film.

A common critical approach is that the film's reassertion of the privilege of white supremacy is the real focus of a narrative written, directed, and promoted by Southerners Thomas Dixon, Griffith, and Woodrow Wilson. According to Stokes, Wilson facilitated the film's popularity, notably by hosting a private showing of the film at the White House as president. According to these three influential figures involved in the film's making and reception, it would be erroneous to consider *Birth* to be dangerously racist except in an unconscious way.[6] As discussed earlier, in considering

Baldwin's assessment of the film, it is indeed the case that the film's reassertion of the supremacist social order was intended to be not only in the service of the white characters but also for the "sake of the dignity of this temporarily defeated people and out of a vivid and loving concern for their betrayed and endangered slaves."[7] Though one can detect Baldwin's ironic tone in this remark, it is not far from the reverent beliefs of these key Southerners in their representation of their homeland.[8]

Stokes suggests that such a feeble excuse can hardly mitigate protests against the film's racist premises and its ability to incite spectators and rejuvenate membership in the Ku Klux Klan. In keeping with those spectator responses, it is difficult to read beneath the surface of Agee's enthusiastic review of the film. The focus of this chapter is on Agee's *ostensible* inability to come to terms with the film's racist content. Close analysis of his review supports the idea that his position can ultimately be differentiated from that of Griffith, Dixon, and Wilson and perhaps other defenders of the film. The idea that these figures and other defenders are in some way displaying overtly racist attitudes is rejected by them in their defense of Southern whiteness and the privileging of said whiteness. Agee's analysis nonetheless borders on a form of "unconscious patronage," a term that serves as an alternative to the concept of invisible whiteness. Agee even uses the term in his review of Jean Renoir's *The Southerner*, and it is apt when considering *Birth* as well. In the case of *The Southerner*, Agee offers it as a gentle reprimand for Renoir's lack of total command over his understanding of the Southern tenant farmer represented in the 1945 film, which is the focus for Chap. 7.

Aesthetic and historical analyses of *Birth of a Nation*'s production history, reception history, influence, and intent are abundant. This chapter contextualizes Agee's criticism in relation to the larger critical history of the film and analyzes what exactly Agee's comments on the film reveal about the Southern intellectual's response to Griffith's "epic tragic" masterpiece. One premise of this contextualization is that Agee's film reviews predate formal theoretical debates about the contrast between classical Hollywood narrative and European art cinema. His reviews nonetheless anticipate some of the key issues of that debate.

Agee was a Southern white American author, poet, scriptwriter, and film critic. The separation of aesthetic form and racist content with respect to Griffith's film could be more easily expected in the time in which he was writing, though it is not clear that he really did wish to take that easy way out. Agee wrote in a pre–Civil Rights age. Even so, his review of the film is written a full ten years after debates had been publicly played out about Griffith's technical prowess versus the film's dangerous racist content had been played out. Agee was well aware of these debates, as can be seen in his review. Nonetheless, to see him as a champion of a pure separation of form and content as an excuse for praising the film would be misleading. Such an argument risks serious oversimplification of his intent in assessing Griffith's work. It also fails to appreciate fully his understanding of racial relations in the American South. Keys to a deeper understanding of Agee's intent can be discerned through a comparative examination of his review of *Birth* and his other writings. Many of his essays, notes, letters, and texts are directly or indirectly concerned with the racially inflected issues that plague Griffith's film.

Agee's reviews of other films that engage with racial themes, including those coming from the European tradition, suggest that though he praises Griffith's film highly, his formal review of Griffith's *Birth* also hints at the tensions for finding a balanced commentary between a film's artistic form and its social consciousness about race. This concern runs through much of Agee's work. Examples of other films where questions of race discrimination are similar to those encountered in Griffith's *Birth* are discussed in this chapter in order to gain more insight on Agee's precise arguments on visible and invisible whiteness. In a sense, he relies on an invisible whiteness in discussing *Birth*, but Agee's ultimate perspective on the racial content of Griffith's work reads like a reluctant confession. At one and the same time, Agee praises the filmmaker, and as James A. Crank has argued,[9] develops an apologetics for Griffith, essentially asserting that Griffith, like Agee himself, was unable to find meaningful solutions to America's race problems.

By contrast, Baldwin's later critique was a culmination of a large body of works by African American film critics and activists concerning the invisible whiteness that allows the film to escape censure from the perspective of film form versus racist content.[10] Baldwin anticipates the concept of the black spectator who is unable to identify with the characters on the screen, thus emphasizing that subject position and spectator identification came to be a crucial component of the filming techniques of classical Hollywood narrative. Griffith's film sets this need for identification into motion to a large extent.

Notable critics, such as Manthia Diawara, develop critiques of black spectator effect rooted in Laura Mulvey's "Visual Pleasure and Narrative Cinema," as indicated in the opening of his article "Black Spectatorship: Problems of Identification and Resistance."[11] For both Diawara and Mulvey, the ethnic gazes they theorize are equally pitted against the white male gaze of Hollywood studio productions. These seminal theoretical treatments of spectatorship and identification sync well with Baldwin's book-length essay, *The Devil Finds Work*, in which he insists on a visible whiteness that blinds black viewers from appreciating the emotional components of this film.

For white viewers, articulations of whiteness remain invisible as a result of the unconscious or conscious whiteness that informs Hollywood narrative systems. Though many Hollywood films can be considered in light of this dichotomy, *Birth* remains one of the most pertinent examples to analyze and reanalyze due to its unquestionable importance in American film history. As Bernardi and others point out, "[T]he impact that *The Birth of a Nation* had—and continues to have—on cinematic story-telling" should never be minimized.[12]

Yet Agee does seem to challenge the contemporary understanding of the film by appearing to excuse content. He does so through an appeal to innovative form. Like President Wilson and other prominent Southerners, Agee claims that the film is a testimony to the poetic genius of an original filmmaker and is an authentic portrayal of the struggles of the Southern United States in the period of the Civil War and postwar Reconstruction. As many critiques of the early reception of the film recount, not only was the film one of the first to be shown at the White House, it was also praised by Wilson in unqualifiedly positive ways.[13]

Agee's solid support of the film, in line with that of other Southern intellectuals, raises the question of whether his critique of the film or indeed his film criticism in general can be seen as nefariously racist or not. Is it more accurate to see Agee's appreciation of Griffith's film as a deeper engagement with the Southern intellectual's distress over the ambiguous use of Negrophobia in order to reassert white supremacy? Or should it rather be viewed as the critic's blind acceptance that cinematic storytelling of an innovative nature is easily and necessarily separable from the racist content of the film? Griffith establishes that the cinematic storytelling of Hollywood cinema will always rely on a confirmation of invisible whiteness and that this is largely as a result of the extent to which Griffith weds the two inextricably together in this pivotal film.

It would be unwise to read Agee's critiques of D. W. Griffith in only a surface way, as to do so contributes to a perpetuation of Griffith's influence on cinema without a deeper understanding of how that influence might be appreciated. His influence and its role in the Hollywood industry transformed a nascent national cinematic industry. Innovations in cinematic storytelling with respect to race that can be seen in the works of contemporary black filmmakers, such as Lee Daniels, Ava DuVernay, Barry Jenkins, Steve McQueen, and many others, can be further enabled only if one steps back and reexamines how popular film criticism approached supremacist themes and, by extension, issues such as casting and representation of black characters.[14] Even a study of black filmmakers of earlier periods, such as Oscar Micheaux, could be analyzed in alternative ways by considering more deeply to what extent critics such as Agee determined the parameters of spectator response to films based on racial themes.

Parsing Agee's critique of *Birth* uncovers more about the specific whiteness of the South from which this film emerges. In this manner, the film can be put into context and one can question the easy dichotomies between invisible and visible whiteness that control so much of the spectator's response to Hollywood cinema. As Daniel Bernardi remarks in "The Birth of Whiteness: Integrating Race into the Narrator System," the impact that Griffith has had on cinematic storytelling is undermined by segregating "his contribution to the craft of narrative filmmaking from [the film's] racist imagery."[15]

This position resonates with Agee's assessment of the film. W. H. Auden's harsh comment in his October 16, 1944, "Letter to the Editors" of *The Nation* was that it would be a sad day when *Agee on Film* became "the subject of a Ph.D. thesis."[16] Auden's assessment is crucial because there is so much one can misunderstand about Agee's work if one remains controlled by the dichotomies of film form and content or by visible and invisible whiteness. Agee's criticism could be easily misconstrued in this manner. All the more reason to reopen the analysis of his real intent in writing his review of Griffith's film.

AGEE ON *BIRTH OF A NATION* AND D. W. GRIFFITH

David Wark Griffith died on July 23, 1948. Agee's principal writings on Griffith come in the form of a tribute, which reads like an obituary and which was published in *TIME* magazine on August 2, 1948. The second piece of writing is in the form of a film review and was published in *The Nation* on September 4, 1948.[17] In the film review, Agee states that "to watch his [Griffith's] work is like being witness to a melody, or the first conscious use of the lever or the wheel."[18] He stresses that Griffith achieved what no other man has achieved and that one of his greatest gifts was his ability to create permanent images.

If we consider the "permanent image" in the context of the American mythologies discussed in Chap. 2, it is a short leap to attributing these permanent images as *visualizations* of the mythologies in question. Agee's filmmaking collaborations with Helen Levitt, Sidney Meyers, and others, discussed later in this chapter resonate interestingly with his remarks here and with the experiments in the highly visual and unguarded documentary film work in which they were engaged. Simultaneously with his review of *Birth*, Agee was collaborating on *In the Street* (1948) and *The Quiet One* (1948), films that went beyond documentary realism. The films were innovative attempts to create images that could convey meaning in a poetic, lyrical fashion without the need for words. As Joseph Wranovics points out in his "The Makers of *In the Street* and *The Quiet One*," when Helen Levitt was asked to explain what was going on in her photos, her response was "just what you see."[19]

Shades of this filmmaking experience seem to have crept into Agee's critique of Griffith's artistry when he claims that the "most beautiful single shot that I have ever seen in any movie is the battle charge in *Birth of a Nation*."[20] Agee suggests that the shot is like a "collective dream" and argues that it perfectly captures what the Civil War was like for veterans who remembered it but that it could equally serve as the realization of the war for children who might imagine it fifty years from the time of his writing this review. He even insists that when he saw that shot, he felt that his imagination about what the Civil War must have been like had been corroborated.

One important aspect of high praise for this image from the film is that Agee asserts that the image goes beyond realism and nourishes memory and imagination. While he admits that his praise is entirely subjective, he concludes the opening section of his review by claiming that the "deepest and clearest" aspect of Griffith's genius, was capable of "intuitively perceiving and perfecting the tremendous magical images that underlie the memory and imagination of entire peoples." Agee thus appeals to the idea that the images created by Griffith caused spectators to recognize that "art can draw upon" the deepest levels of human imagination and memory.[21]

While Agee suggests and later quotes Charlie Chaplin as stating that the entire Hollywood industry owes its existence to Griffith, he further remarks in this review that Griffith's experience as a filmmaker was also singular in that he worked in an unspoiled medium and for an unspoiled audience.[22] This claim implies that after this point, the industry became spoiled, as did the spectators. There is a particular irony in this position in that it is largely agreed that the filmmaking techniques of the industry were set in place by *Birth* and that, by extension, spectator responses to what was shown on the screen were henceforth controlled by the deep levels of their memory and imagination to which this film appealed. As many argue in the critical appreciation of the film over the years, the acceptance of the invisible whiteness underlying the myths of American white supremacy is one of the givens that the film both promoted and instilled in its audiences across the nation. As discussed earlier, Susan Courtney traces the birth of the Great White Spectator through a close reading of the film and in particular its finale, in "The Mixed Birth of 'Great White Masculinity' and the Classical Spectator."[23]

In the paragraph following Agee's remarks on the dreamlike images of the film, he compares Griffith's films to other fundamental documents of the Civil War, notably the photography of Mathew Brady, known as one of the earliest American photographers of scenes from that war. The similarity between certain images in the film and Brady's photographs borders on the uncanny. Agee also mentions Lincoln's speeches and Walt Whitman's war poems. What is striking is that at this point in American cinema history (1948), the prominence of cinema is uncontested. By placing Griffith's film in context with these eminent figures, Agee seems intent on suggesting that Griffith's film surpasses the expectations of classical Hollywood narrative that it has set in place as a norm and that it joins the ranks of other artistic and indeed patriotic endeavors. Agee ends this comparison by claiming that the film is not the "greatest" but rather the *one* "great epic tragic film." It is equal, he asserts, "to the best work that has been done in this country."[24] That he refers to it as a tragic film is crucial to notice in going beneath the surface of his praise. Though he agreed that the film speaks to a restoration of custom in the Reconstruction South, he still evokes the tragic nature of how racial difference functions within that context.

It appears that Agee deemed such hyperbole necessary, as in the next section of the review he turns explicitly to the controversy surrounding the film. Agee condemns the widespread tendency to boycott the film or to show only excerpts. He laments the fact that so many critics had claimed that Griffith turned the film into an "anti-Negro film." It is in this section of the review that one begins to get a sense of Agee's purpose in announcing that the film is capable of evoking the memory and imagination of entire peoples.

Agee argues that even if it were an anti-Negro film, a position he vehemently rejects, it should still be shown in its entirety. As Stokes, Everett, and others have chronicled, protests against the racism of the film are well documented, and in his book *The Birth of a Nation: A History of "the Most Controversial Film of All Time,"* Stokes features a photograph of one of the many protests against a showing of the film, taken in New York City in 1947. Since Agee's review was written only one year after this historic protest, this image no doubt weighed heavily on Agee when he was writing.[25]

Agee claims that these protests are "vicious nonsense" and that in general protests against Griffith are unjust because the director had gone to "preposterous" lengths to be fair to the Negroes "as he understood them and he understood them as a good type of Southerner does."[26] Agee ends by stating that though he does not necessarily agree with Griffith, he nonetheless thinks that the attacks against Griffith are unwarranted. Agee considers that the desire for fairness on Griffith's part far outweighs the capacity of his critics to be equally fair, honest, understanding, and compassionate when viewing his film.

While it might be tempting to read Agee's position here as an apologist for racial hatred and an advocate for film aesthetics over racist film content, that argument becomes problematic when weighed against his letters to his lifelong friend, Father James Harold Flye, in the years leading up to the 1948 review. As Crank has argued, the letters as well as other unpublished documents attest to the fact that Agee had a very complex understanding of white-black relations in the Southern United States. The most telling letters are from May 15 to September 19, 1945, and involve a discussion begun between Father Flye and Agee on the subject of Donald Davidson's 1945 article in *The Sewanee Review* titled "Preface to Decision."[27]

Agee's essential argument in these letters is that he has sympathy for both sides of a difficult debate. He understands Flye's and Davidson's positions that the rights of a Southern white man are compromised if he is *legally* required *not* to discriminate against a Negro. He also understands and more forcefully supports the idea that every human being has the right not to be discriminated against due to their race or religion. He regards the "right to hate as a deadly wrong."[28] He asserts in his letter of the May 21 that such basic human rights are "too fundamental" to be mitigated as being legal, moral, or social concerns.

Here Agee responds in some way to Davidson's suggestion that sociologists believe the "Negro Problem" can be solved by abstracting the problem of racially inflected histories in America. He ends this exchange of letters with Flye by agreeing that the "Negro Problem" cannot be solved through legislation and by specifying that custom cannot be cured by law, which is at the crux of Davidson's argument as well. Crank argues that Agee's conclusions lead to a sense of self-disgust on Agee's part. In his article Crank delves further into Agee's unpublished response to Davidson.[29] Agee's ultimate conclusion in these letters is that the "Negro Problem" will never be resolved until the parties concerned are able to recognize the vast differences between custom and law and until legislators can recognize that law will not eradicate the "maniacal rage" of both Southern whites and Negroes.[30]

A closer look at Davidson's article makes it clear that his argument echoes the one Baldwin finds in *Birth of a Nation*, though on a less emotionally manipulative scale. Aside from claiming that Southerners accepted the entry of Negroes into America on condition that they remain slaves, Davidson asserts that the South would have eventually "emancipated the Negro slaves of its own accord." He essentially asserts that the South accepted the Constitution's Thirteenth Amendment, which emancipated the slaves, but that the Fourteenth and Fifteenth Amendments were "planted in the Constitution by fraud and force."[31]

Davidson further argues that the amendments granting citizenship and suffrage to African Americans were made possible only by the "puppet governments" of the Reconstruction and that the Southerners' duty to care for the Negro populations that had been emancipated was usurped from them by corrupt (or, in Griffith's argument, mulatto) Northerners.[32] Like Baldwin, Davidson intimates, though in nonironic fashion, that the Southerners needed to restore a particular kind of social order based on custom rather than law in order to protect their black populations. To fail to do so brought about a greater risk of violence between the races to the detriment of the African American. Though Baldwin does not use the same terms as either Davidson or Agee, it is clear that custom is intimately linked to the American supremacist mythologies that inform *The Devil Finds Work*, *The Fire Next Time*, and indeed most of Baldwin's essays and novels.

Therefore, the most intriguing point made by Agee is his review of *Birth* is that Griffith understood the Negro as any "good Southerner" would. The question then becomes: What does Agee mean by calling Griffith a "good Southerner"? How does he interpret the political and cultural struggle following the end of the Civil War and the various attempts to control American memory through revisionist accounts? Crank's conclusion, based on his close reading of Agee's unpublished response to Davidson, is that Agee agrees that imposing law upon custom would lead to violence in the South. Agee says as much in his letter of September 19, 1945.[33] Oddly enough, just after making this concession to Davidson, Agee turns directly to personal concerns in this letter. It's as if to suggest that his sense of frustration about discussing the "Negro Problem" has gone as far as it can go.[34]

AMERICAN HISTORY, MEMORY. AND THE WAR

As Stokes points out, "*The Birth of a Nation* was released in the semi-centennial of the ending of the American Civil War, and would become a major factor in the political struggle taking place over the control of the American memory relating to the war itself."[35] Stokes suggests that the aftermath of the war and the desire to shape how it would be viewed historically was heavily wrapped up in perpetuating the myth of the Lost Cause. Though Baldwin never uses the term "Lost Cause," one can find threads of empathy between his positions and Agee's through recognizing the extent to which that myth controlled thoughts about race in the period when classical Hollywood narrative storytelling techniques tarose.

The principal tenets of the myth involve reconstructing the real causes of the war and placing more blame on the abolitionists as a primary cause for the war as well as an increased insistence that slave owners were more benevolent than history had depicted them in prior periods. The "Lost Cause" also suggests that the real victims in this war were the states and the destruction of their sovereignty and that white Southerners were the most victimized party of all.[36] As mentioned, the imposition and corruption of the Fourteenth and Fifteenth Amendments is part of that victimization. Davidson mentions corporate businesses profiting from the Fourteenth Amendment in order to declare themselves legal individuals to the detriment of social and economic stability in the South.

Overt sympathy for the ex-Confederacy gave rise to "a dominant view of the Civil War based on a rereading that was deeply sympathetic to the South," according to Stokes's summary. He notes that the rise in the number of films sympathetic to Southerners after 1911 may have enticed Griffith to "backdate" his source material, Thomas Dixon's *The Clansman*, to include more episodes dealing directly with the Civil War itself. He posits that Griffith's *Birth* was probably the most important film promoting the myth of the Lost Cause. This argues for the fact that the film, while revolutionizing film technique and giving birth to classical Hollywood narrative techniques, was also embedding myths inherent to the privileging of American white supremacy. Despite the film's heavily racist content, whiteness is rendered invisible due to this entwining of new narrative methods of storytelling and the invisibility of whiteness.[37]

Agee's review of the film, written thirty years after the film appeared and eighty-three years after the Civil War ended, may very well have been swayed by these revisionist histories, which, as Thomas Cripps has argued, ultimately caused the most suffering to the African Americans and by extension, to African American spectators of Griffith's film.[38] Agee thus distances himself from Griffith's racist stance by suggesting that the director's critics do not have a full grasp of how a "good Southerner" understands black-white relations in the South. Again as Crank has suggested, we see this kind of apologetics from as early as Agee's short story "Death in the Desert," which was published in 1930, during his junior year at Harvard.

In this story, the protagonist is a hitchhiker who is picked up by a quarrelsome couple and the short story follows the course of his ride with them through the desert. They run across a dying black man who is flagging down their car and trying to get help from them. The husband refuses to pick up the man, creating fictions of what the man has no doubt done wrong in order to find himself bleeding in the desert. The wife berates her husband saying that he should have picked up the n***ger, but her disagreement with her husband's course of action is consistent with their disagreement on everything else that gets discussed during the ride. According to Agee's depiction, it's just another excuse for them to argue with each other. Nonetheless, the protagonist realizes that he too should have spoken up and that "my silence made me confederate in a monstrous wrong."[39] As in Agee's letters to Father Flye, the early protagonist in Agee's writing acknowledges that he dare not speak about a situation that is clearly wrong because he realizes that he is extremely confused about his own feelings with respect to this situation.

In a similar manner, Agee seemingly pardons the miraculous filmmaker Griffith for a position on the war and its aftermath that rests on the high marketability of the Civil War genre but also on his observation that Griffith's primitive poetry, which is displayed in the film, is built on the emotions and rationale of a "good Southerner." Though Griffith went to great lengths to insist on the historical accuracy of his film, many critics, surveyed by Stokes in his overview of the film's critical apparatus, have effectively argued that myth trumps history in *Birth of a Nation*.

As a result, Agee's pardon is ultimately rooted in his belief that, no matter what, custom will prevail over any attempts of reason or law to overcome the tense racial relations of the South. His claim is that Griffith accurately depicts this paradoxical tension. Hence, we see links between Agee's position on the film and Baldwin's much later critique in which he readily praises the film's technical qualities while simultaneously exploring why and how it is so hurtful to "*our*—American—history."[40]

Contrasting Agee's film review of *Birth* with his subsequent tribute to Griffith and *Birth* written one week after Griffith's death, Agee's portrayal of the filmmaker is always loving, for lack of a better word, but far bleaker in the later piece, in terms of the actual life Griffith led. In this latter piece of writing Agee is more focused on laying bare the ways in which Griffith's humble beginnings and his "hurt and astonishment" concerning the spate of protests against cinema's first "colossal" film, his masterpiece *Birth of a Nation*. Agee's tribute reads more like a plea for sympathy for the masterful filmmaker, though it is prefaced with a laudation from Charlie Chaplin and ends with an even more superlative quote by René Clair wherein Clair claims that nothing new has been added to cinema since Griffith made his films.[41] Agee reinforces this quote by asserting that Clair was certainly someone who knew about such things as excellent filmmaking. Praise from a renowned European filmmaker for a director working in Hollywood, it is suggested, is by no means to be taken lightly.

JAMES AGEE: THE AMBIVALENT SOUTHERNER

While Agee is never ambivalent about Griffith's value as a filmmaker and while he also does not embrace the racist attitudes of the film made by Griffith, he does seem to want to hold critics of the film to task for privileging critiques of content over excellence of form. Agee's praise of Griffith mirrors and explicates his own complex relationship to the troublesome racial dynamics of his native South. In addition, it is important to see how this relationship colors some of his other film criticism, his essays, and his literary works.

In "Racial Violence, Receding Bodies: James Agee's Anatomy of Guilt," Crank provides useful insight into why some ambivalence might be detected in Agee's appreciation of Griffith's film despite the obvious praise of Griffith's cinematic genius. Crank argues that Agee unambiguously sympathizes with poor Southern whites but remains strangely silent about the struggles of poor blacks in the South, despite his articulation of anguish over the American Negro's plight in his letters to Father Flye. Crank suggests that rather than interpret Agee's silence as indifference to or disdain for the Negro, it is best to explore his unpublished fiction, letters, and journals. Crank's essay traces many sources from Agee's writing and examines them in relation to Agee's representations of the American Negro. He stresses throughout that Agee's primary guilt with respect to the "Negro Problem" was an outgrowth of his inability to "communicate his complicated feelings over the situation between whites and African Americans."[42]

Crank's thesis is that Agee's depiction of racial violence against black bodies seems ultimately to be a mirror for Agee's own guilt and sense of helplessness, suggesting that in most of the examples he analyzes, Agee systematically creates "a still image" of scenes of violence rather than imagining them from beginning to end, thus allowing for a "movement from body to bodilessness" such that the importance of these scenes seem to be that they allow Agee to reflect on his own inability to express himself about racial violence per se.[43] Crank points to the concept of the "southern white racial conversion narrative," a term that is central to Fred Hobson's work on other Southern intellectual writers, as one that parallels this particular aspect of Agee's work.

In Agee's film criticism and even in his film commentary written for the quasi-documentary *The Quiet One*, further examples of his reluctance to offer solutions to racial problems through the ambivalence of his critiques can be found. Agee's film criticism is more easily liberated from his fear of confrontation with the "Negro Problem," but it is not simply because he uses the easy excuse that form can be separated from content in Hollywood or European filmmaking. Rather, as in his fiction, Agee saw form in all of his writings as something with which he is capable of working and with which he had a right to engage. As Crank puts it, Agee again and again intimates that the solution to the "Negro Problem" is hopeless. He equally intimates that he is particularly inept when it comes to solving the problem, having grown up as a Southerner. His primary compensation is to assert his right to control his artistic form, a right he affords to the filmmakers he evaluates in his film criticism.

If we apply this attitude to Agee's film criticism, we can deepen the analysis of his assessment of D. W. Griffith. Agee's rebuke of Griffith's critics for calling *Birth* an anti-Negro statement seems rooted in this complex "anatomy of guilt" and hints at the more complicated relationship between form and content for filmmaking than merely Agee's participation in an unconscious patronage toward the Negro. As Bernardi also insists in a quote cited earlier in this chapter, segregating narrative craft from racist imagery when analyzing *Birth* would be a gross oversimplification of Griffith's impact on cinematic history. Ingraining invisible whiteness into the fabric of the film is a crucial factor in that Griffith essentially creates a negotiation between the mythologies that will guide future spectators and distorts historical accounts in a new and innovative way that only cinema could achieve.

In other words, Griffith creates the idea of a spectator that is resonant with the one Agee describes in his review of *Birth*, namely a spectator whose memory and imagination will be affected and will revise for themselves the historical epic they are watching precisely because they are not only affected by the myths being entwined in the film language but also because the film language itself is instructing them on how what they are seeing affects their memory and imagination. In her chapter "The Mixed White Birth of 'Great White' Masculinity and the Classical Spectator," Courtney provides another perspective from which to appreciate this phenomenon through her discussion of the differentiation of the gaze and the look and their impact on representations of white masculinity in the film. She first of all establishes that the gaze, as theorized by Kaja Silverman in *Male Subjectivity at the Margins*, is complicit with white male supremacist perspectives.[44] The gaze, while attributed at times to select characters in a given narrative, is ultimately most strongly linked to what the camera sees and therefore to what the spectator is able to see.[45]

Courtney asserts that white male masculinity is embodied by the gaze in *Birth*, and is an overarching and powerful notion of seeing that implies an almost disembodied authority. The gaze is therefore opposed to the "look," which is almost always linked specifically to the body and thus appears more vulnerable. Courtney's claim, following Silverman, is that the gaze is always attributed to white male masculinity while the look is reserved for the black characters in Griffith's film, which establishes a precedent for future classical Hollywood films.

For example, Courtney cites an image of a Negro looking out of the peephole of a doorway when one of the white principals of the film knocks on the door. The shot that follows is an extreme close-up of the Negro's eye. Courtney stresses that most instances of such peeping, which characterizes the looking of the black men in the second half of the film, are almost always off center. What is therefore established is a systematic use of the vision wherein "we do not look with these black men looking so much as we watch them watching. Unlike the classic white male *voyeur*, this black male peeper exposed is represented not as the source of the film's vision but as one of its objects."[46]

Courtney thus establishes an in-depth rule of Griffith's filming that does not simply incorporate close-ups but rather uses them in ways determined by racial difference. After outlining this and other crucial filmic techniques, Courtney closes this subtitled section of her chapter on the birth of the "Great White" spectator by suggesting that the seemingly superfluous scenes of whites observing the grand finale of the film, introduced by the intertitle "while helpless whites look on," are actually part of a construction of a spectator response which promises that we, the passive spectators of the closing scenes, will be transported from a feeling of passivity to a sense of authoritative control over the events taking place on the screen. The spectator of *Birth* is transformed from someone who looks on to someone who can lay claim to the authoritative gaze of white supremacy with which the film ends. As Courtney puts it, "[T]hese remarkable final moments would seem to answer all that has gone before them not only by restoring Ben's masterful vision but also by anchoring it to, and producing from it, a new white order divinely envisioned by him, the film and its spectator."[47]

As has long been the case with critical reception of *Birth*, this newly empowered gaze can be embraced only by the white spectator for whom the privileging of American white supremacy becomes once again tenable. The triumph of the Ku Klux Klan is a form of agency that exacerbates protests against the film. It also cements the vengeful relations between blacks and whites that is the most troubling aspect of spectator response according to Baldwin. He describes it as a "relentless need for something [even] much deeper than revenge [which] comes close to the truth of many lives, black and white."[48] The rise of protests against the film by black and white Americans alike has its own incredible history, as has been chronicled in many volumes and, in particular, in Everett's account of black protest against the film's racist content from as early as the anticipatory protest against Thomas Dixon's theatrical staging of *The Clansman*.[49]

Everett argues that what should be stressed in any analysis of Agee's critique of the film is that there are several facile dichotomies upon which criticism of the film has long relied: namely, the separation of form and content. Everett corrects the implication that African Americans rejecting the racist content of the film equally rejected the idea that the film had any artistic merit. As she puts it, "[O]n the contrary, African American critics of that era understood only too well that the film's artistic merits could function to conflate and obfuscate its more wrenching sociopolitical agenda of fomenting racial discord." She further points out that, "even in their scathing denunciations of *The Birth of a Nation*, several black critics acknowledged the film's artistry in some ways."[50] The film nonetheless gives way to the concept of the ethnic spectator of classical Hollywood narrative for many of the reasons suggested by Bernardi when he states that "the art of *The Birth of a Nation* is its racism, particularly its construction of whiteness through the lens of the black stereotypes and the craft of cinematic technique. In *The Birth of a Nation*, art is ideological, form is content, and cinema is simultaneously moving, artistic, ugly and painful."[51]

Rightly or wrongly, Agee asserts in his review of Griffith's film that the filmmaker believed that *Birth* represented a nation built out of pain and ugliness and that this was the reality of the United States of America after the Civil War. Griffith offers solace to white viewers by restoring white masculinity and by invoking and elevating the myth of the Lost Cause. Neither Agee nor Griffith has solace for black viewers due to their somewhat shared belief that the plight of black viewers is tragically irresolvable. Furthermore, in reducing black viewers to objects of the gaze rather than agencies of the gaze, Griffith sets future Hollywood production against the empowering of the black race. The illusory power of white supremacy is thus folded into the mythologies of Hollywood storytelling, and the talent needed to undo that complicity will need to be considerable. It necessarily demands asking the question of whose stories need to be told, who has the right to tell them, and how should they be represented through cinematic language.

As a final consideration, Agee's seemingly blanket public silence about the representations of African American characters in his film criticism is contradicted by a few telling examples. In these cases, he delivers a harsher judgment than is expected, given his reticence with respect to his condemnation of Griffith's film. In his March 11, 1944, review of the Army orientation film *The Negro Soldier* (Stuart Heisler 1944) Agee remarks that the only problem is that the film is too mild for its subject matter but that it should by all means be seen. He states: "I believe that for many people the screen presentation of the Negro as something other than a clown, a burnt-cork Job or a plain imbecile will be startling and more instructive than we are likely to imagine."[52]

In another review, published July 29, 1944, in *The Nation*, Agee adopts an ironic stance on the representation of African American characters in his reference to the war-time melodrama *Since You Went Away* (John Cromwell, David O. Selznick 1944). Agee criticizes Selznick mercilessly in this review for making a bad film about *the* American family, the Hiltons. The film is essentially about a family who must endure emotional and financial hardship when the father goes away to war. Agee's most sarcastic critique concerns the depiction of the black maid (Hattie McDaniel) who has to take on a union job when Mrs. Hilton no longer has the means to pay for her services. As Agee observes, "once she [the Negro maid] is done she hustles back to the Hiltons to get in her day's measure of mala-propisms, comic relief, mother wit and free labor."[53]

Since Agee's overall critique of the film is its clumsy, shortsighted understanding of American life, it can be asserted that this most scathing critique of the representation of the African American character is a subtle but controlled jab at the precepts of American white supremacy that sustains the spectator's belief in that character's behavior. Agee's disdain for how Hollywood represents African Americans extends not only to film-makers but also to his fellow critics. He condemns critic Arthur Winsten's desultory reading of an American Negro soldier's behavior in a role played in Luigi Zampa's film *To Live in Peace* (1947). Agee upbraids Winsten for his inability to understand what the Italian director intended in this depic-tion and for his psychological insensitivity to the Negro's behavior. The review was published in *The Nation* on December 13, 1947.

In this review, Agee concludes by remarking: "As a native of this coun-try, with probably more experience both of the South and of non-Southerners who think they mean well by Negroes, I am like many other Americans particularly impressed by the whole treatment of the Negro [in the film]; it is the only pure presentation of a man of his race that I have seen in a movie."[54]

Agee's work on the film *The Quiet One*, discussed earlier, is a depiction of a ten-year-old Harlem boy living in a state of dire pain directly inflicted by his unfortunate environment was no doubt ongoing when Agee wrote his reviews of Griffith's work. *The Quiet One* is a vibrant statement con-cerning the need for an honest presentation of a man of his race and comes closer to a public outcry against American critical attitudes toward the African Americans than most films of that period. The concern most at the heart of Agee's perspectives on racial relations in America is the need for honesty above all else, even when it reveals an ugliness at the core.

One can only speculate on how Agee would have responded to the evolving Civil Rights movement, since he died at the age of forty-five in 1955. Looking underneath the surface of his praise for Griffith's *Birth* nonetheless reveals a much more conflicted relationship to racial prob-lems in America than can be gleaned from a surface reading of that review. What appears to be simply an excusing of racial content by arguing excellence of form is a misrepresentation of the darker edges of Agee's perspectives on invisible whiteness.

NOTES

1. I had decided on a title of "But Now I See" for this chapter before I began writing it. The phrase seemed fitting for discussion of a conversion narrative. It was also the phrase that first came to mind when I began closely analyzing James Agee's film criticism and his other works. Then I eventually made my way to Fred Hobson's excellent study, *But Now I See: The White Southern Racial Conversion Narrative* (Baton Rouge: Louisiana State Press, 1999). Though Hobson speaks of Agee only once in his book, his concept of the conversion narrative is invaluable in my reexamination of Agee's reading of *Birth of a Nation*.
2. Michael Rogin, "'The Sword Became a Flashing Vision': D. W. Griffith's *The Birth of a Nation*," *Representations*, Issue 9, *Special Issue: American Culture between the Civil War and World War I* (Winter 1985): 150–195. 150.
3. Daniel Bernardi, "The Birth of Whiteness: Integrating Race into the Narrator System," in *The Birth of Whiteness: Race and the Emergence of U.S. Cinema* (New Brunswick, NJ: Rutgers University Press, 1996), 82–96.
4. Melvyn Stokes, *D. W. Griffith's The Birth of a Nation: A History of the Most Controversial Motion Picture of All Time* (Oxford: Oxford University Press, 2007). 238–249.
5. Stokes, *D. W. Griffith's The Birth of a Nation*, 246.
6. Stokes, *D. W. Griffith's The Birth of a Nation*, 111.
7. James Baldwin, *The Devil Finds Work* (New York: Dial, 1976), 59.
8. Again, a closer examination of the relationship among these three men as well as the fact that this was the first film to be shown in the White House to an enthusiastic President Wilson is succinctly summed up in Stokes, *D. W. Griffith's The Birth of a Nation*, 111. Other sections of the book look more closely at his writing *A History of the American People* (198–200) and its impact on Griffith in the making of the film. Stokes also provides information on the friendship of the three men in their youth, which reinforced their shared views about race as Southerners throughout their careers (32–32).
9. James A. Crank, "Racial Violence", 56.
10. As previously noted, the definitive history of black film criticism on *Birth of a Nation* can be found in Anna Everett, *Returning the Gaze: A Genealogy of Black Film Criticism, 1909–1949* (Durham, NC: Duke University Press, 2001).

11. "Visual Pleasure and Narrative Cinema", *Film Theory and Critcism*, 7th Ed., Braudy and Cohen, 711–722; "Black Specatorship: Problems of Identification and Resistance", Braudy and Cohen, 767–776.
12. Bernardi, "The Birth of Whiteness," 84.
13. Of particular interest here is Michael Rogin's comment that there was a tendency to attribute the racist content of the film to Thomas Dixon's novel, *The Clansman*, as source material and to suggest that "Griffith and its audience did not share Dixon's propagandistic purposes; they were victims of "unconscious racism." That unconscious is visible on the screen in *Birth*, and it invites us not to avert our eyes from the movie's racism but to investigate its meaning (151). Rogin, "The Sword Became a Flashing Vision.
14. One of the seminal texts with respect to a history of representations of blacks in Hollywood and the related casting issues is Donald Bogle, *Toms, Coons, Mulattoes, Mammies and Bucks: An Interpretive History of Blacks in American Films* (New York: Viking Press, 1974).
15. Bernardi, "The Birth of Whiteness," 84.
16. Auden's remark is quoted from a letter to the Editors of the *Nation* from October 16, 1944, reprinted on the opening page of *Agee on Film* (New York: Penguin, 1958).
17. Both pieces can be found in *Agee on Film*. The film review from *The Nation* is found on pages 313–315, and the tribute published in the *Times* is on pages 396–398.
18. *Agee on Film*, 315.
19. "The Makers of *In the Street* and the *Quiet One*" in *Agee at 100: Centennial Essays on the Works of James Agee*, ed. Michael Lofaro (Knoxville: University of Tennessee Press, 2012), 201–223. 204.
20. *Agee on Film*, 315.
21. *Agee on Film*, 314.
22. *Agee on Film*, 396. One relative aspect of Baldwin's *The Devil Finds Work* here is that Baldwin, by following his own evolution as a filmgoer, implies that the spectator begins as a kind of blank slate but becomes "spoiled" by continual exposure to films which play upon the mythologies of the American Dream. These mythologies, as is argued throughout this book, are in turn tainted by white supremacist ideologies.
23. Susan B. Courtney, *Hollywood Fantasies of Miscegenation: Spectacular Narrative of Gender and Race, 1903–1967* (Princeton, NJ: Princeton University Press, 2005), 50–103.
24. *Agee on Film*, 314.
25. Stokes, *D. W. Griffith's The Birth of a Nation*, 250.
26. *Agee on Film*, 314.
27. Davidson, "Preface to Decision," *Sewanee Review*. The letters can be found in *Letters of James Agee to Father Flye* (Brooklyn: Melville House, 1962/2014). Kindle. James A. Crank, "Racial Violence, Receding Bodies:

James Agee's Anatomy of Guilt," in *Agee at 100*, ed. Michael Lofaro (Knoxville: University of Tennessee Press, 2012), 53–74.

28. *Letters of James Agee to Father Flye*. Location 1782.
29. "In the Summer of 1945..." Box 1, Folder 1, Harry Ransom Center, 1928–1968. Austin: University of Texas.
30. *Letters of James Agee to Father Flye*, Location 1802.
31. Donald Davidson, "Preface to Decision," *Sewanee Review* 53, no. 3 (Summer 1945): 394–412. www.jstor.org/stable/27537598. 404–405.
32. Davidson, "Preface to Decision."
33. Agee's unpublished response "In the Summer of 1945," Box 1, Folder 1 Harry Ransom Center, 1928–68, University of Texas Austin. I am reliant upon Crank's reading for this document.
34. *Letters of James Agee to Father Flye*, Location 1805.
35. Stokes, *D. W. Griffith's The Birth of a Nation*, 179.
36. Stokes, *D. W. Griffith's The Birth of a Nation*, 185.
37. For further exploration of the myth of the Lost Cause and its propagandistic effects on American history, the reader may consult Gary W. Gallagher and Alan T. Nolan, eds., *The Myth of the Lost Cause and Civil War History* (Bloomington: Indiana University Press, 2000). The argument from Stokes is from pages 180–184 of *D. W. Griffith's The Birth of a Nation*.
38. My point here is a basic overview of Cripp's "Reaction of the Negro to the Motion Picture, *The Birth of a Nation*," *Historian* 25, no. 3 (May 1963): 344–362. This point is also observed in Stokes, *D. W. Griffith's The Birth of a Nation*, 180.
39. *The Collected Short Prose of James Agee* (Boston: Houghton Mifflin, 1968), 74.
40. Baldwin, *The Devil Finds Work*, 56. My emphasis.
41. *Agee on Film*, 397–398.
42. James A. Crank, "Racial Violence, Receding Bodies," 63.
43. Crank, "Racial Violence, Receding Bodies," 74.
44. Kaja Silverman, *Male Subjectivity at the Margins* (New York: Routledge, 1992), 125–156.
45. Susan B. Courtney. *Hollywood Fantasies of Miscegenation: Spectacular Narrative of Gender and Race, 1903–1967* (Princeton, NJ: Princeton University Press, 2005), 50–103. 88.
46. Courtney. *Hollywood Fantasies of Miscegenation*, 88.
47. Courtney. *Hollywood Fantasies of Miscegenation*, 95–97.
48. Baldwin, *The Devil Finds Work*, 51. In this passage, Baldwin is still focused on Michel Gast's film *I Shall Spit on Your Grave*. However, the decision to speak about this European film focused on racial violence and revenge and then turn directly to a discussion of *Birth of a Nation* is strategic on Baldwin's part. Europe's conception of what constitutes racially inflected desires for vengeance is grotesque and obvious. But so equally are America's home-grown representations of a similar obsession.

49. Everett, *Returning the Gaze*, 60.
50. Everett, *Returning the Gaze*, 71.
51. Bernardi, "The Birth of Whiteness," 95.
52. *Agee on Film*, 80.
53. *Agee on Film*, 108.
54. *Agee on Film*, 284.

CHAPTER 4

"The Colored Angle": Contending Visions of *Imitation of Life*

There is a wonderful expression: seeing through a glass darkly.
Everything, even life, is inevitably removed from you. You can't reach,
or touch, the real. You just see reflections. If you try to grasp happiness
itself your fingers only meet glass.[1]
—*Douglas Sirk*

I want my quack-quack.
—*Jessie Pullman, Imitation of Life, 1934*

Lora Meredith, the ambitious aging actress of Douglas Sirk's 1959 film *Imitation of Life*, exemplifies a woman's limitless desire for fame on her own terms. Defying the men who want to control her, she goes so far as to move from her wildly successful bout of acting in the popular romantic comedies written by her playwright paramour, David Edwards, to performing a role in a "serious" play, complete with its own "colored" angle. The theatrical production apparently contains a subplot concerning race issues that Lora considers important enough for her to risk her assured rise to fame through her regular appearances in the safe domestic comedies to which she had become accustomed.

After hearing about the play, a highbrow drama, she decides to take the role of the social worker. Both her agent, Allen Loomis, and her playwright lover frown on this move until she proves that her instincts were right. Her rousing performance in the drama draws applause and shows that she

© The Author(s) 2018
A. M. Craven, *Visible and Invisible Whiteness*,
https://doi.org/10.1007/978-3-319-76777-2_4

can rise above the comfortable and entertaining theatrical pulp that had lifted her out of her earlier struggles to succeed. Up until this point, her success could still have arguably been attributed to the fame and talent of her lover, David Edwards. She marks her own terms with this social drama and its controversial "colored angle."

In a sense, this surreptitious wink in the plot of Sirk's adaptation of Fannie Hurst's novel *Imitation of Life* could almost serve as a scholarly footnote on the question of genre, classical Hollywood narrative, and the race issues that are at the center of both John M. Stahl's 1934 domestic melodrama, also based on the Hurst novel, and Sirk's adaptation twenty-five years later. With very little stretching, one could contend that "the colored angle" distinguishes both films from the intense focus on feminine gender issues that typically dominate in Hollywood domestic melodrama in the period from the 1930s through the 1950s. Many of the essays in Christine Gledhill's volume on the links between melodrama and the woman's film indeed argue that cinematic melodrama is first and foremost rooted in Hollywood and in the related discussions of gender and class that fuel the film criticism of melodrama.[2]

In particular, Thomas Elsaesser's "Tales of Sound and Fury: Observations on the Family Melodrama" does suggest that melodrama of course does not emerge from a vacuum in Hollywood, but both he and Gledhill effectively argue that the cinematic language developed in relation to the family melodrama does indeed become centralized in early- to mid-1950s Hollywood.[3] Stahl's film falls roughly into the category of melodrama, though the film ultimately converts from melodrama to romantic comedy. This decision plays heavily in the film's successful though regrettable move to render whiteness invisible in the second half of the film. One of the central tenets of this chapter is that Stahl and Sirk both use temper Hollywood's privileging of the male gaze with the need for a dominant female subject position in the traditional melodramatic genres. As has been argued in Chap. 2 of this book, the male gaze is established in the ending sections of Griffith's *Birth of a Nation* of white masculinity as an authorizing force within the classical Hollywood narrative, and this cinematic trope remains unchallenged for many years. Hence the tenuous balance between female subject position and male gaze that both Stahl and Sirk must establish.

Their source material dictates the foregrounding of a female subject position, though Stahl and Sirk ultimately take different directions when reconciling that subject position with the primacy of the male gaze in Hollywood cinema. Based on Fannie Hurst's 1933 novel of the same title,

Stahl's *Imitation of Life* was a groundbreaking film with respect to the casting of blacks and equally with respect to narratives that leaned tentatively
toward humanizing black characters. Though Stahl ultimately respects the
centrality of the gender-based narrative of Hurst's novel, his film has long
served as a focus for essays on both racial and gender conflict.[4]

The intersectional participation of the novel and its film versions in
both race and gender conflicts makes them critical for examining the con-
tending representations of the Hurst narrative by Sirk and Stahl as exem-
plars of contrasting treatments of visible and invisible whiteness.[5] Shifts in
key elements of characterization, narrative detail, and filming techniques
create both a classical Hollywood melodrama that inevitably reaffirms the
unconscious patronage of American white supremacy, as is the case in
Stahl's film, and a borderline art cinema melodrama in Sirk's version.
Indeed, in critical assessments, Stahl's film is more often used as an example for analyzing gender issues and what I have referred to as invisible
whiteness in Hollywood per se. Sirk's version is most often centralized in
criticism that considers the evolution of self-reflexive trends in filmmaking.
Sirkophilia is indeed a crucial base for n*ouvelle vague* critique and the central contributors to the *Cahiers du cinéma* as well as the journal *Screen*.[6]

Both films are nonetheless rooted in American domestic melodrama, in
keeping with their source material, Fannie Hurst's novel, which was taken
to be "sentimental hokum" by its contemporary critics. While her novel
can indeed be studied as a women's novel and equally as a "white" novel,
as Henry Louis Gates puts it, according to Daniel Iztkovitz in his introduction to the 2004 reprint of the novel, *Imitation of Life* in all of its
manifestations conflates the problems of gender equality and visible and
invisible whiteness in ways that bear further scrutiny.[7] Susan Courtney
indeed traces the close relations between a reassertion of American white
masculinity in Griffith's *Birth* as a way of mitigating the threat to white
femininity and this argument is reintroduced in important ways in her
discussion of Stahl's *Imitation of Life*.

Consistent with Courtney's overall argument, she notes in the opening
pages of her analysis of *Imitation of Life* that the most formidable obstacle
for the film's script in passing the Production Code's requirements for
protecting white femininity and for suppressing narratives of miscegenation was that Peola, the near-white daughter of Bea Pullman's black maid
Delilah, was indeed white enough to "pass" for white, and thus the clause
against miscegenation was being violated by the script "in spirit if not in
fact."[8] The ultimate suggestion here is that whiteness is rendered visible in

that Peola has to be considered as essentially black though she appears on the screen as white in color and therefore Hollywood's control over the cinematic representation of whiteness is deemed to be at risk.

Intricate relations hence were set up in Hollywood filmmaking with the appearance of *Birth of a Nation*. I privilege questions of race rather than gender in what follows in order to look more deeply at how the two filmmakers in question define whiteness through cinematic language. According to seminal definitions of cinematic melodrama advanced by Thomas Elsaesser and others, it can be argued that in the 1934 version of *Imitation of Life*, the melodramatic genre is usurped by the more complacent Hollywood genre, romantic comedy, in the second half of the film. The total effect of this transition is a reaffirmation of patriarchal supremacist values that are marginalized in the first half of the film.

The Skeletal Plot and the Skin that Covers It

The plot of Stahl's film follows the narrative of Hurst's novel more closely than does Sirk's film. In Stahl's film, Bea Pullman is a young white widow and mother whom Delilah, a young black mother, convinces to hire her as a maid and cook. Delilah's only condition is that she be allowed to keep her daughter, Peola, with her in her new position as a live-in maid. The potential tragedy and melodramatic aspects of the film are presented through the fact that Peola is an extremely light-skinned Negro and she learns over time that her most basic desire is to pass for white. The central driving plot device in the film is Delilah's secret recipe for pancakes, which provides Bea with a way of becoming a successful businesswoman and allows for a pivot away from the tragic premise of the film.

Stahl's transition in genres happens halfway through the film, just after Delilah refuses to accept an offer to become a stockholder in the burgeoning pancake business Bea has begun based on Delilah's secret pancake recipe. In an unbelievable two-shot sequence, we move from a first shot of Elmer, Bea's business associate, ridiculing Delilah by claiming that she is "once a pancake, always a pancake" for refusing to share profits in the business. Sterling A. Brown targets this moment in the film, which, as Hortense E. Simmons and others have pointed out, refers to a common racial slur linked ultimately to the figure of Little Black Sambo.[9]

The second elliptical shot in the sequence is of Bea Pullman in her new and very fancy apartment, dressed to the nines and surrounded by a bevy of men who are clearly appreciative of her beauty as well as her business prowess. As has been often cited, it was the comment by Elmer which prompted Brown to denounce the film as just another purveyor of invisible whiteness and supremacist values, arguing that it reified Negro stereotypes, despite its claim to raise Negro characters to more human levels of participation in the narrative. Donald Bogle stresses that the Christian stoicism of Delilah's character established a trend for black characters from Ethel Waters to Sidney Poitier who were equally "elevated" by their stoic behavior. Bogle also suggests that "the irony of this stoicism was that it made the Negro character more self-effacing than ever and even more resolutely resigned to accepting his fate of inferiority."[10]

The shift in genre just described evidences supremacist complicity between classical Hollywood narrative and Hollywood's stock genres. Bea's tremendous success, in which Delilah refuses to participate other than passively, has momentarily displaced the relationship of the two women as a central component of the cinematic narrative and therefore has created a vacuum that the entrance of Stephen Archer as a romantic interest rushes in to fill. Accordingly, Delilah takes her place as accommodating servant and confidante to the amorous white woman. The generic shift pushes the colored angle to its rightful place as a subplot, according to Hollywood expectations, and allows invisible whiteness to regain its supremacy.

One can argue that though also challenging the limits of Hollywood classical melodrama and narrative, Sirk creates a different kind of transitional moment for his cinematic adaptation, but it is also a generic one. As noted at the beginning of this chapter, Lora Meredith (Lana Turner), the name given by Sirk to the protagonist paralleling Hurst and Stahl's Bea Pullman is a very determined woman, set on success in her acting career on her own terms. Sirk's generic shift and consequent challenge to Hollywood norms involves an abrupt change in Lora's lifestyle as the viewer sees her moving into a very elegant, obviously expensive home. Dyer remarks that this is the moment in the film when Sirk sacrificed his protagonist Lora Meredith and exposed her superficiality in order to also expose the intransigency of Hollywood with respect to whiteness. Dyer says of the film that "the problem it poses (thus bringing in the suffering element in Turner image) is whether there is anything but imitation in it.[11] As Sirk remarks in his conversations with Jon Halliday, "Lana Turner's life is a very cheap imitation…You can't escape what you are.[12] In effect, Sirk uses Lora's magnanimity toward her black companion/maid to expose the superficiality of white patronage both in American life and in Hollywood representations of that life. At the end of 1959's *Imitation of Life*, Lora is united with her daughter, her loving fiancé, and the daughter of Annie Johnston, her black maid, but she is still only performing the "colored angle" as she comforts Sara Jane, the daughter of her dead colored "friend," Annie Johnston. One might go so far as to say that the colored angle looks good on her.

Critics who look at the films comparatively tend to agree that the filmmakers are bringing something of their own to their adaptations of the novel. Both directors nonetheless partially reinforce the expectations of the melodramatic genre. However, where Stahl disrupts that genre and turns to romantic comedy in order to reaffirm the Hollywood status quo with respect to invisible whiteness, Sirk raises challenges to representations of white patronage. Stahl's film is most often used to look more closely at the evolution of black acting in Hollywood and/or race and gender representation in Hollywood studio production. The criticism that originates in the October 1978 *Cahiers du cinéma* 293 dedicated to Sirk's work takes his style as an exemplar of auteur filmmaking.

Jeremy G. Butler argues in "*Imitation of Life*: Stahl and Sirk" that "the 1959 version of *Imitation of Life* may be read as a critical, disrupted vision of a world that 1930s Hollywood took for granted." Thus suggesting that his status as an auteur singularly responsible for challenging the norms of 1930's melodrama is overstated. His argument is based on a close analysis of the shot sequences in the scene where Delilah/Annie, the black mother, comes to pick up her daughter, Peola/Sara Jane, from school on a rainy day. In this scene the mother discovers that her daughter has been passing for white since the beginning of the school year. Butler concludes by arguing that, in his view, it is the evolution of the genre rather than the imposition of one film-maker's challenge to Hollywood's ideological norms that is reflected in the differences between the two films. As he points out in various parts of his article, "As that one scene evolved, so the domestic melodrama evolved." Further he notes that "[i]t's my belief that the elements of Sirk's style which these writers extol are more a function of the evolution of the genre than of the solitary genius [of Sirk]. One may properly wonder if this stylistic evolution characterizes the genre or comes as the result of an inspired genius *auteur's* reaction against generic conventions of the time."[13] Though Butler's article ends with questions rather than strong assertions and he does call for a more systematic study of the style of the domestic melodrama, Butler resists the idea that the genre can be or has been subjected to an auteur approach or art cinema self-reflexive gesture imposed by Sirk.

Butler's article was published in 1987, when there was perhaps some stake in resisting auteur film theory. He has since contributed enormously on the critical apparatus surrounding the two film adaptations. This early position nonetheless raises the question about whether a director who chose to render whiteness more visible, thus challenging the norms of Hollywood studio production, should be able to get away with desecrating or aiming criticism at an actual structural component of Hollywood—the melodramatic genre.

By succeeding in doing this, by keeping the "colored angle" front and center throughout the film, Sirk inadvertently argues that invisible whiteness controls vital narrative generic structures in Hollywood studio production. An implication of Butler's argument is that, with time, Hollywood might self-correct, might stop being unconsciously racist and patronizing. Criticism in recent years of the whitewashing tendencies of Hollywood and the Oscars does not bear this out.

Given Sirk's definitive impact on auteur theory, Butler's original and strongly argued position, based on very in-depth knowledge of both films, nonetheless seems difficult to maintain. The evolution of melodrama both in Hollywood and Germany as a result of Sirk's profound influence on Rainer Werner Fassbinder must be seen as directly linked to this last Hollywood film Sirk made, which long enjoyed the reputation as Universal Studio's highest-grossing film, despite the director's own discomfort with it.[14] Sirk himself signals that the source material was disturbing and affected his filmmaking decisions in ways that prompted his individual input in contradistinction to studio expectations. He was disturbed by its peculiar American qualities. Sirk points out that "after a few pages [of reading Hurst's novel] I had the feeling this kind of American novel would disillusion me."[15] But as Itzkovitz points out, Sirk chose "not to abandon a style built around highly fraught emotional intensity and narrative excess but to dive in."[16] Sirk tells Halliday in their conversations that he was mostly interested in the Negro angle (the "colored" angle) and that he had to fight against the melodramatic sentimentality of the plot in order to create a film of both white *and* black social consciousness. He emphasizes that what one must capture in the film is the hopelessness of the characters featured in the subplot.

Sirk refers to his approach to the film as one of Euripidean irony, which is to say an irony based on the fact that the "happy ending" he creates for the film is also an irresolute ending, just as the plays of Euripides end with the chorus telling us that there can be no real resolution in the lives of the characters. It is only thanks to the gods that we can, as spectators, escape a cruel ending. Sirk ends his discussion on the making of *Imitation of Life* with the remark that he was ready to leave Hollywood after completing the film, and perhaps before he even began making it. As Paul Willimen indicates, Sirk was challenged by working within the Hollywood system and was frustrated by the intransigency of mythologies privileging whiteness.[17] He became increasingly uncomfortable making films for Hollywood audiences. Whether one agrees with Butler or not concerning Sirk's individual impact on the melodramatic genre, his active and critical questioning of the racial relations depicted in Hurst's narrative is what contributes to making whiteness visible in his adaptation of the novel. Sirk claims that Stahl's decision to make the relationship between two women, Bea and Delilah, revolve primarily around Bea's thriving business took the social significance out of Delilah's role.[18]

While most comparative analyses rightly focus on questions of characterization and casting, particularly of the black characters in the film, Peola and Delilah, Sirk shifts subject positioning and spatial or framing issues in order to bring more attention to the pervasiveness of a white supremacist ideology. Stahl's version minimized these aspects of the source material, and he no doubt did so in order to sustain the main plot line concerning Bea's dilemma with respect to domestic duty, romantic desire, and individual achievement. This was certainly in keeping with studio demands. Claudine Colbert was routinely cast in romantic comedies rather than melodramas (with some notable exceptions, such as *Imitation of Life* in 1934 and *Since You Went Away* in 1943). Casting her as Bea is already a key to understanding that for Stahl and the studio mentality he embodied, romantic comedy and its strong tendency toward comic resolution were necessary to mitigate any disruption caused by the film's racially inflected subplot.

But finally, as was mentioned in previous chapters, the fact that Bordwell's tenets for classical Hollywood narrative have been considered not only in terms of narrative but equally with respect to generic structures, a comparative analysis of Stahl's and Sirk's visions for Hurst's narrative is key to considering how Hollywood structures in general conceal or make invisible a whiteness that ultimately reinscribes supremacist values. A film working against the grain, such as Sirk's, can render said whiteness visible, as he claims was his aim in privileging the "colored" angle. As David Andrews has pointed out, one of the debates concerning Bordwell's categories is whether they are uniquely concerned with narrative structure as opposed to also affecting questions of genre.[19] The chapters that follow will consider this debate from varying perspectives, including the issue of how genre films in Hollywood affected European spectators and filmmakers.

Though Sirk makes some adjustments with respect to narrative, he primarily works toward a modification of the stylistic goals of the American domestic melodrama in *Imitation of Life*. The subject positioning of the protagonists as well as the various expressions of individual desire that control the plots and subplots of both Stahl's film and Sirk's bear this out.

The transition from poverty and struggle to wealth works in significantly different ways for each film. The use of objects and architecture in each film, which has been a steady source of critique in the analysis of the respective mise-en-scène are widely divergent. Hollywood films are coded according to their resolute or "happy" endings. Stahl's ending is not the full resolute ending of a romantic comedy, but it leaves open the possibility that Steve Archer will be patient and wait for the right moment to marry Bea, which was a surprising compromise between Stahl's source material and Hollywood expectations.

The endings of both films under examination cannot be considered to be either resolute or happy. This is the case for the novel as well the films. Stahl's film ends with Bea renouncing her romantic interests in the name of asserting her maternal duty to a confused and admittedly spoiled daughter. In a typical romantic comedy there would have been resolution and Bea would have been allowed to marry Archer without compromising her duty to her daughter. It must nonetheless be noted that such a happy ending is not a requirement for the art cinema film; therefore, Sirk's ending is ultimately less constrained on some levels than is Stahl's. As Sirk himself admits, his "happy ending" is really a study in the hopelessness of the original premise of the film. Considering the various comments on definitions of melodrama can help in approaching the specific difficulties encountered in looking at the endings of each film.

Sirk questioning of the essential narrative with which he was presented in his reading of early portions of Hurst's novel (along with a short synopsis of the plot of Stahl's version of the film) is effected through his use of cinematic excess, thereby creating a visual resistance to the white supremacist ideologies implicit in classical Hollywood narratives on gender and racial conflict. Sirk's shifts in perspective and narrative strategy result in what he considered to be a more realistic portrayal of racial relations in late 1950s America. As he points out, it was important that the Negro be a woman who remained subservient to the main white protagonist financially in order to provide a deeper commentary on the self-identification of the characters in racial and social terms. This is in opposition to the proposition in Stahl's version of the narrative that Delilah could benefit directly as a stakeholder in the corporation of the pancake business, though she refuses to accept this proposition. Delilah's refusal is based, according to the narrative, on her willful choice to accept her subordination as is only right in the white supremacist culture the film portrays.

It is nonetheless crucial that both directors chose to highlight the "colored angle" by beginning their narratives with the initial encounter of the white woman and the black woman, who becomes her potential business partner and servant. In Stahl's version, we encounter Delilah for the first time standing behind Bea's screen door (clearly a backdoor entrance to Bea's home). She has mistakenly understood Bea Pullman's address as the correct one for a job she is seeking. She is clearly in search of a job that offers her a home for her child and herself in exchange for housework and cooking. The last shot of her before she makes a decision to "talk Bea in to hiring her" (from her perspective) is as she is standing on the first floor of Bea's house while Bea tends to her daughter on the second floor. The camera focuses on Delilah behind the bars of the staircase, as if she has imprisoned herself in order to take on this job. The overall impression of this scene is that she has somehow tricked Bea into hiring her (due to Bea's real need for a maid she cannot afford) but also, read "against the grain," that she has had to ingratiate herself in order to succeed in doing so. Ironically, just a few shots before this one, we see a matching shot of Bea "imprisoned" by the same staircase as she dresses her child (Figs. 4.1 and 4.2).

Fig. 4.1 *Imitation of Life* 1934. Universal Studios. Bea Behind Bars 3:34

Fig. 4.2   *Imitation of Life* 1934. Delilah Behind Bars 6:26

A MORE SELF-REFLEXIVE HIRING

Delilah's infiltration of Bea's home territory is in stark contrast to the initial encounter between Annie and Lora, who meet on a crowded beach as Lora desperately searches for her lost daughter, Susie. Annie is the parallel in Sirk's film to the Delilah character in Stahl's film and in the original novel. She and her daughter SaraJane are visually trapped between bars underneath the boardwalk pier with Lora's daughter Susie, as they all wait patiently for Susie's mother to find her. Meanwhile, Lora dashes about, looking over boardwalk railings and finally descending to the lower levels in search of her daughter. Lora is eventually led to her child by Steven Archer, her eventual love interest in the film. In their initial encounter, he takes a snapshot of her and then suggests that she go to the police in order to find her child. From this point on, he functions throughout the film as the spectator and chronicler of her desperation and her superficial nature as he photographs her performance in the role of concerned mother, a snapshot he later titles "Mother in Distress" (Fig. 4.3).

Fig. 4.3 *Imitation of Life* 1959. Universal Studios. Breaking Through Barriers 2:50

Archer plays a fundamental role in the initial encounter between the two women and hence in the racial subplot as opposed to in Stahl's version, where Archer enters the scene only once the film is ready to transition from the melodramatic to the romantic comedy in which it is resolved. Bea is already an eligible, successful, and beautiful object of envy when Archer enters the scene. While both films opt for the initial encounter of Bea and Delilah (Stahl) or Lora and Annie (Sirk) as their opening sequences in order to privilege the racial subplot, Stahl roots the subject position of the narrative more firmly on the figure of Bea by placing the encounter within her home rather than in a public setting.

Delilah enters Bea's home and, one might say, Bea's narrative. Her arrival is a disruption, but one that is in keeping with invisible whiteness. Delilah seeks a job as Mammy and manages to secure that job. The audience is allowed to see her as more than a Mammy only due to the fact the she is accompanied by Peola, her light-skinned daughter, whose existence must be explained in order for her to become part of the narrative.

By having the initial encounter take place in a public setting, Sirk creates ambiguity with respect to subject position in the narrative and therefore initially places the two women, Lora and Annie, on more equal footing with respect to subject positioning. Using Steve Archer as a primary spectator to the encounter creates an extra layer of uncertainty in terms of subject positioning though the film ultimately centers on Lora. Dyer stresses that the key metaphor for this film is acting but that we primarily see Lora "acting" in her real life, the narrative of the film, rather than on a stage.[20]

Despite the incidental nature of these two simultaneous meetings, respectively between Annie and Lora and between Lora and Steve, Lora's story quickly dominates, thanks to Steve's male gaze. He controls the narrative of the scene through his photographs of Lora and his interpretation of what exactly happened on the beach when Lora and Annie make each others' acquaintance. As he puts it: "I liked what you did for Annie and Sara Jane." He construes what could have been taken as a strict business transaction (the hiring of Annie) as an act of charity on Lora's part. The classical Hollywood narrative of the compassionate white woman is privileged but at one remove, since it is anchored through the gaze of Steve Archer.

Archer's desire to put Lora on a narrative pedestal is shown in the photo he first took of her. It is taken from a low angle, so that we as spectators literally look up to her as the caring and concerned mother who is also kind to Blacks. Both cinematic narrative approaches are in stark contrast to Hurst's decision to delay the encounter between Bea and Delilah until after Bea has already been established as the subject from which readers follow the narrative. In the novel, Delilah and Bea do not meet until after Bea has experienced the death of a mother, marriage to the father of her child, and childbirth. The reader is guided from Bea's adolescence to her entry into adult life and it is only in the fifteenth chapter that Bea hires Delilah. Bea even considers that she has tricked Delilah into working for her. After the transaction is completed, Bea thinks to herself that she has "emulated something that she had seen her mother do. In fact, it had been the method by which she [the mother] had secured the services of Selene."[21]

Bea is not called upon to distinguish Delilah's role as Mammy from Mother as directly as are the films' protagonists since Peola is not present at the first encounter. Delilah does speak of Peola and claim that she will not be separated from her. Bea has made the decision to go across the railroad tracks to the shantytown in search of domestic help. In fact, Bea is encouraged to hire Delilah with Peola in tow because she reasons to herself that "the child would ensure the woman's permanence." Invisible whiteness is not disrupted at all in the initial encounter between Bea and Delilah in Hurst's narrative, despite what Delilah will come to represent later on in the novel. This is a strict business transaction and one that Bea prides herself on.

By foregrounding the initial encounter between the black and white woman in the two film plots, Stahl and Sirk nonetheless both step decisively closer to a portrayal of visible whiteness, allowing the black woman's story to intrude on the central plot of a white woman's rise to prominence in the world of business. The subsequent challenge on the part of both filmmakers is to juggle with the structure of the narrative they have chosen as well as with the dictates of the genre afforded them by studio production in Hollywood. Their choice is to maintain a racial conflict as absolutely central and guiding or to push the racial subplot into the background.

Through an emphasis on performance, objectification, and spectatorship, Sirk resists the impulse to let racial conflicts become normalized and therefore resists the impulse to allow whiteness to be rendered invisible. This is in opposition to Stahl, who willingly and one could argue necessarily, according to studio filming dictates, displaces Bea's motivation from one of benevolence toward Delilah to using Delilah as a plot device, a comic interlude. As the film progresses from a story of the shared anguish of two mothers and their duties to their children into a plot of romantic intrigue between a devoted lover and a successful businesswoman, Delilah is increasingly sidelined once Steve Archer enters the scene. Delilah's story is at best an interruption of Bea's life of business and her romantic intrigue with Archer.

Butler's argument that it is the genre itself that evolves rather than Sirk's auteur filmmaking which is the cause of the self-reflexive gestures characterizing the 1959 film are to some extent compelling from this perspective. From a strictly narrative or generic point of view, Stahl could do little more than set the challenge to invisible whiteness by beginning his narrative with the colored angle. He compromises that angle, in keeping with the dictates of the classic melodrama of the 1930s. Though Peola serves in the first half as a tragic mulatto figure, her acquiescence to the role designed for her by the white world, the role of a teacher educated at a colored college, equally neutralizes her role as a threat to invisible whiteness.

Sara Jane, in contrast, cannot be folded into a romantic comedy plot, and this is the ultimate tragedy of her situation. She would be much more fitting in a deconstructive Fassbinder film, as the gruesome confrontation with her boyfriend once he learns she is black suggests. The emphasis on Sara Jane's narrative in the second half of Sirk's film is part of Sirk's decision to resist Hollywood's insistence on an invisible whiteness, though he does provide some subtle and ironic curtsies to invisible whiteness in transitioning Lora and Annie to lives of financial ease. A crucial shared feature of the novel and each film version is that readers and spectators witness the moment when the protagonists begin to experience and enjoy the American Dream, a narrative element that is at the heart of Hurst's novel as well as central to the race and gender critiques of all three works.

Bea Pullman has become a desired object, and her life represents the goal of every ambitious woman. As E. Ann Kaplan puts it, "Claudette Colbert, driven to make money to provide for her daughter, is very quickly positioned as a glamorous object in a luxurious upper-class setting. She and her house become (like the department store window with its idealized mannequins) objects that embody the spectator's desires."[22] Bea has taken the advice of her new business partner, Elmer, and has "boxed" Delilah's pancake flour, the secret recipe for which Delilah has just given her as a present, since she wants to have no part in the corporate gain from Bea's business.

Like Bea, Lora also moved into a spectacular new home, and both Delilah and Annie in their separate film adaptations become more deeply ensconced in their roles as symbols of the white success story for their mistresses Bea and Lora. Though Bea and Lora are the principle objects of desire in these narratives, Delilah and Annie adorn their homes in the guise of discreet, competent servants. Sirk adds an impeccable black manservant to Lora's landscape as well. The manservant is strongly reminiscent of the stereotypical blacks appearing in 1930s films. He is prompt, knows his place, and speaks only in the case of dire emergencies, such as when Annie is ill and in urgent need of a doctor. That the transition to a life of creature comfort and financial ease is an important narrative pivot for each film is in keeping with each film's function as an adaptation.

The opening shot of Stahl's transition to the second half of the film is one where Bea is stunningly dressed and is surrounded by admiring men. She is lauded as one of the best party hostesses in New York City, and, indeed, it seems to come naturally to her. By contrast, Hurst is careful to remind her reader that Bea's success in business did absolutely nothing to ensure her smooth entry into the elite New York social world and even stresses that Bea continually shied away from social engagements because she had never been taught the necessary skills to perform well in such situations. When her powerful business friend, Virginia Eden, invited her to frequent social functions, Bea marvels that "[in] the long years since her marriage, every one of them spent in urban communities, it occurred to her that she held the unique record of having had part in not one social function of any nature whatsoever."[23]

In Stahl's adaptation, it's as if the spectator went out to get popcorn and returned to a different film. Colbert's sophistication is abruptly acquired and serves her well. In keeping with the generic transition, the camera shifts from her to a medium-range shot of a bumbling but elegant Steven Archer standing just outside the door searching for the doorbell. Once she instructs him on how to find it, he enters both into the house and into the narrative as Bea's soon-to-be devoted and well-mannered suitor.

After almost immediately asking her to dance with him, Archer ridicules the owner of the elegant home, deriding her as no doubt an overreaching nouveau riche. He confesses that he was forced to come to this party because his friend Flake, Bea's business partner, wanted him to meet the owner, whom he refers to as the "pancake queen." He wonders aloud if she has thrown this party just to sell pancakes to her guests. He is of course very chagrined to discover that the woman with whom he is dancing is the pancake queen herself and proceeds to fall madly in love. The premise for a stylish romantic comedy has been set into place. That premise is particularly poignant when we hear that Archer's previous romantic interests have all been fictional characters from books such as *Diana of the Crossways*.[24] Just as Delilah has been reified as a symbol of the comforts of home through the endless array of her smiling face adorning the Bea Pullman pancake boxes sold all over the country, Bea has been "boxed" into her role as desirable object for a romantic adventure.

By contrast, Sirk's transition into the American success story that is Lora's works to reinforce the tenacity of the colored angle with which the film began. After an episodic sequence where the years of successful performance in numerous romantic comedies are flashed across the screen, with titles such as *Born to Laugh* and *Happiness*, the camera cuts to a landscape shot of a beautiful country-style home with a moving van in front of it. The use of the pronoun "we" dominates throughout the scene. The "we" is an echo of the earlier use of "our" at the moment when Annie first moves in with Lora in her cold-water flat. Annie suggests at that early point in the film that the money that is made by addressing envelopes will go into "our" kitty, that is, their joint and seemingly equal savings.

In this scene, it is Lora who wants to cling to the "we" as a way of insisting on the move to the new home as a joint venture. When Annie wonders if the move is not too expensive and whether they are spending too much money Lora responds by saying "we can't afford not to," implying that success and the American Dream must be accompanied by the necessary visible trappings. As Sirk himself points out, this scene cements the fact that Annie will be even more financially dependent on Lora than she was before when they were both struggling mothers. He claims that he had to "change the axis of the film and make the Negro woman just a typical Negro, a servant, without much she could call her own."[25] In conformity with the dominance of acting and artifice that infuses Sirk's film, Lora is essentially setting the stage of her success through her insistence that a lot of money must be spent to make that stage believable.

It is in this pivotal scene that Lora confronts her playwright lover, David Edwards, and informs him that she does not want to act in his new production, another romantic comedy, but rather that she has decided to appear in another playwright's new and dramatic production, and will play the role of the somber social worker. As Annie stands in the background fixing David's drink, he remarks that the choice is a ridiculous one, with no fun, no sex, and a controversial colored angle. He suggests that Lora's impulsive desire to miscast herself is too risky and might affect her standing as a romantic comedy star. Though Annie does not say a word, the camera speaks for her, shifting ever so gently in her direction when he remarks upon the controversial colored angle. She is clearly offended but powerless to react. Within the narrative, Annie has become invisible in this transitional scene just as Delilah became increasingly obliterated by her need to serve as comic relief in Stahl's version. Nonetheless, the second half of Sirk's film aims to make Annie and the hopelessness of her situation painfully visible. The invisible whiteness that has long been part of her situation remains invisible in the narrative but ever more visible to the spectator.

All narrative pivots of both films after this point remain consistent with each other and continue to do so throughout. The flight of Peola/Sara Jane; the search to locate her; Jessie/Susie's awkward crush on Steve Archer; the final disowning of the black mother by her only daughter; and the death and funeral of Delilah/Annie are all narrative events used as guiding directives. However, whiteness as a privilege and narrative controller is maintained throughout Stahl's second half whereas whiteness begins to function as an embarrassing spectacle in the second half of Sirk's film.

One cannot conclude that the use of whiteness in the two films indicates an overt racist attitude on the part of the director Stahl, nor does it assure that Sirk can be taken as an effective crusader against American white supremacy, though he does claim that his goal was to make a film with social commentary on the hopelessness of the black mother's situation. The racist assumptions of some narrative conventions are difficult to eradicate. The same might be said for certain generic conventions. Stahl and Sirk are primarily involved in making narrative and generic choices in their films. Though the two directors have divergent aims, their respective films are both Universal Studios productions and it is to the credit of Universal Studios that both films were successful as products of their times perhaps. As has been argued, Stahl sublimates the colored angle in the name of a successful shift from melodrama to romantic comedy to ensure a certain invisibility of whiteness or white privilege. Sirk keeps the colored angle painfully alive to question white privilege, which is a fitting anticipation of the issues which will dominate in the Civil Rights period in the United States.

The argument generally advanced in favor of Sirk's enlightened racial discourse is that he disrupts the seamlessness of the Hollywood narrative through cinematic excess and thus calls attention to whiteness and the complexity of racial issues in Hollywood in a self-reflexive way. Creating an architecture or mise-en-scène that succeeds in bringing such concerns to the forefront cemented his reputation as an auteur and was the foundation for the admiration of the *Nouvelle vague* critics and filmmakers in France who praised his work very highly. Fassbinder, one of the central German New Wave directors, was also profoundly influenced by Sirk's work, as is evidenced in his reviews of Sirk's films.[26]

As Butler suggests, Sirk's filmic decisions may have been determined by the natural evolution of the domestic melodrama, but maintaining this position requires overlooking or minimizing the importance of Sirk's use of objects, extradiegetic mise-en-scène, and other filmic punctuations throughout his film. These types of decisions brought him initial and lasting praise from the European critics and filmmakers. Elsaesser, in his "Tales of Sound and Fury," points out that melodrama thrives on cinematic representation of the object and its effect on the characters. One could argue that Sirk recognizes this element and takes it to its ultimate extremes, thus creating an excess to the genre. As Elsaesser points out, "Pressure is generated by things crowding in on them and life becomes increasingly complicated because cluttered with objects and obstacles that invade their personalities, take them over, stand for them, become more real than the human relations or emotions they were intended to symbolise."[27] Two examples of the use of objects in similar ways are (1) the dolls with which the girls play on the first day that Sara Jane comes back to the house with Susie and (2) the fire hydrant that is in the foreground in the scene when Annie goes to Sara Jane's school to pick her up.

In the case of the dolls, when Susie offers to give the black doll to Sara Jane, Sara Jane violently rejects it because she prefers the white doll, Susie's favorite. Sara Jane eventually takes the black doll but subsequently lets it drop abandoned to the floor as she is shuffled off to the back room for bedtime. The camera zooms quickly into a shot of the black doll with an ominous musical overtone. On the level of the narrative, the two girls are tired and therefore cranky after a long day of playing. Sirk's shot of the doll in excess of the narrative is the first clear signal that any promise of smooth narrative progression will most certainly get disrupted by the conflicts caused by Sara Jane's existence in an invisible white environment.

The second example is more obtuse but is brought into prominence by Sirk's use of color, another aspect of filmic technique in a melodrama that Elsaesser indicates is characteristic of Sirk's style. This particular example illustrates Elsaesser's provisional definition of melodrama as an "expressive code" that "might therefore be described as a particular form of dramatic mise-en-scène, characterized by a dynamic use of space and musical categories."[28] When Annie shows up at Sara Jane's school to bring her boots and a raincoat, the second shot of her entrance to the school is dominated in the foreground by a bright red fire hydrant. Though the hydrant has no narrative function whatsoever, its connotation of danger is present to the scene. As the scene progresses, the hydrant will appear once Annie and Sara Jane are leaving the school, and its presence is reinforced by a continual onslaught of red objects that assault the spectator throughout Sara Jane's hasty and emotional retreat.

In keeping with Elsaesser's comments, the color red is used to stress the seeming point of no return into which the narrative has entered and to reinforce the connotative threat of danger presented by the hydrant and by Sara Jane's dangerous attempts to pass for white. In these and other ways, the colored angle maintains its central position as participating in the narrative excess of the film. The seamless narrative that controls Sirk's film absorbs this excessive meaning on a surface reading. Read against the grain, the film both presents and critiques this episode in which Annie discovers that Sara Jane has been "passing" at school. Sirk's trademark as auteur is indeed rooted in the assertion that such excesses to narrative create a more self-reflexive effect. By contrast, Stahl composed his shots with care, but it is a shot composition that is almost always consistent with forwarding the narrative rather than establishing a meaning outside the diegetic space of the film, as is the case with Sirk's use of objects or shot composition.

A potential exception to this rule might be gleaned from Stahl's use of an arbitrary object as a focus in the initial shot of the film. The film opens onto a close-up of a rubber ducky floating in the bathtub as we hear the voice-over of a young Jessie Pullman saying "I want my quack quack." This shot is quickly folded back into the narrative and indeed punctuates and defines the narrative throughout as the ending of the film suggests. On one hand, the shot defines Bea's primary motivation in the narrative. She wants to give her daughter Jessie whatever she desires, no matter how silly or inconsequential these desires might seem.

The shot representing the object of Jessie's desires, the rubber duck, coincides with the central narrative opening of the film, which is the encounter between Bea and Delilah. If taken as an individual shot, the rubber ducky does indeed function in some ways outside the narrative flow. Stahl's ending nonetheless economizes the shot by using it as the beginning of Bea's narrative to Jessie about how she almost chose romantic intrigue over her maternal duty to her daughter. As the film draws to a close, the camera focuses on Bea, who has just chosen to forsake her chances of marital happiness in the name of her daughter's well-being. As the camera closes in on her face, she begins the story of the day they both met Delilah. She explains to Jessie that she was a little baby in the bathtub exclaiming that she wanted her "quack quack" when Delilah arrived at their home. In essence, Bea recenters the narrative on her daughter's desires as the focal point for the story, thus cementing her choice of maternal sacrifice over romance. The film's opening shot provides closure for Stahl's film and mitigates the viewer's potential disappointment that Bea has chosen not to marry Archer.

Closure works very differently for the novel and each of the two films. While Hollywood studio production of a romantic comedy would normally require that marriage ensue, Stahl refuses this route and thus remains true to his source material. He therefore offers a subtle reminder to the spectator that the narrative is really about family duty and the mother-daughter relationship. The establishing shot of the rubber ducky is used to make this connection concrete. Hurst's novel is more brutal and exacting in that the last moment of the novel shows Bea entering her own home to witness the manifestations of a budding romance between her daughter and Frank Flake, the man with whom she was in love. Flake was eight years younger than Bea, which had always caused her concern, so the reader is somewhat prepared for this surprise. Nonetheless, having had Bea as the subject position from which the reader has witnessed all events throughout the novel, it is expected that the reader would be disappointed when Bea observes that the image of Jessie and Frank in love and about to embark on a new life together is fitting. Bea's observation saves the protagonist from herself and reasserts the theme of maternal sacrifice as the central one.

In both cases, the colored angle has been far removed from emphasis and is completely immaterial to the closure of the novel or the 1934 version of *Imitation of Life*. Any living remnant of this subplot, namely Peola, has been eradicated. Peola has sacrificed her desire to pass for white, having realized that she will never be able to combat the invisible white world around her fully. In Hurst's novel, Peola has married a white man but has acquiesced to invisible whiteness by being sterilized before her marriage. She bows to the social order which dictates that miscegenation involves the sinful polluting of the white race with colored blood.[29] In Stahl's film, Peola has accepted her role as a second-class citizen and returned to the colored college she originally scorned. These narrative resolutions allow invisible whiteness to prevail.

Elsaesser's reading of Sirk's ending elucidates the extent to which the ambiguity of the closing shot refuses a resolution that denies the centrality of the colored angle and therefore criticizes the mythic supremacy of invisible whiteness. The film ends on a shot of Steve, Lora, Susie, and Sara Jane in the funeral hearse with Sara Jane leaning on Lara's shoulder and everyone wearing a "happy" smile. As mentioned, Sirk explicitly remarked that his happy ending was not believable, and this is so for the reasons Elsaesser evokes. As he suggests, while Sara Jane is being brought into the fold and has apologized for her rejection of her mother, she has not renounced her desire to be white and may well go back to her job singing in the nightclubs where her semblance of whiteness is not questioned.

To build on Elsaesser's analysis, the physical proximity of Lora and Sara Jane, with Steve and Susie looking on as silent and admiring spectators, suggests that no matter how many mistakes Lora has made or how much she has lost with the death of Annie, she still remains the central lever of power in the narrative. She is still invisible whiteness personified, as Dyer intimates in his analysis of Lana Turner's performance in the film. Dyer rightly points out that though Lora claims that no one has ever treated Sara Jane as if she is different, the very structure of the society in which Lora participates discriminates against Sara Jane.[30]

Lora is no more enlightened on this point than she has been throughout the film. Her invisible whiteness is thus rendered painfully visible through this last magnanimous performance. According to a narrative that privileges invisible whiteness, a narrative informed by the mythology of American white supremacy, Lora will save Sara Jane from needless suffering, a fact the careful spectator cannot accept. And if the spectator has somehow missed the irony of this happy ending, Steve Archer is once again invoked as the male spectator whose eyes remain focused on Lora. His smile is perhaps the only genuine one in this final shot since it seems to suggest his tacit approval of Lora, the benevolent white woman, ready to spare Sara Jane from experiencing pain.

Through close analysis of the structural distinctions between the two films, I establish an instance of intersectionality with respect to Bordwell's categories and visible and invisible whiteness. Sirk's deconstructive strategies with respect to the classical Hollywood narrative attracted the attention and praise of the *Nouvelle vague* critics, and this chapter incorporates discussion of their appreciation of Sirk's films in my analysis of *Imitation of Life*. As is argued by most who engage in the classical Hollywood versus art cinema debates, the *Nouvelle vague* was instrumental in triggering the categorical film distinctions between Hollywood and art cinema.

NOTES

1. Sirk's comment on his filmmaking choices in *Imitation of Life*, quoted in Jon Halliday, *Sirk on Sirk: Conversations with Jon Halliday* (London: Faber and Faber, 2010/1971), Kindle edition. A similar reference to this quote is given in Paul Willemen's seminal article, "Distantiation and Douglas Sirk," *Screen* 12, no. 2 (Summer 1971): 63–67.
2. Christine Gledhill Ed., Home is Where the Heart is: Studies in Melodrama and the Woman's Film, (London: British Film Institute), 1987.
3. Thomas Elsaesser, "Tales of Sound and Fury: Observations on the Family Melodrama," in Christine Geldhill, ed., *Home Is Where the Heart Is: Studies in Melodrama and the Woman's Film* (London: British Film Institute, 1987), 43–69. Gledhill's echoing argument is in pages 1–5 of her introduction.
4. As pointed out by Daniel Iztkovitz in his introduction of the 2004 reprint of the novel (critical response to the novel surprised Fannie Hurst because it signaled a shift in her thinking and writing from a simple appeal to women readers towards a politics of race. Due to her popularity, this shift proved to be unsettling to her critics. Fannie Hurst, *Imitation of Life*, ed. Daniel Itzkovitz (Durham, NC: Duke University Press, 2004), vii–xlv).

5. Notable but certainly not exhaustive treatments of the 1934 film include Sterling A. Brown's seminal review "Once a Pancake" in *A Son's Return: Selected Essays of Sterling A. Brown*, ed. Richard Yarborough. (Boston: Northeastern University Press, 1996), 287–290; Susan Courtney, "Picturizing Race: On Visibility, Racial Knowledge, and Cinematic Belief" in *Hollywood Fantasies of Miscegenation: Spectacular Narratives of Gender and Race, 1903–1967* (Princeton, NJ: Princeton University Press, 2005), 142–169; Richard Dyer, "Four Films of Lana Turner," in Lucy Fischer, ed., *Imitation of Life* (New Brunswick, NJ: Rutgers University Press, 1991), 186–206; Anna Everett, *Returning the Gaze: A Genealogy of Black Film Criticism, 1909–1949* (Durham, NC: Duke University Press, 2001); bell hooks, "The Oppositional Gaze: Black Female Spectators," in *Black Looks: Race and Representation* (Boston: South End Press, 1992), 115–131; Tom Ryan, "Obsession, Imitations and Subversiveness, Part Two: Imitation of Life," *Senses of Cinema* 77 (December 2015). http://sensesofcinema. com/2015/feature-articles/imitation-of-life-adaptations/; and Miriam Thaggert, "Divided Images: Black Female Spectatorship and John Stahl's Imitation of Life," *African American Review* 32, no. 3 (1998): 481–491.
6. Notable contributions here would be the article by Willemen, "Distantiation and Douglas Sirk," 63–67; Laura Mulvey, "Notes on Sirk and Melodrama" in Gledhill, ed., *Home Is Where the Heart Is*, 75–82; and the *Cahiers du cinéma* special issue on Douglas Sirk, *Cahiers du cinéma*: Douglas Sirk, Jacques Demy, Ruy Guerra, (avril 1967), 189.
7. Fanny Hurst, *Imitation of Life*, Ed. Daniel Itzkovitz, (Durham: Duke University Press), 2004. Henry Louis Gates' comment on the back cover of the reprint notes that "Although it is a 'white novel' *Imitation of Life* is certainly a part of the African American canon."
8. Susan B. Courtney, *Hollywood Fantasies of Miscegenation: Spectacular Narratives of Race and Gender, 1903–1967* (Princeton, NJ: Princeton University Press, 2005). 145.
9. Hortense E. Simmons, "Sterling A. Brown's Literary Chronicles," *African American Review* 31, no. 3 (Fall 1997): 443–447.
10. Donald Bogle, *Toms, Coons, Mulattoes, Mammies, and Bucks* (New York: Viking Press, 1973), 82.
11. Dyer, "Lana: Four Films of Lana Turner," 203. Dyer also emphasizes that her change in living quarters is accompanied by a change in wardrobe, making the character Lora more and more like the real-life star, Lana Turner.
12. Halliday, *Sirk on Sirk*. Location 2612.
13. Jeremy G. Butler, "Imitation of Life: Stahl and Sirk", *JumpCut: A Review of Contemporary Media* 32 (April 1987): 25–28. 26. https:www.ejumpcut. org.

14. Halliday, *Sirk on Sirk*. Location 2681.
15. Halliday, *Sirk on Sirk*. Location 2599. The following quotes from Sirk in his conversations with Halliday are in sequence starting from location 2599 to 2625.
16. Itzkovitz, *Imitation of Life*, xxxiii.
17. "Distantiation and Douglas Sirk", Screen, Volume 12, July 1971, 63–67, 64.
18. Halliday, *Sirk on Sirk*. Location 2606.
19. In "Art Cinema as Institution Redux: Art Houses, Film Festivals and Film Studies," *Scope: An Online Journal of Film and Television*, October 18, 2010, David Andrews specifies in his opening that one distinction between Bordwell's and Neale's treatment of art cinema concerns whether it should be considered as strictly linked to narrative or also to genre.
20. Dyer, "Lana: Four Films of Lana Turner," 203.
21. Hurst, *Imitation of Life*. Both quotes in this section are on page 75.
22. E. Ann Kaplan, "Mothering, Feminism and Representation: The Maternal in Melodrama and the Woman's Film 1910–1940," in Gledhill, ed., *Home Is Where the Heart Is*, 131.
23. Hurst, *Imitation of Life*, 219.
24. It is interesting to note that Diana of the Crossways, the protagonist of the 1885 George Meredith novel of the same title, was a fiercely motivated woman who was determined to live independently after failing to get her husband to follow her in her ambitious efforts to succeed in the world of society.
25. Halliday, *Sirk on Sirk*. Location 2606.
26. R. W. Fassbender, "Six Films of Douglas Sirk," in Fischer, ed., *Imitation of Life*, 244–250.
27. Elsaesser, "Tales of Sound and Fury," 62.
28. Elsaesser, "Tales of Sound and Fury," 51.
29. Hurst, *Imitation of Life*, 247.
30. Dyer, "Four Films of Lana Turner," 205.

CHAPTER 5

Having Forsaken Hollywood: Samuel Fuller's "Art House" *White Dog*

Looking back, I should have thrown my body over barbed wire to stop
White Dog *from being made.*
—*Don Simpson, Paramount Studios*

If you don't like the films of Sam Fuller, then you just don't like cinema.
Or at least, you don't understand it.
—*Martin Scorsese[1]*

Douglas Sirk parted ways with Hollywood and America after 1959, but he left behind *Imitation of Life*, one of the largest-grossing films in the history of Universal Studios. American mythologies of supremacy and the privilege of invisible whiteness troubled him while making the film. These concerns inevitably led to his decision to highlight the racial subplot in *Imitation of Life*. Sirk subjected what he considered to be the injustices of such mythologies to his unique ironic style or, as he himself put it, he represented the subplot of the Negro characters in this film "through a glass darkly."[2]

Twenty-four years later, another filmmaker, Samuel Fuller, left Hollywood for reasons directly relating to racial issues. In contradistinction to Sirk's case, Fuller left behind a film that never even made it to the box office. The film, *White Dog*, was not even publicly shown until long after its making. Fuller was essentially forced out of Hollywood after the shelving of his film *White Dog* (1982) for its purported racist message. As Fuller puts it, "[T]he studio used me as a scapegoat for their lack of determination and

© The Author(s) 2018   91
A. M. Craven, *Visible and Invisible Whiteness*,
https://doi.org/10.1007/978-3-319-76777-2_5

Fig. 5.1 *White Dog*. Paramount. Deadly Danger Just around the Corner 57:54

courage … Moving to France for a while would alleviate some of the pain and doubt that I had to live with because of *White Dog*.[3]

Fuller's bizarre protagnoist, a dog trained to attack black people, is equally scapegoated throughout the film as a danger to society through no fault of his own but rather, as a result of his training. (Fig. 5.1) The controversies surrounding the making of *White Dog* have long been fodder for discussions about intersections between racist concerns in Hollywood studio production and Hollywood narrative and generic conventions. The aim of the studio from the outset was to make a blockbuster thriller, which they claimed Fuller failed to produce.[4] That the film met its fate on the basis of limited target viewings and predistribution discussions adds to its unique status as one that was condemned without even being seen. As Fuller pointed out, "Shelve the film without anyone seeing it? I was dumbfounded. It's difficult to express the hurt of having a finished film locked away in a vault, never to be screened for an audience."[5]

The anticipation of audience reactions and ultimately the intersection of studio expectations as opposed to the projected anxieties of special political groups, notably the Beverly Hills-Hollywood chapter of the National Association of the Advancement of Colored People (NAACP), were largely the cause of the suppression of the film. Fuller's style, his adaptation of the narrative, and the threats posed to invisible whiteness by his independent directorial choices resonate throughout the controversy. These three factors were ultimately more an imposition on the generic demands of the studio rather than an affront to the NAACP.

Indeed, once the film was shown in art house circles and eventually released by the Criterion Collection on DVD in 2008, close analysis of its techniques were more widely available, and the position that it was not a racist film but rather a failed Hollywood blockbuster gained traction. The *implicit* contention at the time of its making was that Fuller's *White Dog* threatened to compromise the complicity between invisible whiteness and Hollywood conventions.

Protests by the NAACP were a convenient excuse for suppressing the film, as Fuller himself suggests when he claims the studios used him as a scapegoat. Considering the importance of this film for racial issues and Hollywood studio production, it is important that one look at all perspectives which led to the call for its suppression and how they belie a fear concerning Fuller's style in the studio atmosphere of the early 1980s.

This was Fuller's first studio production in sixteen years, and he viewed the producers with whom he worked as largely inferior to those he had worked with in earlier eras, such as Darryl F. Zanuck. Analysis of the film itself as well as of the controversy surrounding it suggests that *White Dog* is one of the earliest examples of what Jeffrey D. Sconce refers to as the American Sm(art) film, a film that is made in American studio and independent contexts but that nonetheless succeeds in questioning the central tenets of Hollywood studio production, be they technical or ideological. *White Dog* is thus a crucial example in considering the intransigent nature of racist assumptions in Hollywood conventions and studio demands. If one places it into the context of sm(art) film theory, the reasons for its suppression come into sharper focus.

Critical analysis of *White Dog* suggests that it was only the production and distribution contexts that brought continued attention to this film. This early position led to an underappreciation of the film's value as an artwork and as a valuable political statement on race and the prevailing American mythologies of the supremacy of whiteness. *White Dog* needs and deserves to be studied more explicitly in terms of its actual style and content. What is it about the style and Fuller's directorial choices that led to the film's suppression? Does the debate concern its ideological and political intent or its stylistic ability to undermine the complicity between privileges of whiteness and Hollywood conventions?

In "Irony, Nihilism and the American 'Smart' Film," Sconce outlines the burgeoning phenomenon of films that employ strategic gestures of irony and that invite the disgust of contemporary critics due to the films' supposedly amoral and apolitical stances—their nihilism and apathetic indifference. Sconce's primary argument about these films is that as examples of American "smart" films, they are not at all apolitical or apathetic but rather films that use irony as a "semiotic intervention into politics."[6] Sconce claims that such films capitalize on the space intersecting Hollywood, indie cinema, and "what *cinéphiles* used to call 'art' films." He argues that these films exude an "ironic disdain for the personal politics of power, communication, emotional dysfunction and identity in middle-class white culture."[7] Sconce further stresses that the films' dependence and simultaneous critique of Hollywood is one of their crucial components.

Both the history of production and the content of *White Dog* place it in a position to be seen according to Sconce's descriptions. Based on a segment of Romain Gary's novel *White Dog*, published first in English in 1970 and originally as a short story in *Life* magazine, the rights to a script treatment were bought by Robert Evans, and the film project floated through Hollywood for several years, landing first in 1975 with writer Curtis Hanson and director Roman Polanski. The film was eventually picked up again by producer Jon Davison. In 1981, when Paramount Studios needed to fast-track a few production jobs before the Writer's Guild and directors' strikes were to begin, Michael Eisner, then president of Paramount Studios, chose *White Dog* as film to be fast-tracked, seeing in it a "thriller with a social message, one that suggested that hate was not innate not learned."[8]

Since Hansen had already worked on the script treatment in the film's prior life, he readily suggested Sam Fuller as a scriptwriter and director who could understand the material and work quickly and bring the project to completion in a timely manner. Hanson was asked to work with Fuller in order to make sure studio objectives were achieved, in terms of both timing and ideological content. Producer Jon Davison was happy with the choice of Fuller, seeing in him a director who had "been dealing with serious racial issues his whole career and his whole life."[9] While Davison was concerned with the difficulty of advertising the film, he seemed confident that Fuller could work well with the material.

Though the source material, Gary's novel, is much more complex than the storyline Fuller chose for the film, Fuller opted to concentrate on the kernel of the novel, that is, the discovery by Gary and his wife Jean

Seberg of a white dog, though the dog is indeed white in color, he is also a "white dog" in that he is trained to attack black people. Like Fuller, Gary centers his novel on the discovery of the dog, but follows this narrative detail with multiple observations on the questions of racial imbalance in America. Fuller narrows his scope by limiting his treatment within the film to the discovery of the dog by a young actress, Julie (Kristy McNichol), who after being threatened with rape in her California hillside home, is saved by the dog only to find out later in the film that the dog is an attack dog specifically trained to attack blacks. Despite the protests of her boyfriend, she decides to have the dog trained at an animal trainer's compound, so that he can be cured. The principal person interested in curing the dog is a black man named Keys (Paul Winfield).

Despite some tragic setbacks, such as the dog's escape from the compound and his subsequent killing of a black man in a church, the film ends with the hope and belief that the dog has indeed been reeducated. However, in the final moments of the film, when the dog attacks the white owner of the animal trainer's compound, Carruthers (Burl Ives) those hopes are dashed. the reasons for teh attack against Carruthers remain ambiguous. Fuller specifically states that he chose to change the ending of Gary's novel, which he considered racist, since in the novel's ending, the dog's black Muslim trainer is a racist who deliberately trained the dog into a reverse racist mode, teaching him to attack whites rather than blacks. Fuller's choice to insist on the ambiguity regarding the final attack is in keeping with art cinema techniques which do not seek total closure in their endings. I return to a closer analysis of this ending in a discussion of Fuller's techniques later in this chapter.[10]

Davison's and Hansen's confidence in Fuller was severely undermined by others, such as Robert Price, executive director of the Black Arts Defamation Coalition, which proves that celebrity whiteness was quite toxic at this time. Price commented in a letter to the editor of the *Los Angeles Times* that blacks were being made to "suffer such indignities as Paramount's upcoming *White Dog*." Price was explicitly protesting against the idea that a film about racial discriminiation against African Americans could be directed by a whote man was an injustice to black filmmakers. When Fuller engaged directly with Price, indicating that one does not have to be black to write the truth about blacks, Price suggested that the whole project was flawed because it proposed to bring a second-rate novel (written by a white man) to the screen (directed by a white man), when there were many quality novels that dealt with the same psychological issues written by blacks.[11]

When the decision was nonetheless made to go ahead with the project, one provision from the studio directors was that the subject of racism per se should never be addressed in the film. Paramount was, as previously mentioned, most interested in producing a film to rival Spielberg's *Jaws* or an uplifting film about the love between a girl and her dog. It deemed the racial angle was deemed to be included in a standard Hollywood thriller. Just as the "colored angle" of Hurst's *Imitation of Life* had to be downplayed in a studio-produced film adaptation, so the colored angle needed to be, in fact, excised from *White Dog*.

Neil Mitchell, in his review of the film states that this approach was decidedly wrong-headed and that "Hollywood has often been uncomfortable, misguided or plain backward in its dealings with race." His remarks coincide with the 2014 release of the Blu-Ray version of *White Dog*, suggesting that judgments of the film increasingly recognize the problematic decisions made concerning racial issues during its original production.[12]

Michael Eisner, Jeffrey Katzenberger, and Don Simpson were the Paramount producers overseeing the project most directly. In their capacity as keepers of the box office gates, they made the decision to hire two private consultants, David L. Crippens, vice president of KCET, a division of the Los Angeles Public Broadcasting Services, and Willis Edwards, then newly elected director of the Beverly Hills-Los Angeles NAACP. Despite Fuller's increasing ire caused by the intervention on his film set, Edwards and Crippens enjoyed unlimited access to the set. While Crippens purportedly did not see any evidence of racist content in the film, Edwards asserted that "unintended" racist readings might incite violence or give supremacist spectators ideas about training their own "white dogs." As Edwards put it, "[W]hen you train a white dog to kill black folks that gives the KKK and other white supremacist organizations ideas."[13]

According to Dombrowski, even Paul Winfield, the black actor playing the animal trainer Keys, hinted that Edwards was being something of an opportunist in attacking Fuller's intent.[14] Larry Gordon's obituary for Willis Edwards in the July 15, 2012, *Los Angeles Times* suggests that Edwards's motives may have been questionable in this regard. He records that Edwards was a respected Civil Rights fighter but was also known as a "fixer." According to the obituary Edward's reputation was also challenged by Arsenio Hall in later years. Hall claimed he had been threatened by Edwards if he did not give money to the NAACP.

In a 2002 profile of Edwards entitled "The Fixer" by John L. Mitchell, Mitchell remarks that "you couldn't help but admire Edwards' brashness.

And you couldn't help but understand the contempt he sometimes generated."[15] It is impossible to prove a motive so many years after the fact, but it is clear that for Fuller, Edwards's sudden appearance on his set and his license to question Fuller's intentions was extremely unwelcome. As Fuller put it, "[W]hat right did this man have to snoop around, making a nuisance of himself, no matter how honorable the objectives of his organization?"[16]

The film's subject matter was a controversial one in the tense Civil Rights violence that characterized the period between the writing of Gary's novel to the production of the movie in the early 1980s. At the time, dogs routinely trained to attack black people, as such dogs were in the days of slavery was not as unbelievable as it is in contemporary times. The subject of Gary's novel as well as the protagonist of Fuller's film is indeed a dog trained to attack blacks. In what follows in this chapter, I analyze the choices Gary and Fuller made in treating this subject matter and how or why their choices might be considered racist or not. For the moment, the subject matter is important as it was useful in creating a compelling reason for shelving the film. On the basis of the ideological argument about Hollywood studios and their responsibility not to advocate incendiary racist material, the decision to suppress the film can be justified. Through the arguments of Edwards as well as what Fuller considered to be the cynicism and incompetence of Katezenberger, Simpson, and Eisner, the film only opened to limited viewings then was shelved, despite a very positive response to it from European viewers.

Indeed, a close analysis of the film's aesthetics argues for a total lack of racist content and in fact for the brilliance of the film as an attack on American white supremacy and racism. Nonetheless, the strategic argument against racial hatred was unable to overcome the studio mechanisms that strove to suppress a film capable of revealing the Hollywood narrative and generic conventions which perpetuate the privilege of invisible whiteness. Even NBC's decision to run the film on television was shut down as a result of Edwards's protest.[17]

Eisner suggested, however, in an article that "the film sits on a shelf not because I was afraid of controversy but because I was afraid no one would go see it."[18] Edwards used his position in the NAACP to threaten boycotts due to job discrimination in Hollywood for black people. As a result of a number of studio-related issues, primarily technical in nature, Eisner ultimately decided to shelve the film due to a fear that it would get unsatisfactory returns at the box office, not because of its racist content. As Fuller rightly judged, the studio used both him as director and the convenient critique of the film by the leader of a black organization to save itself from what it feared would be a box-office failure.

Fuller's film does indeed anticipate the American smart film of the 1990s since its ironic view of Hollywood film production is interwoven with its treatment of Gary's complex attack on American white supremacy in the 1960s both serve to create varied levels of spectator response. In Sconce's terms, the film's style divides its audience. It is inevitably viewed differently by those capable of reading Fuller's semiotic attack on racism as well as Hollywood's complicity with said racism and those who would be viewing the film on a surface or narrative level.

This second set of spectators would understandably be disappointed and maybe even bored but also potentially incited to violence, which vindicates Edwards to a certain extent. To appreciate the film and the intentions of its director, one needs to look more closely at how its attack on white supremacy is differentiated from Gary's attack. Its style, it must also be recognized, accomplishes an attack on racism perhaps too sophisticated for a mainstream American white middle-class audience in 1982 to accept or appreciate.

The purpose is not to denigrate mainstream American audiences in 1982 but rather to suggest that decisions made about the shelving of the film were indeed based on *projections* about how spectators, both black and white, would receive the film in America. Those projections are grounded in invisible whiteness and perhaps an inability for the studio to gauge the reactions of black spectators. The fear of black spectators' possible violent reactions to the film seemed unwarranted since even initial responses at preview screenings in Denver placed positive response to the film at 75 percent. The film was also very enthusiastically received in Europe, where audiences had broad familiarity with art film expectations.[19]

Its first mainstream U.S. viewing in 1991 at the New York Film Forum yielded equally favorable reviews at a time when, according to Sconce, American smart films were on the horizon. The DVD release in 2008 and the Blu-ray release in 2014 have allowed for the film finally to be judged on its filmic merits and aesthetic qualities. In short, Fuller's film style created a narrative ambiguity that thwarted studio expectations in 1982, especially among producers perhaps unfamiliar with or indifferent to Fuller's career-long treatment of racial issues. Anyone familiar with the films *Steel Helmet* (1951) or *Shock Corridor* (1963) would have found it difficult to believe Fuller was capable of making a racist film.[20]

The irony of the film's suppression was that if Hollywood producers had watched it more carefully, there would have been larger issues with which to contend, namely Fuller's use of extradiegetic space to target Hollywood studio production. As Jan Dara points out, the multiple controversies and suggestions for script changes on the part of consultants and producers makes it difficult to know how much of these extradiegetic touches are Fuller's responsibility.[21] The film creates a metanarrative of disgust with Hollywood that rings true to Fuller's accounts of his life in Hollywood production. Fuller's filmmaking, particularly in films directly involved with racism and its dangers, are extremely instructive in understanding how the part of his style that is supplemental to his fulfillment of Hollywood narrative, studio, and generic conventions constitutes a critique of American invisible whiteness in the industry.

This critique can be found in many of his films, but the key to examining *White Dog* as a central film is that it was not being judged on the basis of what it was but rather on what producers, directors, black activists, and others deemed it capable of *becoming*. As has been argued, anticipation of its controversial force plays a pivotal role in the decision to shelf it. The reasons for the film's initial rejection and its eventual embrace by art house critics lies in the question of how Fuller's style managed to pull at the seams of a seamless Hollywood style.

Fuller's style was routinely appreciated as macho, violent, and *primitive* largely as a result of his training as a news journalist and due to his public persona. As Dombrowski emphasizes in her introduction to *If You Die I'll Kill You* (2008), Luc Moellet's seminal article praising Fuller for his primitivism set a trend for both praise and condemnation of Fuller's work. Dombrowski traces the thin line that exists between Fuller's public persona and his actual filmmaking practice in order to contextualize terms associated with his film career, such as "primitive" or "maverick."[22] Oddly, his admirers and detractors seem ready to praise or condemn him for the same attributes. Michael Gates claims his defenders, primarily the European critics, "would argue that Fuller is the most American of all directors and that, *auteur* theories aside, he is an undeniable film stylist, with a unique, if at times primitive vision of the Universe. An American universe." Gates equally suggested that the film "excited his admirers and ignited his opponents."[23]

Why *White Dog*, a film commissioned for a studio that clearly endorsed the aesthetic principles of the classical Hollywood narrative, would be suppressed in that context and eventually become a cult classic for art cinema aficionados lies precisely in blended aspects of both aesthetic realms. The result is a film that anticipated *perceptions* of incendiary racism by an audience accustomed to Hollywood norms. Audiences were already strongly affected and outraged by the inflammatory racist issues of the time—that is, the African American audiences which Edwards claimed would be offended by what they perceived to be the message of the film.

Also, white audiences would potentially have taken offense at the depiction of the dog's original owner, who appears at the end of the film and proudly admits to being the one who trained the dog to attack black people. Gary's account of meeting with the dog owner is more explicit in its critique of Southern white Supremacy and informs the scene of confrontation between Julie and the old man who lives in a trailer park. Gary refers to him as Grandad Kruschen, because the man resembles a man who used to appear in an ad for Kruschen Salts, advertising ways of remaining healthy in old age. Kruschen is accompanied by his two innnocent and happy looking grandkids, and all of them clearly miss their dog.

When Gary sarcastically praises the old man for his "remarkably trained dog," he quickly realizes that his sarcasm is:

> Way off the mark. I expect him to behave like one of those cliché southern heavies in the movies, but the fact is that I am dealing with a completely honest, decent and straightforward person—and that is exactly what makes the whole thing so horrible. If only he could be a villain, I would feel a lot better. But the impression of American niceness, even goodness, the son-of-a-bitch radiates, leaves us no excuses, no alibis. His conscience is clear, his eyes unflinching.[24]

Gary stresses the real invisibility of whiteness in a culture whose ideological base is rooted in the primacy of supremacy. Though he fully grasps what he encounters in the exchange, he ends his frustrated tirade against the man's belief in his own goodness by claiming that that *visibility* is greatest revolution of the twentieth century and that remarks such as "you can't understand, you are not a Negro or you can't understand you are not an American etc. are nothing but racism. There are no places outside the bounds of the eye and the mind any longer."[25]

Fuller's depiction of the dog's original owner manages to convey Gary's sentiments precisely and also the invisible whiteness embraced by the man. By placing this episode at the end of the film, Fuller has nonetheless trained his audience for a rejection of the position held by the owner. The audience rejects the man's ideological stance because they have been looking at the world through the dog's eyes throughout the film. Whiteness is rendered visible through this sequence.

Indeed, Fuller's enitre career shows that he was intent upon casting black actors in roles that could just as well have been played by whites from a narrative perspective. Though *White Dog* postdates Bogle's *Toms, Coons, Mulattoes, Mammies and Bucks* (1974), and Fuller does not comment on Hari Rhodes's performance in *Shock Corridor*, he also notes the intelligent and complex acting of James Edwards in films such as *Steel Helmet* only to conclude that, unfortunately, the portrait of the "Good Sensitive Postwar Negro" was too scary for the Hollywood and American public in 1950 and so James Edwards was denied the kind of stardom enjoyed by Sidney Poitier.[26] Fuller's decision to cast Edwards in a significant role in *Steel Helmet* is yet more proof that Fuller resisted not only racist themes in Hollywood but also resisted casting and representing blacks in demeaning and stereotypical roles.

In short, Fuller's antiracist approach in his films, which is largely accepted in contemporary evaluations, suggest that he was ahead of his time. The restoration of his legacy is largely dependent on art cinema critics and audiences. These groups would not be reading only against the grain of the narrative motivation but also with an eye to discerning the trademarks of an auteur. They actively look for an antiracist sentiment in *White Dog*, in keeping with one aspect of Fuller's trademark style. When the film was finally released in America in the art house cinema the New York Film Forum, this is indeed what they found. As Janet Maslin stated in her *New York Times* review of the film just after the 1991 viewing, "In light of the finished film, which is a fascinating oddity and the clearest indictment of racism as one might ever see, this furor seems all the more remarkable."[27]

Maslin singles out one of the values of the film as being located in its self-reflexive Hollywood minutiae. Other critics such as Lisa Katzmann equally stress the value of the film when read against the grain. As Katzmann points out, the film is an antiracist statement though its ending suggests that "racism is an incurable condition for those afflicted by it." While she realizes that this is not an upbeat ending typical of Hollywood production, it is "wholly consistent with the dark moral vision that is Mr. Fuller's trademark."[28]

The Criterion collection DVD release elicits similar praise for the film from J. Hoberman and Armond White, whose articles are reprinted in the booklet accompanying the DVD.[29] The 2014 release of the Blu-ray version yields the same high praise. What is regrettable is that a film so articulate on the subject of racism in America could be suppressed for so long and that its suppression is completely linked to the question of how Hollywood-trained audiences could have had access to a film that exposes the supremacist assumptions of a classical Hollywood narrative through its cinematic excess. Visible whiteness or certainly the visibility of supremacist assumptions in the generic and narrative conventions of studio production in Hollywood is disturbing and ultimately unprofitable.

White Dog is one of Fuller's few films not based on his own yarns but rather on the novel written by his friend Romain Gary, who was French consul general in Los Angeles at the time of their first meeting, Which occurred when Gary demanded that Fuller make some changes in the prologue of the film *China Gate* (1957), as he viewed its representation of France as too harsh. Despite their standoff and Fuller's ultimate disagreement with what he considered to be Gary's end to *White Dog*, the two men bonded on the basis of what they each considered to be a basic honesty and commitment to their own principles.[30]

Given his somewhat paradoxical relationship to Gary and his person versus the views he expressed in his *White Dog*, it is even more crucial to analyze the ways in which Fuller made the film his own property—his own "new-born baby," as he put it.[31] Stylistic oddities become therefore more important for the making of this film. Fuller's cinematic language, while true to the *themes* introduced by Gary in his novel, are entirely his own addition to those themes. It also can't be forgotten that Fuller was a director brought in at the last minute for a project that production studios wanted fast-tracked.

Fuller's tendency to defy Hollywood norms constitutes one crucial stylistic consideration. His films typically possess a creative exaggeration or "weirdness" that fits with the maverick or primitive labels attached to him. Dombrowski asserts that one of the most important aesthetic signatures for Fuller's works was his "propensity for weirdness." "Weirdness," denoted in Fuller's scripts with a "W," indicated to others working on the set that Fuller absolutely had to be consulted on that particular part of the script. It signaled his intention to film the sequence with a radical disregard for classical conventions.[32]

Fuller's career encompassed both Hollywood studio productions and independent productions. According to most accounts, his early producers, such as Robert L. Lippert and Darryl Zanuck, were very protective of his scripting and directing.[33] As is clear from the production fiasco of *White Dog* Fuller's reputation for being an outsider to Hollywood studio production by 1982 had been compounded despite his many productive years in Hollywood studio production. As Todd McCarthy wrote in a July 1, 1981, article "Film's Theme: Can a Dog Trained to Attack Only Blacks Be Cured?," this was to be Fuller's first Hollywood studio production in sixteen years.[34] In short, he was a director schooled in and capable of functioning successfully in the context of studio norms, but as his career shows, he could take them or leave them. As McCarthy suggests, he had "left them" for some time.

This is the key to the controversy. In *White Dog*, Fuller both took them and left them. He constantly used and abused generic conventions to order to build his own ideas. In what follows, I make use of Dobrowski's introductory analysis of Fuller's film style, as it is one of the most succinct and comprehensive overviews available.[35] Most of the techniques she outlines can be found in *White Dog*, though I return to the film explicitly in order to show how those techniques are used.

First, one of Fuller's signature departures is from classical Hollywood analytical editing, which is a form of editing intended to provide continuity and seamless access to plot and character motivation. Fuller replaced this stock-in-trade Hollywood technique with long-take master shots. His purpose in insisting on these master shots was to replace narrative clarity by emotion while shooting particualr scenes. Fuller's practice was to do only one or two takes of a given scene through a master shot; therefore, continuity editing became a nightmare in postproduction since the editor did not have recourse to a shot from a separate angle on the scene to mask any mistakes that may have occurred during a shot.

One normal use for shot-reverse-shot sequences in analytical editing is to explain and mitigate the emotions and thoughts of an individual character and to ensure clarity of character motivation. The principle tendency in *White Dog* is to feature exaggeratedly close-up exchanges between the dog and the human beings with whom he interacts. Repetition of this type of sequencing lulls the viewer into identifying principally with the subject position of the dog rather than other characters throughout. Classic Hollywood narrative demands an early identification with a character through these camera strategies. As Kaja Silverman and others have established, the male gaze of the white masculinity is usually privileged.[36]

In the case of *White Dog*, though the dog's gaze is privileged, other options for identification with character subject positions are a naive and vulnerable young female protagonist; This bolsters the claim on the part of some critics that the film could be considered as a melodrama.[37] Keys, the young complex and intelligent black animal trainer determined to cure the dog, is a third possible subject position with which a spectator could identitfy. The limited shot-reverse-shot sequencing of the film foregrounds the subject positions of these three characters for the most part. Julie's boyfriend, fashioned on Gary, the author of the original source material, warns her against putting up posters in the neighborhood to try to locate the dog, who has wandered temporarily from her home, the boyfriend asserts a protective and affectionate "ownership" over Julie. The relationships between Julie, her boyfriend and the dog become complicated when the dog becomes equally possessive of Julie and threatens to attack the boyfriend each time he physically engages with Julie in any way.

The white male gaze is essentially emasculated by the dog and the viewer, bounced among the three possible subject positions—the dog, the woman, and the black man—throughout the film. About halfway through the film, the boyfriend is, in fact, largely absent. This privileging of unconvential subject positions is initiated in the film's first shot. The film opens with a dark medium shot. Only the red taillights of what turns out to be Julie's car are visible in the night landscape. The disorientation of this shot is sutured over when the viewer eventually deduces that the shot is a reverse shot from the dog's perspective. The first visual exchange of glances between girl and dog follows, all within the long take described by Dombrowski as characteristic of Fuller's style.

The irony of the insistence on identifying with the dog was that he was actually a postproduction creation composed of shots of five different dogs.[38] Nonetheless, it retroactively establishes the subject position of the dog as protagonist of the film. In an effort to search for other subject positioning in order to suture over the discomfort caused by this realization, the viewer moves from genre to genre, one of which notably is the melodrama, where the woman's point of view is traditionally centralized.

Another moment when Fuller's weird insistence on privileging the dog's point of view is emphasized is during the scene where Julie is indeed being "paid back" for being so naive as to think she can live alone in the hills. Her boyfriend's predictions prove true, and a rapist enters her home. The scene of the rape is cross cut with a scene of the dog "watching" the John Ford war film *They Were Expendable* (1945) and the dog's subsequent attack of the rapist when he hears the noise of the rape.[39]

As mentioned earlier, in Fuller's use of fragments of genres to build his own ideas, several interesting issues can be elicited from his choices, both narrative and filmic, in this scene. As Fernando F. Croce comments in his review of the 2008 DVD, "Unlike its purebred German shepherd protagonist, *White Dog* is something of a mutt: Part marauding-animal horror movie, part *Afterschool Special*, part tragic-sardonic agitprop."[40] First, the scene of a rape as an addition to the original source material is Fuller's, but it enhances the paradox of the attack dog's presence. Even though the rapist is a white man, the dog proves that his training and early loyalty to Julie is an advantage for a society is which invisible whiteness is prized. The dog is trained to protect white womanhood, the prize of the white supremacist society, as the mythology of the ideology goes, from *Birth of a Nation* and before.

That crucial intertitle in *Birth* which asserts that white Northerners and Southerners are willing to unite together to protect the white race from contamination by black bloodlines is echoed in the rape scene. Though at this point in the film it has not been ascertained that the dog is an attack dog and, even worse, a white dog, trained to attack black skin. The dog's violence toward the rapist is prized in a society where the jewels of white supremacy must be defended. One might argue that the dog would have attacked even if his new mistress had been black, but the film later mitigates this position by having the dog attack Julie's black girl-friend. Racial issues have not yet been addressed in these early moments of the film.

Another aspect of Fuller's films overviewed by Dombrowski is that they function in an episodic manner comparable to the techniques of art cinema. Julie's recovery from the trauma of the rape will be much more rapid than will be her recovery from the later discovery that her dog has been trained to be a racist attack dog. The generic demands for a contemporary melodrama would no doubt chronicle the traumatic recovery of a young woman from rape. Questions about the limitations imposed on her desire for a free lifestyle in the mountains of California are quickly cast aside in order to shift ground back to the racial elements of the story Fuller inherited from Gary and Paramount studios.

In Jan Dara's review, he notes that *White Dog*'s protagonists, Julie and the dog, echo other character configurations, notably in *Pick-up on South Street* (1953), where a young woman attempts to save a man who plays outside the rules. In the case of *White Dog*, the male character is replaced by the dog, giving the dog an even greater prominence as protagonist in the film. As Fuller points out in an interview with Michael Gates in 1983, "Anyway, the clinch is this: At the beginning of the film I had a clinch. The dog is to be treated like a man. Through the whole thing."[41] Fuller further elaborates in this interview as he describes his shot sequencing with the dog character as typical shot-reverse-shot sequencing for establishing a human being's thoughts and motivations. As he further emphasizes and Dombrowski reiterates, Fuller draws his inspiration from the scene when the dog escapes from the animal training center from the classic prison-break generic convention.

In his article on sm(art) films, Sconce also notes that strategic gestures that characterize this group of films are often used to bifurcate the audience into those who can pick up on the stylistic excesses and those who, if exposed to a generic or narrative convention, need to be led all the way through it. They are unwilling or unable to accept such conventions *in fragments.* In the case of the dog's role as protagonist of the film, misperceptions of racism in the film stem from a significant number of viewers who might not understand or accept this smirking irony for what it is, a critique of that viewer's own cultural moment.[42] Fuller's claim in many interviews was that he had made a film that blacks would love and that racists would hate.

The potential bifurcation of the audience between surface viewers and those trained to recognize the irony of the cinematic excess of the film was embedded in the Hollywood minutiae that causes Maslin to praise the film in a quote cited earlier. For example, the dog is fed a hamburger several times to reward him for his progress toward total cure. This choice of reward evokes mythologies of the American Dream. In similar ways, the prevalence of red, white, and blue throughout the film is a recognizable connotation linked to American culture. Critics ranging from McCarthy, Katzmann, to Rosenbaum stress Gates's point that "America, with her bigotry, pride, power, avarice and destructive capacities, provides the canvas for Fuller's primary color painting of life as a battle zone."[43] In the article "His Master's Vice," Rosenbaum even refers to *White Dog* as the best American movie of the year 1991 and contrasts his viewings of the 1991 Film Forum version and the version shown on television when the film first came out on cable. Rosenbaum notes that in the cable version some discrepancies are evident between Fuller's original intentions and studio tampering. In order to make the film safer for American consumption in 1982, studio tampering was deemed necessary. Rosenbaum's prime example concentrates on the scene where a black man is attacked in a church. The man is killed and the dialogue comments on this explicitly in the original release and also in the Criterion Collection re-release of 2008. The 1991 version changes the dialogue to indicate that it is not certain the black man will die, as this was presumed to be too provocative for an American viewing public.[44]

Other Hollywood minutiae in the film do not have as pervasive a cultural relevance to American culture in general but are rather more connotative of *Hollywood* culture. For example, there are references to the robotic character R2D2 in *Star Wars* as a threatening substitution for real animals such as Lassie or Flipper the dolphin, and the warm fuzzy feelings they evoke. Several of these references could very well be related back to Fuller's own forty-year career in Hollywood, particularly with respect to references to the actor John Wayne. At one point, Carruthers tells Julie in a bravado though unconfirmable fashion that it was his very own hand that was filmed as a cutaway from John Wayne's performance in *True Grit* (1969), a film that won Wayne the Oscar. There is a self-reflexive wink here to the fact that the protagonist of the film *White Dog*—that is, the dog—is also a character constructed through postproduction editing. This further implies that John Wayne himself, the icon of American whiteness as well as the supremacist assumptions that girded his heroic stature in Hollywood Westerns, is also a postproduction product.

Fuller states that he avoided casting John Wayne for *Steel Helmet* because though he loved Wayne personally, "he became a star because audiences were sold on fantasy, which unfortunately sells better than fact. Entertaining as they are, those heroes that Wayne played just didn't exist in reality."[45] If one combines this explicit reference concerning a fragmented John Wayne to the film that the dog was watching during Julie's rape, a film that belies John Ford's disdain for John Wayne's record of deferments during World War II, it is difficult to believe that Fuller is not in some roundabout way commenting on his own disdain for the fantasy heroism associated with white supremacy and unfortunately embodied by an actor like John Wayne.

Another ostensible attack on Hollywood occurs when a black man drives a garbage truck into the window of a department store marked Oscars. After having been attacked by the dog, the black man loses control of the truck, which crashes into a window filled with lifeless mannequins. Is this a deliberate attack on Hollywood's Oscars ceremonies or not? It is difficult not to imagine that Fuller is making some ironic comment on the "window dressing" of the Oscar ceremonies in Hollywood, though I have found no explicit reference proving that this was his personal touch. Given the heavy amount of studio intervention in this film, there is no substantial proof one way or the other.

A final metafilmic reference is to François Truffaut, a director with whom Fuller enjoyed very cordial relations. His praise for Truffaut in *A*

Third Face is unequivocal. This is consistent with Fuller's referencing of Truffaut in the Venetian gondola scene in *White Dog* when Julie must finally face the fact that her dog had been trained to attack black skin. As the film shoot of the commerical in which Julie has landed a role begins, someone remarks on the uneven quality of the lighting, and another person claims that Truffaut would find the flicker effect produced by this uneven quality to be formidable, this last word spoken with a French accent. It's as if Truffaut is being offered up as an alternative to the crassness of filming an advertisement about Venice in an American studio. Given that Fuller leaves Hollywood in a huff just after *White Dog* was shelved, one can surmise that he, like Sirk, was in some ways already on his way out and just needed a last nudge. Truffaut and the cinematic world of France became a distinctly viable escape route for the frustrated Sam Fuller. Given Fuller's great admiration for Truffaut—"I liked this shy man, his warmth and thoughtfulness coming through immediately"—the aside about Truffaut reads as a deliberate addition by Fuller and evokes not only the tensions between art house cinema techniques and Hollywood techniques but Fuller's personal relationship to those two worlds as well.[46]

Though coincidental, it is perhaps even more fitting that Fuller would be charged with making a film based on a Frenchman's perspectives on American white supremacy though this adaptation of *White Dog*, Gary's novel. Despite Robert Price's attack on Gary's second rate novel and his disdain that a white American director should be making such a film, Fuller's altercation with Price counters the claim that just because a person is white does not mean they cannot speak the truth about racism in America.

Even though Fuller admittedly finds Gary's ending to his novel racist, he defends the idea that a white man can speak meaningfully about racism in America. In Fuller's view, even a Frenchman should have the right to enter this debate. Despite what position one takes in the debate, Price raises an issue that continues to raise questions about cinematic representation of the African American plight which still resonate in contemporary debates. Gary also brings attention to that issue in his novel *White Dog* when he speaks about black capitalism. As he states:

> Talk about black capitalism … They sure want all of it for themselves. Now at least, I understand why black intellectuals were so hateful and resentful and often beastly when Bill Styron's *Confessions of Nat Turner* turned out to be such a success. Although their arguments sometimes bordered on delirium, yet they were absolutely right. It was not a matter of a good book, bad

book, truth, fiction. It was much more final than that. It was theirs. It was a
matter of black ownership. Bill Styron had robbed them.
    You can't say capitalism is dead in America.[47]

While Price and Fuller are sparring about the rights and abilities of
Americans, white or black, to represent white supremacy or American racism, Gary takes one of the bleakest looks at American white supremacy he
can in his novel. He is constantly reminded that the French, when looking
at the "black problem" in the United States, "don't have a fucking idea
what they are talking about. You've got to be an American to understand." This statement from his African American friend Balard, who has
chosen to expatriate to France, is quoted verbatim in Gary's novel, and is
followed by Gary's reaction: "I close my eyes. That's what I keep hearing
from every white southern politician."[48]
    Gary's comments about not only the discovery and existence of the
white dog is quasi-fact, quasi-metaphor, but his analysis of the larger contexts of his wife's involvement with the Black Panthers as well as American
reactions to the death of Martin Luther King Jr. are woven into the picture
in the novel. Fuller's film *White Dog* is dedicated to the author of its source
material, Romain Gary and indirectly to his wife Jean Seberg. Both Gary
and Seberg might be seen as having been destroyed by the American gov-
ernment's crusade against the Black Panthers. It is difficult to imagine that
the controversy surrounding the film's distribution, coming only a ten
years after the suicide of the characters to whom it is dedicated, was not in
some way affected by this contextual nexus.
    While there is no direct evidence to suggest that Fuller's film was
shelved for any reasons other than the ones cited in the research discussed
in this chapter, it is also important to realize that Fuller was unwittingly
dealing with material that was perhaps still incendiary due to the controversies surrounding the Seberg-Gary scandal ignited by her involvement
with the Black Panther movement. Therefore, the context of shelving this
film was larger than Fuller could have foreseen.

NOTES

1. The quote from Don Simpson is from Lisa Dombrowski, "Every Dog Has
   Its Day: The Muzzling of Sam Fuller's *White Dog*," *Film Comment* 44, no.
   6 (November/December 2008): 46–49. Scorsese's comments are taken
   from the foreword to Samuel Fuller's autobiography *A Third Face: My Tale
   of Writing, Fighting and Filmmaking* with Christa Lang-Fuller and Jerome
   Henry Rhodes (New York: Applause, 2002).

2. Jon Halliday, *Sirk on Sirk. Conversations with Douglas Sirk* (London: Faber and Faber, 1971). Kindle Edition. Location 2681.
3. Fuller, *A Third Face*, 493.
4. This genre-specific idea ranges as far as French critiques of the film, such as Bruno Icher, "*White Dog*. Canin le barbare," *Liberation*, June 1, 2014. The central source for well-researched evidence on production details of this film are in Lisa Dombrowski, *If You Die, I'll Kill You* (Middletown, CT: Wesleyan University Press, 2015), 176.
5. Fuller, *A Third Face*, 492.
6. Jeffrey D. Sconce, "Irony, Nihilism and the New American 'Smart' Film," *Screen* 43, no. 4 (2002), 352–353, 369. https://doi.org/10.1093/screen/43.4.349.
7. Sconce, "Irony, Nihilism and the New American 'Smart' Film," 352–353. Another crucial text for this topic is Murray Smith and Thomas Wartenberg, eds., *Thinking through Cinema: Film as Philosophy* (London: Wiley-Blackwell, 2006).
8. A brief outline of production details is provided in J. Hoberman, "Sam Fuller, Unmuzzled," published in the *Criterion Collection DVD* release of the film in 2008. A fuller account is given in Lisa Domborwski, "Every Dog Has Its Day: The Muzzling of Sam Fuller's *White Dog*," *Film Comment* 44, no. 6 (November/December 2008). Eisner's remark is quoted in Dobrowski's article, 47.
9. Dombrowski. "Every Dog Has Its Day." 47.
10. Samuel Fuller, "The White Dog Talks—To Sam Fuller," originally published in *Framework*, issue 19 (1982), was republished in the booklet accompanying the 2008 DVD film release. In a fictional interview with the white dog protagonist of the film, Sam Fuller informs the dog that he changed the ending because he considered Gary's ending to be racist. DVD release booklet. 22.
11. Dombrowski, "Every Dog Has Its Day," 48.
12. Neil Mitchell, *White Dog*, March 29, 2014, "Electric Sheep: A Deviant View of Cinema," www.electricsheepmagazine.co.uk.
13. Quoted in Dombrowski, "Every Dog Has Its Day," 176.
14. Dombrowski, "Every Dog Has Its Day," 177.
15. John L. Mitchell, "The Fixer," *Los Angeles Times*, November 3, 2002. http://www.latimes.com/la-tm-edwards03nov03-story.html.
16. Fuller, *A Third Face*, 491.
17. "NBC Drops Plans to Show Film *White Dog*" announces an abrupt plan for cancelling a showing of this film, January 19, 1984, *New York Times*. The article states that Edwards had called the decision to air the film "unfortunate." http://www.nytimes.com/1984/01/20/movies/nbc-drops-plan-to-show-film-white-dog.html.
18. Quoted in Dombrowski, "Every Dog Has Its Day," 49.

19. Dombrowski, "Every Dog Has Its Day," 176.
20. Fuller in fact accuses the NAACP of not doing its homework for failing to notice his antiracist positions in these films. Fuller, *A Third Face*, 491.
21. Jan Dara, "*White Dog*," Coffee, Coffee and More Coffee, December 3 2008, http://www.coffeecoffeeandmorecoffee.com/archives/2008/12/white_dog.html.
22. Dombrowski, "Every Dog Has Its Day," 6, suggests that it was Luc Moullet, in the March 1959 *Cahiers du cinéma* article, who first referred to Fuller as a "primitive" director. Of interest in this looking in more depth at the relations between Moullet and Fuller is Sam Dilorio, "The Woodcutter's Gaze: Luc Moullet and the *Cahiers du cinéma* 1956–1959," *SubStance* 34, no. 3 (2005): 79–95.
23. Michael Gates, "Slam Bam Sam," *Reader*, (Los Angeles California), December 2, 1983, Interview, 7–13. 7. Available in *Cine-Files*, University of California: Berkeley Art Museum and Pacific Film Archives. https://cinefiles.bampfa.berkeley.edu.
24. Romain Gary, *White Dog*. (Chicago: University of Chicago Press, 1970), 47.
25. Gary, *White Dog*, 50.
26. Donald Bogle, *Toms, Coons, Mulattoes, Mammies and Bucks* (New York: Bantam Press, 1973), 205–206. Fuller's decision to create Edwards's role in *Steel Helmet* is further proof of his anticipatory rejection of black stereotypes in Hollywood cinema.
27. Janet Maslin, "A White Dog as a Metaphor for Racism," *New York Times*, July 12, 1991.
28. Lisa Katzmann, "*White Dog* Is Set Loose at Last," *New York Times*, July 7, 1991.
29. J. Hoberman, "Sam Fuller: Unmuzzled," 5–8, and Armond White, "Fuller vs. Racism," 10–15, in *White Dog. Supplement, The Criterion Collection*, (Paramount), DVD, Spine 454.
30. Fuller, *A Third Face*, 353.
31. Fuller, *A Third Face*. 492.
32. Dombrowski, *If You Die I'll Kill You*, 21–22.
33. Fuller provides numerous personal accounts of his close working relationships with these two directors in Section III of his *A Third Face*, 233–244.
34. Todd McCarthy, "Film's Theme: Can a Dog Trained to Attack Only Blacks Be Cured?," *Variety Magazine*, July 1, 1981, 24. https://cinefiles.bampfa.berkeley.edu/cinefiles/DocDetail?docId=11096.
35. Dombrowski, *If You Die I'll Kill You*, 10–23.
36. Kaja Silverman, *The Subject of Semiotics* (New York: Oxford University Press, 1983), Chap. 5, which focuses on this issue through the theory of suture theory, is the seminal text for considering how the male gaze functions in narrative techniques.

37. Philip French, "On Sam Fuller's Powerful Attack on Racism," *The Guardian*, April 26, 2014. French refers to the film as an "allegorical melodrama."

38. Gates, "Slam Bam Sam," 13.

39. Though it is clear that even multiple viewings of the film draw the viewer's attention to the cross-cut of a dog watching a battle scene with an impending rape taking place close by is weird, it is Dombrowski who identifies the name and director of the film. *If You Die I'll Kill You*. 176.

40. Fernando F. Croce, "White Dog," *Slant Magazine*, December 12, 2008. https://www.slantmagazine.com/film/review/white-dog.

41. Jan Dara's comments in the December 8, 2008 site "Coffee, Coffee and More Coffee." Michael Gates quotes Fuller in "Slam Bam Sam," 13.

42. Sconce, "Irony, Nihilism and the New American 'Smart' Film," 369.

43. "Slam Bam Sam." 7.

44. Jonathan Rosenbaum, "His Master's Vice [*White Dog*]," *Chicago Reader*, November 29, 1991. https://www.jonathanrosenbaum.net/1991/11/his-master-s-vice/.

45. Fuller, *A Third Face*, 292.

46. Fuller, *A Third Face*, 433.

47. Gary, *White Dog*, 253.

48. Gary, *White Dog*, 228.

CHAPTER 6

Rainer Werner Fassbinder's "Western," *Whity*

I'm all for making simple things. But they have to be beautiful too.
—*R. W. Fassbinder*

Fassbinder said that he loved my movies and that he wanted to meet me.
A screening was set up so that I could see one of his films, a Western. It was
a terrible movie and I told him so in a teasing way. He took it warmly.
—*Samuel Fuller*

In *A Third Face*, Samuel Fuller describes his first encounter with Rainer Werner Fassbinder, which took place during a personal screening of the 1970 film *Whity*.[1] Fuller and Fassbinder watched the film together and then discussed Fuller's reaction to the film. Fuller was in the process of filming *Dead Pigeon on Beethoven Street* (1972) on location in Germany, which made the encounter possible. Fuller already had established a reputation as a director of Westerns and quasi-Westerns such as *Run of the Arrow* (1957), *40 Guns* (1957), and *I Shot Jesse James* (1949).[2] Like the Berlin critics at the premiere of *Whity*, Fuller failed to see any inherent value in Fassbinder's film. As Marc Siegel remarks in "Somewhere, a Tenderness: On Fassbinder's *Whity*," the film was a total failure at the Berlin Film Festival of 1971 and was never shown in cinemas.[3] In the course of the men's various encounters during that period of only a few months, Fuller nonetheless came to recognize Fassbinder as a visionary over time with

© The Author(s) 2018
A. M. Craven, *Visible and Invisible Whiteness*,
https://doi.org/10.1007/978-3-319-76777-2_6

whom he felt destined to become friends. Fuller would be denied this pleasure when Fassbinder's life was cut short at age thirty-eight.

Fuller berated critics for labeling Fassbinder as an anti-Semite, a charge that arose and stuck to the filmmaker as a result of certain characterizations in his theatrical script *Garbage, the City and Death* (1974–1979).[4] According to Fuller, the charge was unfair. He saw Fassbinder as an artist who simply wanted to show people the truth. Fassbinder himself was infuriated and hurt by the critical misapprehension of the play, as recorded in an interview with Helga Schlumberger on February 28, 1978. In that interview Fassbinder explains that scenes from the play were based on his own childhood experiences witnessing his father's work as a landlord and that the views of his characters could not be necessarily taken as similar to his own.[5]

In a parallel manner, Fassbinder holds American white supremacy up to a negative light in *Whity* despite the fact that the characters' experience could never have been his own. Indeed, some of the early critiques of *Whity* might very well stem from the harsh light in which Fassbinder cast supremacist myths, especially when he claims that even the violent actions of his main black character at the end of the film cannot be seen as correctives to white supremacy. As Christian Braad Thomsen puts it in his overview of an interview with Fassbinder about *Whity*, "As long as the oppressed unconsciously adopt the norms of the system that oppresses them, then their rebellion will only reproduce what they are rebelling against."[6] In the case of *Whity*, the title character might be seen to be reproducing the norms of the supremacist system.

Key questions dominate in light of the fact that the film was rejected at the time of its making. By dedicating himself to a stylized examination of the Western and the Southern Plantation melodrama, has Fassbinder reproduced and endorsed the ideological underpinnings of those genres, as many early critiques imply? Or as revisionist critiques after the release of the 2000–2001 DVD version of the film suggest, has he managed to put them on display, rendering them more visible and therefore more available for in-depth examination and analysis?

Little did Fuller realize that he would be subjected to the same critical rejection as was Fassbinder with his 1982 film *White Dog*. Fassbinder's intentions with respect to a critique of American white supremacy in *Whity* were similar to Fuller's critique of racism in *White Dog*. Just as Fuller was accused of breaking some crucial Hollywood conventions, so Fassbinder's deep questioning of those same generic conventions led to the suppression of his film. The public rejection by German audiences is important, but the 2000–2001 DVD release and more contemporary reactions to the film are crucial as well.[7] *Whity* has been variously labeled as a kraut Western or as a Southern Plantation melodrama. It has also been highly praised for its provocative style, but the bulk of the positive reviews were published after the release of the DVD version rather than at the time of the film's initial showing at the Berlin Film Festival.[8]

Tobias Nagl and Janelle Blankenship's suggestion is that *Whity* is a "crude generic hybrid, part Euro Western, part southern racial melo-drama."[9] They remark that the film "provoke[d] controversial reactions to its sensationalist treatment of racism as a form of psychopathology." They even go so far as to compare it with Fuller's *White Dog* in this respect. Both Fuller and Fassbinder both focus on said psychopathologies in order to deconstruct cinematic treatments of white supremacy. Both films are dependent on the assertion that audience reaction to supremacist genres is simultaneously a form of recognition of and denial of the fact that the films actually possess said supremacist attitudes.

Whity indeed enjoyed a fate similar to that of *White Dog*. Shown at the Berlin Film Festival of 1971, the film was never released theatrically, as critics saw it as an "utterly secondary experience" and as one that failed to engage effectively with the political complexities of the postwar Germany.[10] The critical assumption was that it was not a failure but, rather, part of Fassbinder's purpose. Pricilla Layne has convincingly argued that the film evidences an avid interest in *cross-cultural appreciations* of the German Left. Her focus is on its intersection with blaxploitation. Given the prox-imity in time between the making of *Whity* and Fassbinder's *Niklashausen Journey* (1971), which has significant overlaps in terms of cinematic excess with *Whity*, her argument is convincing.

These associations are articulated primarily in recent recuperative criti-cism, and any possible comparisons between Fassbinder's comparative scrutiny of American white supremacy and the German Left were not recognized by critics at the film festival German audiences were therefore unable to identify with the issues being treated in the film as they were more interested in German political conflicts than they were with American racial struggles. Hence the film was not released for larger public con-sumption, aside from showings on Pro 7 TV, until the DVD version of the film appeared. According to Marc Siegel, it was the first Fassbinder film to be released in the United States on DVD.[11] It is with the study of this ver-sion that assessments such as those of Nagl and Blankenship begin to take precedence over charges of *Whity*'s irrelevance and neglect of German politics. In their article, Nagl and Blankenship additionally assert that though *Whity* is one of Fassbinder's most underrated films, it "(together with *The Niklashausen Journey* [1970]) [is one of the] most interesting productions when it comes to the politics of the New German Left and its responses to the Black Power movement."[12]

Of primary interest here is that the Black Power movement, which is referenced in *The Niklashausen Journey*, can be taken as the first effective rebellion against the norms of white supremacist structures in Hollywood and elsewhere in America. Contrary to initial assessments of *Whity*, the later critiques, such as Layne's, stress the value of the film as an exploration of said structures while simultaneously tracing new ways of understanding its link to the weakness of the German Left, according to Fassbinder as well as to his interest in the Black Panther movement.

For example, Priscilla Layne on *Whity* cited above, and Page Laws both suggest in different ways that the racial tensions of the United States are, to some extent, mirrored in *Whity* but that the film might be potentially read as an allegorical treatment of the politics of the German Left.[13] Part of this current chapter considers both Fassbinder's use of the film as a larger framework for studying racism and its treatment by the German Left without forgetting the personal factors prompting Fassbinder to make the film. Fassbinder's use of Hollywood generic and narrative structures are most central to my concerns, however, since it can be argued that Fassbinder discovered a visible language of white supremacy by dissecting the invisibility of those Hollywood structures.

The narrative of the film is simple almost to exaggeration, though a longer script was used in the initial filming. According to Thomsen, many references and sequences were omitted in the actual filming, which he suggests led to a misunderstanding of the film's original intent.[14] Ben Nicholson (Ron Randell), of the landed gentry, lives with his family, which is composed of his wife (character, Katrin Schaake); Davy Nicholson, a mentally handicapped son (Harry Baer); Davy's twin brother Frank Nicholson (Ulli Lommel); Marpessa, a quasi-stereotypical Mammy figure who is purportedly the mother of Whity (Elaine Baker); and the mulatto son of Nicholson, Whity (Günther Kaufmann). Whity plays the role of domestic servant or slave throughout the film. In order to test his family, Ben Nicholson convinces his acquaintance Tomas Blanco to pretend to be a doctor in order to announce that Nicholson's life is in danger and that he does not have long to live. Once Ben's family has been convinced that he is dying, Nicholson shoots the "doctor" in cold blood and claims that he shot him because the man had raped his wife. Nicholson obviously wants to avoid having any witnesses to his subterfuge. The shooting was nonetheless witnessed by Hanna (Hanna Shygulla), a singer and prostitute in a local saloon. She is bribed by Nicholson and corroborates his story in order to avoid being killed as well. A good portion of the film involves the family waiting impatiently for Ben's supposed death and even trying to influence Whity to help them hasten that death to benefit their own causes. Whity embraces his role as slave to the point of absurdity. The infighting of family members who hope to benefit from Ben Nicholson's death puts him at the center of attention since they each hope to convince Whity to help them rather than other family members.

Like many others in the town, Whity is in love with Hanna, who constantly cajoles him to rebel against the torture of his servitude and leave town with her. In the final moments of the film, he indeed makes the decision to free himself by killing all members of the family and then escapes to the desert with Hanna, only to anticipate a certain death for both of them, through thirst and starvation. The opening and closing shots of the film are repetitive in that the opening shot shows Whity's "black body in a white suit lying face down in the mud, clutching a red rose."[15] The sense of defeat and inevitability of this scenario is not fully explicated until the film's closing shots, where we again see Whity falling to his death. This technique of the ending echoing the beginning parallels another film to be explored in Chap. 9, Rachid Bouchareb's *Two Men in Town* (2014).

The stereotype of the hero riding into the sunset is disrupted in the ending shots of both films, as will be discussed in relation to *Whity* in this chapter (Figs. 6.1 and 6.2).

Fig. 6.1   *Whity*. KirchMedia. Close-up on Whity Fills the Landscape 0:13

Fig. 6.2 *Whity.* KirchMedia. Landscape Ending in the Desert 1:33:36

Despite its simplicity, the narrative is heavily enhanced stylistically and cinematographically. Fassbinder's personal motivations as well as the potential allegorical critiques of the German Left that have been asserted by critics play a role in accurately assessing the film's value as a commentary on American white supremacy. Fassbinder's disintegration of the Hollywood genres and narratives claim to criticize racial prejudice on the surface but risk unconsciously reaffirming them in the mind-set of the spectator. To assess the extent to which this film can be seen to render whiteness visible, one must analyze the comparative uses of the genres in Fassbinder's role model films, in particular, Raoul Walsh's *Band of Angels* (1957). The debate about whether Fassbinder is emptying stereotypes in order to deconstruct them or whether he reaffirms them is more accessible through an examination of his actual sources.

Katrin Sieg's analysis of 2002 Branwen Okpako's video installation *Do I See Something You Don't: Subversion and the Subversion of Racial Fantasies,* suggests that the installation offers "a refashioning of racist mythologies and nostalgic longings for white domination" rather than a simple critique of American racism that has led to an underappreciation of Fassbinder's ultimate intent in making the film. Okpako's installation is a three-screen perspective on Fassbinder's *Whity* that insists on ignoring many narrative aspects of the film and concentrating on slowing down and highlighting the ways in which cinema has the ability to "suture spectators to racial pleasures encoded in specific genres." One key to considering how Fassbinder's film might be read in this way is indeed through a glimpse at Raoul Walsh's

Band of Angels. No doubt Fassbinder was able to discern Walsh's bleak message while still being mesmerized by the stylistic and narrative control of Hollywood to which *Band of Angels* is subjected. Walsh's film offers a sober message on the slave trade in America but does so in a gandiose Hollywwod way, complete with a happy ending suitable to classical Hollywood narrative. Just as Okpako unpacks Fassbinder's project to "render whiteness grotesque," so Fassbinder has shown a microscopic lens on Walsh's representation of racism.[16]

That Fuller considered *Whity* to be a terrible movie attests to the fact that Fassbinder's goal was not simply to re-create a Hollywood genre film. Rather he wanted to examine the cinematic language and mythologies that enabled the supremacist values underpinning the genres of the Western and the Southern Plantation genres to thrive.[17] Fuller's eccentric though still uniquely American style placed limits on his ability fully to reject the genres and narrative lines that formed his own work. By contrast, Fassbinder's access to such American values was perhaps limited in that he was a German filmmaker and therefore was viewing American cultural myths underpinning the Western only through a glass darkly.

While Fuller could not critique Fassbinder for his desire to show people the truth, he was also perhaps not in the position to understand Fassbinder's critique of American white supremacy. Though Fuller viewed Fassbinder as a kindred spirit, they nonetheless experienced American racism differently, one through lived events and upbringing and the other uniquely through the cinematic lens. Thomas Elsaesser rightly suggests that there are "significant American attitudes of conservative radicalism" that only directors such as Raoul Walsh or Fuller were able "to bring out."[18]

Though it is not completely apparent what is implied by the term "conservative radicalism," I interpret it as being a radical approach to the underpinnings of American's conservative tendencies that one finds in both the films of Fuller and Walsh. Raoul Walsh's *Band of Angels*, a Southern Plantation melodrama that served as a central source for Fassbinder's film, according to interviews, is crucial to analyze in exploring this concept further.[19] One can find elements of John Ford, Fuller, Sergio Leone, Nicholas Ray, or even the novels of German Euro-Western writer Karl May in certain aspects of *Whity*, but Fassbinder singles out *Band of Angels* as an influence.[20] According to Thomsen, the idea that Fassbinder's gangster films and his Western are *parodies* of Hollywood films is mistaken since Fassbinder is rather drawing out and overemphasizing the clichés of these genres. In his exchange with Thomsen, Fassbinder insists that his purpose is to recuperate the true content of some of the genres he examines from their rampant commercialization, which has led to an erasure of their significance.[21] This argues against the idea that Fassbinder is simply reinforcing the power of these supremacist mythologies but is rather rendering them more visible to the discerning spectator.

Speaking both of Fassbinder and Godard, Thomsen remarks, "Godard and Fassbinder have an anguished love for the Hollywood movie, which represents the tradition they have grown up with. Apart from that they have a common knowledge, experience and political perception on the basis of which they must intellectually reject as well as what they are emotionally tied to." He further suggests that as long as the new cinema language they are seeking has not been found, they must use the old one and hence their return to the cinema language of Hollywood.[22] In this equation, Fuller must be seen as one of the creators of that old language though not necessarily as a believer in the mythologies some of that language encodes.

FASSBINDER'S AMERICA: HOLLYWOOD AS A WINDOW OR DARK LENS

In discussing the making of *Whity* directly, Fassbinder claims that what was most important to him was indeed *not* to make a Hollywood film. He rather wanted to place himself outside his own circle of collaborators and to see through a double prism what he claimed was the tyranny of the outside to which victims succumb and in turn seek to perpetuate.[23] Fassbinder suggests that all victims are subject to their sense of alienation caused by outside and overpowering forces in their lives. He equally intimates that a victim's response to these overpowering forces is to seek to become the oppressors themselves. In the case of *Whity*, the tyranny of the outside is presented by the cold and unfair world of racism. That Fassbinder focusses on the theme of American white supremacy enhances his own externality since Hollywood is a world he has experienced from the outside and cinematic representations of white supremacy must be read by him through that outsider's perspective. Choosing to focus on themes of white supremacy in America in *Whity* is Fassbinder's attempt to deconstruct the codes and myths of Hollywood cinematic language. His desire to get at the truth of white supremacy in America required a close scrutiny of the Hollywood genres which rely upon the myths which perpetuate such supremacy. It also demanded that he keep strong control over his own production practices in order to develop a precise critique of American studio practices.

Notably, during the filming, Fassbinder purportedly subjected his actors to a cruel regime. Not only are the film spectators watching the cruelties of life on the Southern plantation played out, they are equally watching actors being subjected to the demands of a unrelenting torture coming from the outside in the form of the film's director.[24] In his article "Somewhere a Tenderness: On Fassbinder's *Whity*," Martin Siegel discusses this in terms of Fassbinder's desire to create an "outside" from which to discuss multiple forms of victimhood in the film. Fassbinder claimed to have learned a great deal about his personal world through using this tactic. Inadvertently, it seems to have created a supplementary commentary on his Hollywood film viewing experiences. It is this question that is revisited by Okpako in her video installation. She completes an exercise begun by Fassbinder, that is, to "work through the cinema's abilities to suture the spectator's to racial pleasures encoded in specific genres."

Created by a director of great talent primarily on the basis of his viewing experiences of classical Hollywood narratives, *Whity* thus remains a deconstruction of American racism but once removed. Inspired by Hollywood but critical of its status quo, the film preserves a delicate balance between the generic and narrative structures of the Hollywood films while putting those structures under a microscopic lens. This reinforces the idea that it not the narrative which maintains the authority of white supremacy in the Hollywood film but rather the details inherent to the Western or Southern Plantation genres which support and perpetuate such mythologies. Despite his many visits to America and his fascination with its culture, Fassbinder's access to the sordid nature of many of its foundational myths is nonetheless through the language of the cinema. It's remarkable that he was able to penetrate the truths of those myths so deeply, having recourse only to the distorted lens of Hollywood's highly constricted narratives and genres.

Fassbinder chooses to oscillate between the Western and the Southern Plantation melodrama in order to insist that a full appreciation of how Hollywood worked to maintain the invisibility of whiteness is made apparent through such an oscillation. As Richard Dyer specifies in *White* (1997), both the West and the South constitute "myths of origins" for the United States. In keeping with Dyer's overall project, these "myths of origins" are to be understood as linked to the need to maintain the invisibility of whiteness as a form of privilege. He nonetheless contrasts the West and South as frontiers constituting two genres of national origins, though one of these frontiers embodies success and the other failure. In both cases, visible or invisible whiteness are at issue. One might even posit that Westerns reinforce the desire for an invisible whiteness in the United States whereas Southern Plantation melodramas bemoan the fates of those men who were not able to keep whiteness invisible. They failed in their attempts to stave off the attack on the purity of whiteness in the foundational myths. Dyer claims that "the South seems to be the myth that most consciously asserts whiteness and most devastatingly undermines it, whereas the West takes the project of whiteness for granted and achieved."[25]

Dyer equally refers to the Western as a man-led and woman-inspired genre, and in this configuration, Fassbinder's choices for gender representation in *Whity* are already key factors in his deconstruction of the genre. The character Whity is an object of desire for both male and female characters, and cross dressing is a key feature for Frank Nicholson, one of Ben Nicholson's sons. Other gender-related issues are integrated in the plot. The pretense propagated by Ben Nicholson that he has shot the man he hired to pretend to be a doctor because Nicholson claimed the "doctor" had raped his wife plays on the trope of saving the honor of white womanhood.

Whether *Whity*'s critics were correct in claiming that Fassbinder failed to make his points about race with precision in his film or not, they can certainly never suggest that he has not perfectly dissected the cinema language which has kept American supremacy alive and authoritative in Hollywood studio production and in the films have been inspired by them. One could argue that this cinema language can be found in the spaghetti Westerns of Sergio Leone, the samurai films of Akira Kurosawa, and the entire lineage of deconstructive Westerns from Samuel Fuller to Quentin Tarantino. Political perspectives may vary, for better or for worse, in these diverse examples, but the cinema language that maintains them is still used.

Indeed, Fassbinder explicitly distances himself from the spaghetti westerns of Sergio Leone, stating that he, unlike the Italians, was not attempting to copy a Hollywood film but rather to construct a film according to his own personal reception of Hollywood films. He represents what he sees when he watches these films, albeit through a glass darkly. In effect, *Whity* is Fassbinder's mirrored representation of what he sees when he watches *Band of Angels*.[26] As Fassbinder has pointed out, he strives for simple but beautiful films because "it's my opinion that each viewer has to flesh them [the stories of the films he makes] out with his own reality. And he has an opportunity to do that when a story's very simple."[27] Whity's storyline is indeed very simple, composed of the narrative expectations of a Hollywood Western and yet infused with a young director's enthusiasm about the beauty of Hollywood and all its attendant cruelties.

The reception of *Whity* in 1971 and revisions of that reception over the years attest to an evolution in critical awareness of the racial assumptions about these central Hollywood genres. The American directors who inspired Fassbinder's film also were part of an internal evolution in terms of representations of invisible whiteness in Hollywood. The self-reflexivity of Westerns is not exclusive to European directors, as can be seen in films such as Fuller's *40 Guns* (1957) and the contemporary though controversial Tarantino film *Django Unchained* (2012). Nonetheless, Fassbinder's film announces the sharp divide between the art cinema's tendency toward fragmented genres and reconstructed nonlinear plots from an outside perspective. Classical Hollywood narrative's seamlessness and the desired invisibility of its ideological underpinnings is undone by Fassbinder through what he refers to as his stylistic creation of alienation in the film. Through a radical slowing of the pace of the film, Fassbinder suggests that viewers reading against the grain of the Western genre can see the cruelty underneath the generic conventions involved.[28]

So Much Cruelty: The Making of *Whity*

Fassbinder's interest in revealing the cruelty of the Western and Southern Plantation melodramas is indeed deeply personal and reflects on his own need to understand the nature of cruelty and victimization. As has been pointed out by Thomas Elsaesser, the 1971 film, *Beware of a Holy Whore*, made directly after *Whity*, is a crucial companion piece to *Whity*. Beware is essentially a self-reflexive film about the making of Whity. By fully appreciating the relationship between the two, one can deduce that *Whity* is a kind of play within a play or, in more common terms, a baroque Western. The film is purportedly a self-reflection on the making of *Whity* and the personal acts of cruelty involved in the making. Athenaide Dallet goes so far as to suggest, in her article "Invalid Representations and Despotism in the Theater," that Fassbinder has broken his own rule of letting the audience flesh out his story according to his or her own reality.[29]

In Dallet's discussion of the film, she introduces the concept of "acting for" which she argues is an acceptable way of seeing theatrical and cinematic practice. Actors imitate certain actions necessary to the narrative of a play of film but their actions are only imitations, not real actions. For example, when an audience sees someone killed on the screen they know that the person being killed is not really being killed. Fassbinder's own despotic and cruel direction in the making of *Whity*, however, breaks this separation between real and imitated actions when he for example, forces the actress (Katrin Schaake) to slap her real-life husband Ulli Lommel repeatedly and for real in the shooting of one scene in the film. Lommel plays the part of Frank Nicholson in the film and Schaake punishing him is necessitated by the narrative. Nonetheless, the enactment of the violence against Lommel is brutally physical and real, as Fassbinder insited it should be during the filming of the scene. Dallet asserts that the actor is no longer *acting for* the audience, who would not be capable of sanctioning such violence, and therefore the scene violates theatrical and cinematic practice in the traditional sense.

While questionable in terms of ethical artistic practice, Fassbinder does assert allegorically through this directorial style that there is no "outside" to racial violence to which the victims can appeal and so their only recourse is to continue to combat it rather than succumb. This idea runs parallel to Fassbinder's observation that until a new cinematic language can be created, one must continue to combat the language of classic Hollywood cinema, despite a desperate longing for it to embrace and save those whom it victimizes, Fassbinder included.

Nonetheless, Fassbinder does not attempt to pit Hollywood narratives and genres against European art cinema aesthetics. Making *Whity* seems to have taught Fassbinder that such an approach eventually proves futile, as is echoed in many of his interviews. He equally despairs of the efficacy of the political critiques mounted by various Left-leaning groups in Germany, which he describes as "depressingly ineffective."[30] With the making of *Whity*, he concludes that European art cinema is not the antidote to Hollywood. Similarly, in *Film Culture in Transition: European Cinema Face to Face with Hollywood* (2005), Elsaesser delineates the five primary axes of differentiation between Europe versus Hollywood in order to set the framework for arguing against the commonplace assumption that European art cinema is "implacably" opposed to Hollywood, as has long been maintained. The axes specified by Elsaesser are the cultural, the institutional, the political, the economic, and the spatial.[31]

Whity can indeed be seen as distinct from a Hollywood film on most of the axes delineated by Elsaesser: the cultural (it's a unique work of art, not an entertainment product; the political (it has no protectionist political policies); the economic (it is artisanal and independently funded); and the institutional (it was only shown in a festival setting and box-office returns were not a consideration). However, on the level of spatial considerations, Fassbinder aims to reproduce the world of *Whity* in a Hollywood manner. He wants to capture the "state of mind of American empire" rather than root his film in a spatial imagination in keeping with his own nation-state. This led to some misperceptions about the film's intent, no doubt. It is nonetheless this paradoxical approach that makes the film revealing in terms of visible and invisible whiteness.

Band of Angels was a key influence on the directions Fassbinder took in filming *Whity*. Matching the narrative concerns of Walsh's film was not a priority for Fassbinder. He was more concerned with matching the sense of space usually associated with a Western or a Southern plantation melodrama. *Band of Angels* focuses on a young woman Amantha (Yvonne de Carlo) who is the daughter of a plantation owner. Her father has a reputation for benevolent treatment of his slaves. Amantha has been raised as a privileged child, adored by the slaves of the plantation and educated in all the best schools. She is engaged to a Northern abolitionist preacher, and her future is assured. However, her father dies and his slaves are sold to pay some of his debts. Amantha is surprised to discover that she herself is the issue of her father and a mother who was one of her father's slaves. She therefore qualifies as officially black, and subsequently she is eligible to be auctioned off as a slave as well. The fact that she is a "white" Negro assures that her buying price will be high. She is bought by Hamish Bond (Clark Gable), a wealthy plantation owner, ostensibly, as the plot continues, to save her from being bought by a crueler or more sexually depraved master. He sets her up as a "guest" in his New Orleans home, and she is served by his prior light-skinned slave mistress, Michelle (Carolle Drake).

Eventually a romantic relationship develops between Hamish and Amantha, and he offers to free her so that she can escape to the North. She is finally unable to leave him since she realizes that she is in love with him. Set against the backdrop of the beginning of the Civil War, the film has several convoluted plot twists. One involves Amantha's attempts at passing for white during later portions of the film. Her behavior is admonished by Bond's educated slave Rau Ru (Sidney Poitier), who claims she is abandoning her true roots. In a later episode she encounters her former fiancé, the upstanding abolitionist. He tries to attack her sexually and feels that he is licensed to do so since he is now aware that she is of mixed race. Meanwhile, Bond is out setting fire to his own property to protect it from being taken over by Northerners. He prefers self-destruction of his property over the idea that Northerners might gain possession of it.

Bond eventually confesses to Amantha that he was a very prosperous slave trader of the worst kind, and he tells her that he is trying to atone for his sins. Bond's confessional story of his past also reveals that he saved Rau Ru's life when Rau Ru was a baby during one of his slave runs. He decided to educate Rau Ru as a way of atoning for his sins. Rau Ru hates Bond for his kindness though he discovers in the final sequences of the film that he is most likely Bond's son, issue from a union of Bond and one of his slaves. This implies that Rau Ru is heir to some of Bond's most precious property, most notably the plantation La Pointe de Loup, which is the setting for the second half of the film. An important undercurrent to this film is Bond's need to redeem himself for his role in the perpetuation of the slave trade and for his participation in a decidedly white supremacist American culture.

Band of Angels was directed by Walsh, a prolific filmmaker whose reputation indeed rests on his successful genre films. Dave Kehr emphasized this aspect of Walsh's legendary status in his article "Crisis, Creation and Compulsion: The Great Genre Director Raoul Walsh and His Cinema of the Individual."[32] Despite the fact that Walsh has never enjoyed a reputation as iconic and mainstream as that of John Ford, some of his films, such as *White Heat* (1949), *High Sierra* (1941), and *The Roaring Twenties* (1939) are indisputable Hollywood classics worthy of any all-time greats lists. A relatively obscure production, *Band of Angels* has been called everything from a very pale imitation of *Gone With the Wind* (1939) to "one of the best movies about race ever made in this country."[33] No matter what Fassbinder's ultimate intentions were in the making of *Whity*, it is clear that he is more in agreement with those critics who praise *Band of Angels* highly than he is with its detractors. He claims in his interview with Thomsen that it was of the most beautiful films he had ever seen.[34]

When *Band of Angels* came out in 1957, the production of films featuring miscegenation themes was prolific, according to Courtney. This wave of films followed in the wake of Hollywood's lifting of the Production Code's segregationist/miscegenation clause as well as the success of Robert Rossen's *Island in the Sun* (1957).[35] Other notable films in this period were John Ford's *The Searchers* (1956), Orson Welles's *Touch of Evil* (1958), and Douglas Sirk's *Imitation of Life* (1959). While mixed-race couples of varied ethnic backgrounds were popular in Hollywood at this time, the films that directly questioned the deeply entrenched mythology of American white supremacy and the need to protect the white race from contamination by black blood were most subject to scrutiny. *Band of Angels* is indeed a film which questions that mythology.

In closely comparing *Band of Angels* and *Whity*, one must not only look carefully at the style adopted for this film by Walsh and the way in which that style is mirrored by *Whity* but also consider the political situation of the victim in both films. Both films create ambiguous positions concerning just *who* is the victim, and this is a key to Fassbinder's intentions under the influence of Walsh. On a surface level, *Band of Angels* engages in a number of surprising and innovative stances with respect to the myth of white supremacy and its victims. For example, the motivating factor for the main male character, Hamish Bond, is to question the supremacist myths that supported him in his quest for power as a slave trader. He casts himself as a victim to the power these myths provided him as a youth. He later claims that blacks will be paying for the transgressions of the white man for hundreds of years. The statement feels somewhat prophetic in that the time period of the film's narrative is roughly 100 years before the time of the making of the film. In 1957, when the film was made, the civil rebellion in the United States was on the horizon and its pain was in some strange sense foreshadowed by Hamish Bond's avowal of the shame of American white guilt.

The critique of white supremacist mythologies in *Band of Angels* is also encoded in the character of Rau Ru, the educated slave played by Sidney Poitier. Rau Ru regularly expresses his "rage at white men's kindness" rather than accepting it as anything other than what he believes it to be—a disgraceful and maddening hypocrisy, thus providing another perspective on victimization in the film. The highly educated slave is nonetheless a victim of his master's kindness. Donald Bogle's masterful chronology of films featuring black actors and actresses is an important reference here. Though Bogle only mentions *Band of Angels* in passing, he does mention it in connection with Poitier's claim to fame as "the modernized version of the black brute. But always, as if to save Poitier's image and the white supremacist scriptwriter's neck, the features concluded with Poitier's goodness and humanity reassured, and once more audiences discovered him to be on the side of the angels."[36]

In other words, Poitier, despite his characterization as a victim of white supremacy that he rails against, aids and abets the filmmakers and characters alike in turning this film into a Hollywood romance. Amantha ultimately chooses to go away with her beloved Hamish Bond rather than accept the path to freedom Bond has made possible to her. Though Walsh remains faithful to Hollywood's need to maintain the supremacist narrative intact, it is disturbing to see a young, beautiful, and vibrant mulatto woman going off to an obscure and uneventful future with a much older former slave trader.

The film does focus nonetheless on Bond's attempts at atonement as evidence of white guilt and the self-interested whitewashing of the racial mistakes he has made. It also allows for Poitier to speak some powerful words against the hypocrisy of white America. Walsh transgressed Hollywood supremacist lines when he created such a powerfully repentant male protagonist as Bond. No matter what he had done, Hamish Bond was in principle protected by the privilege afforded to white male characters in classical Hollywood narrative. That he refuses to take advantage of that privilege makes him a unique white male character in 1950's American cinematic narratives. Nonetheless, the protagonist, consistent with other individuals figuring in Walsh's films, could never usurp Hollywood's supremacist narrative tendencies effectively. That he is loved and chosen by one mulatto woman provides for an erasure of any complex commentary on racial impropriety, redeems his spotted past and salvages the romantic plotline for Hollywood prosperity.

Thus, once again, the genre expectations and narrative plotline of one of the most underrated but nonetheless concise films about race made in America saves the reputation of the reluctantly supremacist protagonist through the love of a mulatto woman. This happy ending is tied inextricably to a genre other than the one on which the film depends in its early phases. In addition, it conveys the message that white supremacy, for better or for worse, is a founding myth that permeates Hollywood production. By focusing on the Southern Plantation melodrama, Walsh echoes Dyer's separation of the Western from the southern genres. The idea of victimization becomes all-encompassing and limited to no specific characters. Whether this was Walsh's intention in making *Band of Angels* or not, this is the message that Fassbinder *as spectator* takes from the film. He then incorporates this into the making of *Whity*. We are all victims of white supremacy according to Fassbinder's reading of Walsh's film.

From the perspective of Fassbinder's love affair with Hollywood, *Band of Angels* clearly seduces him through its lavish sets and spatial orientations. The various critical appraisals that fault Walsh for his *ostensible* need to rival the epic film *Gone with the Wind*, while extremely useful in tracing the similarities between *Band of Angels* and *Gone with the Wind*, overlook the fact that Selznick's film never raises any questions or concerns about the *fact* of white supremacy. Whiteness is completely invisible in the classic Hollywood narrative of this film. Despite his care in consulting with black interest groups, Selznick faced criticism for this film. As Anna Everett points out, Melvin B. Tolson's article, published on March 23, 1940, showed that many black critics saw it as a subtle lie about racial realities in America rather than the barefaced lie of *Birth of a Nation*. Tolson's argument is that this made the film more insidious in terms of how audiences would respond to it.[37] This observation may seem contradictory to earlier points concerning the fact that the Southern Plantation melodrama is a genre that bemoans the failures of invisible whiteness, though this contradiction is somewhat resolved when one considers the reception of *Gone with the Wind*.

What is *shared* by the Walsh and Selznick films is precisely the use of lush and elaborate landscapes that are in keeping with spatial dimensions in Hollywood films and, in turn, Fassbinder's interest in re-creating those visual landscapes. Property ownership is of central concern in both the Western and plantation melodramas, and the value of land is precisely encoded in the use of extensive landscapes shots. *Whity* tends to evoke the great outdoors without always representing it visually, which creates a disturbing effect on a spectator familiar with the genre and its primary visual elements. *Whity* is filmed in more claustrophobic interior spaces and fragmented external spaces.

For example, the outdoor staircase that serves as an entry to the Nicholson home is featured in a shot when Ben Nicholson returns home. He is greeted by his loving wife and though this generically familiar return to the home and wife evokes the great outdoors from which the hero returns, the shot remains very tightly framed and focuses almost exclusively on the staircase. With almost every shot inside these interiors, the open plains are evoked but not necessarily illustrated. The space of the saloon and the space of the barn where the young mentally deficient son spends time with Whity all evoke but do not show the spaces conquered by the white masculine powers of the Old West. It's as if the characters are indeed shown trapped inside a generic conceit, the inner bowels of the Western genre, rather than being able to range freely through the landscapes that Hollywood had dictated for it.

The only truly expansive space is shown at the end of the film, the vast desert through which Whity and Hanna wander when it is clear that they will die from thirst and starvation. Their escape to "freedom" from the oppressors is visualized as literally barren. While beautifully filmed, the landscape in *Whity* suggests despair rather than the hope inspired by the lush landscapes of Hollywood Westerns. As if to emphasize this point and almost to reverse the temporal order of a generic Western, the opening scene of *Whity* evokes that same desert space by showing us an image of Whity lying facedown in extreme close-up. From a narrative perspective, this foregrounds the desert space where he will eventually die, but his inert body obscures the spectator's ability to see the expanse of the landscape.

Landscapes are pointedly denied their ability to represent either escape or the power acquired through property ownership. In the diegesis, Whity's death, visualized in the opening shot of the film, foreshadows the lack of all hope of freedom from the white supremacist mythologies controlling the Western genre. As Geoffrey Blondeau suggests at the end of his brief analysis of the film, Whity can neither put up with his situation of servitude nor can he escape it. He remains destined to revolt, and when he kills the entire Nicholson family in order to escape with Hanna, the thin line between senseless terrorist acts and revolt is palpably represented.[38] Whity is both victim and victimizer. Thomsen's approach is similar when he claims that "as long as the oppressed unconsciously adopt the norms of the system that oppresses them, then their rebellion will only reproduce what they are rebelling against."[39] There is one significant shift in this closing shot that echoes the opening one. It is a characteristically Western genre landscape shot and is incredibly beautiful. It nonetheless shows the cruelty underneath that beauty in that it's as if, in the shot, the Western genre is laid bare in all its beauty and its cruelty.

Futility of escape is also present in *Band of Angels* but is handled differently. Hollywood landscapes are fully visible and capitalized upon. They are nonetheless challenged and even systematically maimed in later portions of the film. The opening scene shows two slaves running across vast fields. They are being chased by barking dogs and the white guards of the plantation. When they are caught and brought back to their master, he does not allow them to be whipped. Instead, their punishment is to dig up weeds in the family cemetery. This is a sequence in keeping with the demands of the Southern Plantation melodrama.

The scene quickly shifts to the young Amantha Starr standing in front of her mother's grave, which is situated just in front of the house rather than in the cemetery to which the slaves have been sent. She asks her father why her dead mother is not buried in the graveyard to which the slaves have been sent to do weeding. Rather than revealing to Amantha that her mother was a Negro and therefore could not be buried in the regular cemetery, the father responds by saying that he wanted to have the mother buried nearer to the house, closer to the interior. Land is here used in both potentially liberating and constricting ways.

This paradoxical use of land as both liberating and constrictive is even more pronounced when one considers that land seems to constrict all of the characters who might be considered the victims of this film: Hamish Bond, Amantha Starr, and Rau Ru. No matter how large and lush the landscapes seem, nor how much they indicate Bond's extensive wealth, the sea both limits those landscapes and serves as a symbol of a means of escape. The slave trade was indeed controlled through travel by ships, and portraits of ships are everywhere evident in the mise-en-scène. When Amantha is treated to a shopping trip, accompanied by Michelle, Bond's former mistress, Michelle offers Amantha her freedom by giving her a ticket to take a steamboat North. When Amantha rushes to catch the steamboat, she is stopped by Rau Ru at the gates to the ship. Though Rau Ru detests Bond for his kindness, he still considers himself to be in his service, which includes rounding up runaway slaves.

In this scene we see a perverse reversal of the opening scene of the film in that Rau Ru, when he stops Amantha from running away, is working in the service of his master, Hamish Bond. But rather than taking off across the vast and expansive landscape that usually connotes freedom in a Western, Amantha is desperately headed out to the water. To compound this, the final escape by Amantha and Bond is an escape to the very ships that brought in the slaves in the first place. The ending of the film coincides from a narrative perspective with the beginning of the Civil War. Amantha and Hamish will no longer be able to support their current situation as beleaguered Southerners in a long and brutal war.

Like the character Whity, the desire for freedom is ironically visualized as a retreat into the bowels of the white supremacist mythologies that control the lack of freedom accorded to any of the characters from the outset. Fassbinder makes these parallels more understandable in his comment about the ending of *Band of Angels* and the significance of the amorous couple's escape. He explains that this is an ending where in principle everything is great. Then he raises the rhetorical question: But is it really? He further suggests that a good director can make happy endings that still have some unsettling effects on spectators. He concludes by saying that the viewer somehow knows that everything is not all right.[40]

A last example might be evoked to consider the lack of possibility for freedom from racial oppression treated in these two films. In the first exchange between Whity and his ostensible mother, the black-faced slave/ cook, the woman is simultaneously singing a gospel song and chopping off the head of a fish. At this point Whity informs her that he does not want to hear her singing Negro songs, and she spits at him. He very eloquently wipes off the spittle with a very white glove. Michael E. Grost has pointed out that spitting is a common trope in Raoul Walsh films, and we indeed see an instance of spitting in *Band of Angels* when Amantha is stopped by Union soldiers who are trying to provoke her so that they can punish her under legislation against treating Union soldiers with disrespect.[41] Fassbinder is using the surface visualizations of Walsh's film to explore questions of captivity and freedom, and both instances of spitting indicate defiance over obedience.

The outside created by Fassbinder in this film, to which his characters and his acting troupe and the spectators themselves must respond, is rooted in the intractability of American white supremacy, which is itself primarily a racially inflected expression of the universality of self-interest. Fassbinder himself is victim to the outside he has created, as he states in speaking of his love-hate relationship with Hollywood.[42] In articles by Page Laws and Tobias Nagl and Janelle Blankenship, the general suggestion is that Fassbinder was himself a bit of a slave to the black body on display. If one studies comparative features of the bodies of Sidney Poitier and Günther Kauffmann in *Band of Angels* and *Whity*, one can indeed conclude that the screen space of both films insists on the capture of these bodies for display (Figs. 6.3 and 6.4).[43]

As Katrin Sieg suggests in her analysis of the 2002 Okpako installation about *Whity*, cited earlier, the fact that Fassbinder essentially slows down the pace of this display has been read as both illuminating the gratuitousness of such a display but also articulating its ambiguity. Is Fassbinder's insistence on a slower pace a way of deconstructing the violence of such images or a way of confessing his own enslavement to them? Both are possible, and to say that these interpretations can coexist suggests that while Fassbinder wants to articulate the racist underpinnings of American white supremacist genres, he also does not provide solutions to their tenacity.

Fig. 6.3 *Whity*. KirchMedia. The Black Male Body as Fetish Object 37:38

Fig. 6.4   *Band of Angels*. Warner Brothers. The Black Male Body as Fetish Object II. Rau Ru Performs for the White Masters 51:03

Articles that focus on the personal nature of the making of *Whity* do illuminate one of the crucial issues for the importance of this film, which is that Fassbinder saw his own tendancy towards cruelty revealed beneath the surface of Hollywood supremacist genres and narratives. He saw some ugly truths about his own relation to those cruelties though the dark mirror provided by Hollywood. But as Fuller pointed out, Fassbinder's interest in telling his spectators the truth did not spare anyone. Fassbinder certainly did not seek to spare himself. One could argue that Fassbinder might have been tempted to see himself in the character of Hamish Bond, a shamed slave trader who despaired of ever being able to escape his past. Nonetheless, Walsh's Hollywood fable lulls us into thinking that Bond has somehow managed precisely to escape that past through the love of a mulatto slave played by a white actress. The initial critical rejection of *Whity* affected Fassbinder's film legacy for quite some time. Despite that, the film and its companion piece, *Beware of a Holy Whore*, represents a painful moment of self-recognition for Fassbinder as well as his brutally honest articulation of white supremacist privilege. Despite *Whity*'s harshness, reading it more closely reveals much about the incurability of American white supremacy.

NOTES

1. Samuel Fuller, with Christa Lang Fuller and Jerome Henry Rudes, *A Third Face: My Tales of Writing, Fighting and Filmmaking* (New York: Knopf, 2002), 452.
2. Susan B. Courtney places *Run of the Arrow* in a spate of films made in 1957 just after the suppression of the miscegenation clause. It is therefore in part a film that features a mixed-race relationship but also follows a quasi-Western genre. Courtney, *Hollywood Fantasies of Miscegenation: Spectacular Narratives of Gender and Race, 1903–1967* (Princeton, NJ: Princeton University Press, 2005), 193.
3. Marc Siegel, "Somewhere, A Tenderness: On Fassbinder's *Whity* (in English and German, 2002)," Zugewinngemeinschaft:5, Werkleitz Biennale., ed. Florian Zeyfang (WerkleitzGesellschaft e.V. 2002) 3–4. https://www.academia.edu/11047055/Somewhere_A_Tenderness_On_Fassbinders_Whity_in_German_and_in_English_2002_?auto=download+1.
4. For a full analysis of the controversies surrounding the play and its evolution from writing to performance, cf. Andrei S. Markovits, Seyla Benhabib, and Moishe Postone, "Rainer Werner Fassbinder's *Garbage, the City and Death*: Renewed Antagonisms in the Complex Relationship between Jews and Germans in the Federal Republic of Germany," *New German Critique* 38 (1986): 3–27.
5. The interview "I've Changed Along with My Characters" was first published in the German edition of *Playboy* magazine and can be found and reprinted in Michael Töteberg and Leo A. Lensing, eds., *Anarchy of the Imagination: Interviews, Essays, Notes*, trans. Krishna Winston (Baltimore: Johns Hopkins University Press, 1992), 17.
6. Christian Braad Thomsen, *Fassbinder: The Life and Work of a Provocative Genius*, trans. Martin Chalmers (Minneapolis: University of Minnesota Press, 2004/1997), 77.
7. Released under Kirchmedia GmbH and Company, Fantoma Films (2000). Dates for the release are confusing since most sites that mention the DVD give a date of 2001, though the date on the cover of the actual DVD is 2000.
8. For positive recent critiques, cf. Jim Clark, "Jim's Reviews," *Jclarkmedia. com*, May 14, 2004, where Clark claims that the film is one of the most fascinating and important Westerns ever made. Also see Douglas Messerli, "Rainer Werner Fassbinder," *World Cinema Review*, September 1, 2016. It is Mersserli who refers to the film as a "kraut" Western.
9. Tobias Nagl and Janelle Blankenship, "So Much Tenderness: Rainer Werner Fassbinder, Günther Kauffmann and the Ambivalences of Interracial Desires," in Brigitte Peucker, ed., *A Companion to Rainer Werner Fassbinder* (West Sussex, UK: Wiley-Blackwell, 2012), 516–541. 528.

10. The first of the comments originates from critic Alf Brustellin and the second observation from Anna Kuhn. Quoted in Siegel, "Somewhere, A Tenderness," 1–2.

11. Siegel, "Somewhere, A Tenderness," 1.

12. Nagl and Blankenship, "So Much Tenderness," 528.

13. Priscilla Layne, "Lessons in Liberation"; Page Laws, "Rainer Werner Fassbinder and *Der Weisse Neger*. Fassbinder and Kaufmann's On and Off Screen Affair as German Racial Allegory," in Marcia Diedrich and Jürgen Henricks, eds., *Black to Schwarz: Cultural Crossovers Between African Americans and Germany* (East Lansing: Michigan State University Press, 2010), 245–264.

14. Christian Braad Thomsen and Martin Chalmers, *Fassbinder: The Life and Work of a Provocative Genius*, trans. Martin Chalmers (Minneapolis: University of Minnesota Press, 2004/1997), 79.

15. Siegel, "Somewhere, A Tenderness," 1.

16. Katrin Sieg, "Remediating Fassbinder in Video Installations by Ming Wong and Branwen Okpako," *Transit Journal* 9, no. 2 (2014), 1–29. 24.

17. It should be noted that I am speculating that *Whity* was the film Fassbinder and Fuller watched together, since neither of them mentions it by name in any sources that I have read. Given the timing of their encounter, it seems a safe assumption to make.

18. Thomas Elsaesser, *European Cinema: Face to Face with Hollywood* (Amsterdam: Amsterdam University Press, 2005), 246.

19. Fassbinder explains his attraction for *Band of Angels*, one of the most beautiful films he had ever seen, in "Quatre entretiens avec Rainer Werner Fassbinder," interview with Christian Braad Thomsen (Berlin 1971) and published in *Positif: Revue de Cinéma* (Paris: July–August 1976), 183–184.

20. Further discussion of these influences or resemblances can be found in Andrew Higson and Richard Maltby, eds., *"Film Europe" and "Film America": Cinema, Commerce and Cultural Exchange, 1920–1939* (Chicago: University of Chicago Press, 1999), 488.

21. Fassbinder, "Quatre entretiens," 62.

22. Thomsen and Chalmers, *Fassbinder: The Life and Work of a Provocative Genius*, 73–74.

23. For more on the concept of the tyranny of the outside please refer to Thomas Elsaesser, *Fassbinder's Germany: History, Identity, Subject*, (Amsterdam: Amsterdam University Press), 1996. Elsaesser argues that "the perspective 'from without' is the view of the group on the couple, and thus also reflects the collectivist, anti-family ideologies and aspirations which Fassbinder professed to share with the rest of his generation during the 1960's and the early 1970's." 31.

24. Peter Berling gives an insider's account of the filmmaking process and also signals that the film *Beware of a Holy Whore* was actually a self-reflexive film fictionalizing the making of *Whity* in "The Making of Whity" in Robert

Katz and Peter Berling, *Love Is Colder than Death: The Life and Times of Rainer Werner Fassbinder* (New York: Random House, 1987), 207–226.

25. Dyer, *White* (London: Routledge, 1992), 35–36.
26. Fassbinder "Quatre entretiens, " 61.
27. From "At some point films have to stop being films," "A Conversation with Hans Günther Pflaum about *Fear Eats the Soul*" in Michael Töteberg and Leo A. Lensing, eds., *The Anarchy of the Imagination: Interviews, Essays, Notes,* trans. Krishna Winston (Baltimore: Johns Hopkins University Press, 1992), 11. Hereafter *Anarchy of the Imagination*.
28. Fassbinder, "Quatre entretiens," 61.
29. Athenaide Dallet, "Invalid Representations and Despotism in the Theater," *Journal of Dramatic Theory and Criticism* 13, no. 8 (Fall 1998): 19–26.
30. The interview with Helga Schlumberger in which he speaks directly to this issue is "I've Changed Along with My Characters" and was first published in the German edition of *Playboy* (April 1978): 53–68. It is reprinted in *Anarchy of the Imagination*. An abbreviated online version is available under the title "I've Changed Along with My Characters" at https://032c.com/fassbinder.
31. Elsaesser, *European Cinema*.
32. Dave Kehr, "Crisis, Creation and Compulsion: The Great Genre Director Raoul Walsh and His Cinema of the Individual," March 22, 2011. http://www.movingimagesource.us/articles/crisis-creation-compulsion-20110322.
33. Dan Callahan, "Fighting Good Fight, the Swashbuckler Becomes a Hero," *New York Times*, August 5, 2010.
34. Fassbinder, "Quatre entretiens," 61.
35. Courtney, *Hollywood Fantasies of Miscegenation*, 193. Also cf. Henry Popkin, "Hollywood Tackles the Race Issue" *Commentary* 24, no. 4 (1957): 354.
36. Donald Bogle, *Toms, Coons, Mulattoes, Mammies and Bucks* (New York: Viking Press, 1973), 256.
37. Anna Everett, *Returning the Gaze: A Genealogy of Black Film Criticism, 1909–1949* (Durham, NC: Duke University Press, 2001), 291–292.
38. Geoffry Blondeay, "Whity-Il était une fois du cinéma-la passion du cinéma" https://www.iletaitunefoisducinema.com/critique/1083/whity.
39. Christian Braad Thomsen, *Fassbinder*, 77.
40. Fassbinder, "Quatre entretiens," 61.
41. Micheal E. Grost, *The Films of Raoul Walsh*. http://mikegrost.com/walsh.htm. This is a regularly updated site that I consulted from January 2017 to August 6, 2017. In dialogue with the author of this site by email, I have established that the site will be continuously updated.
42. Fassbinder, "Quatre entretiens," 61.
43. Page Laws, "Rainer Werner Fassbinder and *Der Weisse Neger.*" Nagl and Blankenship, "So Much Tenderness."

CHAPTER 7

Cream Rises to the Top: Jean Renoir's *The Southerner*

And years later, when I was taking those film studies courses, one of my teachers, strangely enough, said that no European was capable of making a movie about America, giving as a prime example, The Southerner, *directed by a Frenchman. I nearly choked.*
—*Charles Burnett*

Physically, exclusive of the players, it is one of the most sensitive and beautiful American-made pictures I have seen.
—*James Agee on* The Southerner

Unlike Fassbinder, Jean Renoir experienced both America and Hollywood filmmaking firsthand in his midcareer. His fascination with American Southern culture informs his films *Swamp Water* (1941) and *The Southerner* (1945) (Fig. 7.1). Many critics have long argued that Renoir's Hollywood films, particularly those focused on American settings and subject matter, are substandard. Recent criticism has argued for a reassessment of that judgment.[1] Without directly addressing American racial tensions, Renoir appears to have been incredibly insightful about those tensions.

For example, renowned independent African American filmmaker Charles Burnett comments in an interview that one of his positive early influences in filmmaking was Jean Renoir's American-made film *The Southerner*. Burnett claims he was drawn by how the film commented on black lives: "It's a rarity to see Blacks given the same type of justice and

© The Author(s) 2018
A. M. Craven, *Visible and Invisible Whiteness*,
https://doi.org/10.1007/978-3-319-76777-2_7

Fig. 7.1 *The Southerner.* Hakim and Loew. Sam Tucker Forsakes His Cow to Save His Friend Tim. Cream Rises to the Top 1:26:03

humanity [as Whites]—I think that is what attracted me to the film."[2] Likewise, in his review of *The Southerner*, James Agee praises it as one of the best American-made films of his experience. Nonetheless, as a born Southerner, Agee also suggests that the film rings false with respect to the reality of Southern life and its hardships and suggests that the artist's responsibility is to be true to the realities of the people represented in a film. He equally contends that failing in this endeavor causes a risk of expressing "unconscious patronage."[3]

Renoir took a decided risk in making *The Southerner*. The inquiry into the nature of supremacy and its characterization of Southern manhood is a vital component of this film. Given the complexity of *The Southerner*'s production and the wide range of interpretations about its ultimate intent, Agee's and Burnett's reactions to it serve as useful examples in considering such concerns. They also allow for an evaluation of how that representation is orchestrated by a talented filmmaker. As a Frenchman, Renoir's own upbringing and his inherited national mythologies remain distinct from the American ideologies that inform his film. He nonetheless gained the respect and tributes of two born Southerners, Agee and Burnett. Agee's assessment of the film indeed begins with a salute to the independent producers, David Loew and Robert Hakim, who "gave a good man [Renoir] a real chance in Hollywood."[4]

As opposed to Fassbinder's "emphatic deployment of inter-textual reference and self-reflexivity" to deconstruct processes of Hollywood cinematic production, Renoir chooses to apply his own European filmmaking techniques to the treatment of American subject matter.[5] Previous chapters have focused on how genres and principle narratives emerging from Hollywood, though challenged at times by filmmakers such as Fassbinder, Fuller, and Sirk, ultimately both control and depend on concepts of invisible whiteness. In the case of Renoir, one could argue that invisible whiteness is granted but is nonetheless subjected to an alternate scrutiny due to the techniques of filming he employed. Detailed analysis of *The Southerner* nonetheless requires a discussion of the mythological components of American supremacist ideologies, notably the agrarian myth, which serve as important narrative components of the film. Though Renoir's film does not actively question the concept of invisible whiteness, his filmmaking techniques bring it into focus by distorting the ways in which it was traditionally represented in films before 1945. The film was praised in some U.S. circles but condemned by organizations in the South, such as the KKK. It nonetheless won the Best Film Award in the Venice Film Festival in 1946. As Renoir himself puts it, "[T]o my relief the film was a success."[6] He was aware of the extent to which he was bucking studio expectations in order to make this film.

Renoir's fascination with the American South, evidenced most notably in *The Southerner* and *Swamp Water*, created a richly resonating representation of American life. Despite his relief, the film received mixed reactions, including a call for censoring it from critics who claimed it profoundly insulted the lives and identities of Southerners. In the article "Banned in Memphis: The Dark Days of Lloyd T. Binford, known from Coast to Coast as the Toughest Censor in America," Michael Finger traces the extraordinary career of Binford.[7] In Binford's capacity as head of the Memphis Censor Board, he ordered that Renoir's *The Southerner* be "binfordized" due to the fact that it gave a negative portrayal of life in the South. Despite the fact that he was a harsh critic in the extreme, going so far as to ban all Charlie Chaplin films among other absurdities, Binford's critique of Renoir's depiction of the South is at the root of critical assessments of the film.

Indeed, though Renoir's visions are born from an admiration for the beauty of agrarian life in the South, his critics suggest that he has entered into sacred lands and waters, places of national conflict upon which no foreigner should comment. Ralph Tutt points out, that despite Leo Braudy's claims to the contrary, *The Southerner* was "a Hollywood dream in the guise of realism."[8] Roger Viry-Babel insists that the film is a questionable search by a Frenchman for a true American image.[9] Just as Romain Gary was constantly reminded that he could not critique America because he was not an American, Renoir's films on American contexts have a history of being rejected by French and American audiences alike on the grounds that they desecrate American national myths from the outside.

Despite the fact that Charles Burnett was attracted to *The Southerner* at an early age since he saw in it a fairer treatment of the African American, the film takes an approach to the representation of invisible whiteness similar to Fritz Lang's approach in *You Only Live Once* (1937). Like Lang, Renoir does not ever explicitly approach racial conflict, but he does manage to capture something about the inherent privilege and arrogance of whiteness in America. Both émigré directors realize important limitations on their abilities to comment about racial conflict in America, yet both succeed in creating representations of the privilege of invisible whiteness and the role it plays in fomenting racial strife. Indeed, as Ben Dooley has pointed out in the case of *Swamp Water*, reading Renoir's American-made films as racial allegories is strongly tenable.[10]

Fassbinder shows in the making of *Whity* that the nexus of myths that together constitute the overarching concepts of American white supremacy can be gleaned through the cinematic language of Hollywood genres and narratives on their own account, without recourse to a direct lived experience of America. As a result, Fassbinder gives access to analysis of these genres and narratives through the cinematic language of his film *Whity*. He encodes how they reproduce, control, and maintain the invisibility of whiteness, particularly in the Western and Southern Plantation genres. Richard Dyer, Robert Reich, and Jane Tompkins, among others, have also dissected the myths at play in those genres and their representations of white masculinity.[11]

Dyer argues that Westerns and Southern Plantation films encode invisible whiteness in these geographical areas as the areas are defined by the genres respectively.[12] Dyer also insists that despite class difference or geographical context, the mere fact of being white constitutes privileged status in Hollywood cinematic representation. As he stresses, whites in America "are systematically privileged in Western society ... It is this privilege and dominance that is at stake in analyzing white racial imagery."[13] In his chapter on lighting, he goes so far as to suggest that whiteness is not only a racial feature but is additionally a representation that can be cinematographically enhanced through lighting and camera angles. As he suggests, "[T]he aesthetic technology of the photographic media, the apparatus and practice par excellence of a light culture, not only assumes and privileges whiteness but also constructs it."[14]

Similarly, Jane Tompkins gives crucial insight into how invisible whiteness is encoded into the cinematic genre system in her book *West of Everything: The Inner Life of Westerns* (1993). She focuses only on Westerns and is concerned with problems of the male gaze and the Western genre's effect on women spectators. Her remarks are nonetheless pertinent for one of the central issues in *The Southerner*, namely, how the agrarian myth depicts gender difference and, more important, how it comments on the nobility of whiteness and its labors. As she points out:

> The feeling of being "in a Western"—the kind of experience that is and the effects it has—are what I am attempting to record. Westerns play, first and last, to a Wild West of the psyche. The images, ideas, and values that become part of an audience's way of interpreting life come in through the senses and are experienced first as drama. To comprehend how they've shaped people's attitudes and behavior, to understand them in an intellectual or conceptual way, one must begin with their impact on the body and the emotions.[15]

Tompkins stresses that the emotions and ideologies of the Western have been internalized throughout the American male's childhood as well as through adolescent reading and viewing experiences. Similarly, the main critique against *The Southerner*, despite its many supporters, seems to be that Renoir has not managed to capture the authentic pain and suffering of the white Western/Southern hero. He has instead created an overly idealistic image of what the agrarian life demands of a man, as emphasized by Tutt. Tompkins argues that Westerns do indeed indulge the male spectator's identification with protagonists of films in this genre. In what ways is Renoir's film *The Southerner* both fulfilling and breaking with audience expectations, and to what extent does his French perspective come into play?

Core American values embedded in the agrarian myth are one example of the values that must be reinforced by the cinema if audience expectations are to be met in Hollywood production. Robin Wood outlines American ideologies linked to the agrarian myth and their value in defining the prevailing genre categories. In "Ideology, Genre, Auteur," Wood traces the dichotomies of urban and rural life as well as the gender divisions so crucial to understanding how families like the one depicted in *The Southerner* function cinematographically. The focus throughout the film is on the Tucker family, Sam; Nona, his wife; his Granny; and his two children, Sis and Jotty. Their struggles and triumphs are set against a variety of other characters so that Renoir can remain faithful to some dictates of the Southern or the family farm dramas of the New Deal period. For example, in an opening voice-over, Sam Tucker's friend Tim introduces himself as a "town man" and identifies Sam as a sharecropper turned tenant farmer. Tim is one of the shadow characters who provide the contexts for Sam to triumph or fail.

Robert Reich's categories are strikingly similar to those enumerated by Wood. Though Reich intends them as a commentary on the mythologies that permeate American political life, he derives them from an opening story of George, the good and dutiful small-town American Everyman. He compares George to Gary Cooper in *High Noon* or Jimmy Stewart in *It's a Wonderful Life*. He then divides George's story and the myths it represents into four morality tales. In his *Tales of a New America: The Anxious Liberal's Guide to the Future* (1987), Reich uses these four morality tales— the Mob at the Gates, the Triumphant Individual, the Benevolent Community, and the Rot at the Top—to explore the composition of American identity politics and suggest solutions to political gridlock.[16] One can recognize in them the myths of which Baldwin speaks in *The Fire Next Time* when he claims that "the American Negro has the great advantage of having never believed that collection myths to which white Americans cling."[17] In essence, Baldwin argues that invisible whiteness is an ideological construct that can be deconstructed. While Reich focuses on these tales as essential for understanding American culture, Baldwin intimates that they particularly relevant for white American culture.

Two of these tales, the Triumphant Individual and the Benevolent Community, can be seen as relevant to *The Southerner* with the Mob at the Gates pertinent to any discussion of *Swamp Water*. While not exactly aligned, these morality tales are variations on the theme of the agrarian myth and the myth of the Lost Cause so crucial to understanding the representation of American life given to us by Renoir in the films under discussion. Caroline E. Janney identifies the first three of the six tenets of the Lost Cause (pertinent to my argument) as follows: (1) Succession of the South and not slavery was the real cause of the Civil War; (2) slaves were actually "faithful to their masters and to the Confederate cause." In addition, they were not equipped to survive as free citizens and therefore had to be protected and taken care of by their masters; (3) the Confederacy was not defeated because their cause was not just but rather, because of the military strength of the Union Army. Tenets 4, 5, and 6 involve the sanctity and saintliness of the Confederate soldiers as well as the most saintly of leaders, Robert E. Lee, and, last, the support by the noble Southern women who had to be protected from the violence of the war. These myths, when placed in conjunction with Renoir's intentions in his film, can help in understanding the multiple interpretations of the film over time. The agrarian myth is most directly related to Renoir's source material and will be dissected further in context of the film, though the myth of the Lost Cause provides some insight into why native Southerners and, in particular, the KKK might have been unwilling to accept the portrait of the Southerner drawn by Renoir.

The Southerner's focus is on Sam Tucker as a man who takes on the challenge of farming his own land rather than being forced into a factory job or continuing to work as a tenant farmer at the service of others. He aspires to being the Triumphant Individual with the help of his wife and his two children as well as his mother and eventual stepfather. Hoping to find a Benevolent Community in the form of his closest neighbor, Henry Devers, he discovers instead a bitter old man who does not wish him well. As the episodes of struggle play themselves out, it becomes clearer that Devers is bitter precisely because he sees in Sam a younger version of himself. But Devers is also well aware that he has sacrificed his hope, his energy, and his family in his confrontation with the hardships of agrarian life and he has lost. For Sam to succeed where he has failed is not acceptable to him and is in fact so abominable an idea that he actively works against Sam at every turn, raiding his vegetable garden and refusing to give Sam milk when Sam desperately needs it.

THE TUCKER FAMILY CHALLENGES AND RENOIR'S FILM PRODUCTION CHALLENGE

The plot of the film, based on George Perry Sessions's *Hold Autumn in Your Hand*, to which I turn more specifically later, appealed to Renoir precisely because it was "really no story, nothing but a series of strong impressions—the vast landscape, the simple aspiration of the hero, the heat and the hunger." Renoir was first introduced to the novel through Hugo Butler's script treatment, and he claimed that his goal in emphasizing the episodic nature of Sam Tucker's story was to bring into relief the level of spirituality attained by Sam and the other characters. Renoir claims that "[b]eing forced to live a life restricted to their daily material needs, the characters a level of spirituality of which they themselves were unaware."[18] Since Reich's moral categories resonate in nonracially inflected ways with respect to the myths actually evoked by the film, they are useful for my purposes.

What Renoir refers to as "spirituality" can be seen to be in alignment with basic components of the agrarian myth that feeds invisible whiteness. This is because the white demographic controlling farming enterprises in the South in the 1940s when both Sessions's novel was written and Renoir's film was made would not need justifying or even consideration. In Bruce J. Reynolds's economic study, "Black Farmers in America, 1865–2000: The Pursuit of Independent Farming and the Role of Cooperatives," there is ample evidence that independent ownership of farmland was a rarity. Pete Daniel specifies that white control of farmlands and practices lasted well into the post–World War II period.[19]

Sam's spirituality is thus rooted not only in the agrarian myth but also in the white domain in which that myth was played out. It is illustrated in three main challenges that face Sam. First, Sam risks all in order to farm his own land, which is indicative of social mobility in that the land he and his family intend to farm is of a higher quality than other patches of land in the area. It is also more difficult to farm. In the novel itself, when the Tuckers arrive at their new farm, Sam's Granny says of the land "she's black all right … We're black-land folks now and you can put that in your pipe and smoke it."[20] Reluctant as she is to be dragged along on this quixotic journey, she recognizes valuable land when she sees it and recognizes that Sam is aiming to go up a notch or two on the social ladder.

Second, Sam aspires to a certain image of white masculinity in his efforts to tame the river and its creatures, in particular, the very large cat-fish known as Lead Pencil. Since Devers has been attempting to catch for a long time, the idea that one might actually succeed in catching the legendary fish becomes a real challenge and proof of one's masculinity. The quest to conquer Lead Pencil illustrates that asserting one's masculine strength and superiority was a kind of pastime or sport, though the river also represented a source of food and sustenance for Sam's family. Sam's confrontation with the river finally becomes a more serious test of his white masculinity when the river's flooding later in the film makes it necessary for him to sacrifice other benefits in order to save his friend Tim, the town man, from drowning.

Though the agrarian myth is most directly associated with taming the land, in both the film and the novel, the river is central to the challenges facing Tucker. One of Renoir's trademarks is indeed the centrality of rivers from *Boudhu Saved From Drowning* to his masterpiece, *The River*. As Braudy suggests, "[W]hat a river means in a particular [Renoir] film, then, tells us more about that film and the ideas of its characters, than about some general view Renoir has about rivers."[21] This is definitely the case in *The Southerner* since the river is one of Sam Tucker's first challenges when he moves to his new farmland. The river continues to be a challenge throughout both the Sessions' novel and Renoir's film. Sessions indeed describes Sam as "a river man. And while he could have drawn a precise map of this river's course in detail, he did not, preferring to go on thinking of the river as something dark and cool and undulant with mystery."[22] Sessions goes on in this passage to reflect upon Sam's sense of confidence about his ability to conquer the land he had just chosen to farm. Sam reasons that because the land is reseeded by the river each winter, he has a good chance of conquering that land due to his ability to grapple with the mysteries of the river.

Sam's confrontation both with the land and with the river are linked to the agrarian myth. The land and the river are both crucial to the decisions Sam must make in order to master his newly chosen territory. His engagement with the river shows that he is able to make noble and wise decisions with respect to other people. Even while confronting the natural powers of the water, Sam must also take into consideration that his neighbor Devers has long struggled with the river and with the catfish Lead Pencil. When Sam catches Lead Pencil, he wisely agrees to let Devers take the credit for the catch in exchange for the use of Devers's garden in order to nourish his family. In abandoning his cow, which is floating downriver, so that he might save his friend Tim, he exhibits a basic humanity that is indeed a sign of the spirituality Renoir claims his characters have achieved. Sam is simultaneously portrayed as a Triumphant Individual but more importantly as a pivotal member of an eventual Benevolent Community that might be built around him.

Sam's willingness to abandon the cow is a particularly powerful example of his newfound spirituality in that it is the cow, donated by his stepfather, that serves as a metonymic symbol of the nobility of white masculinity in the form of responsible paternity. His challenge to conquer pellagra, or spring sickness, that has afflicted his younger child, Jotty, can succeed only if Sam is able to provide him with daily supplies of milk. Sam confronts pellagra, another indicator of the harshness of Mother Nature, as proof of his ability to provide for his family. Pellagra is indeed a necessity of Nature and one that notably has stricken Devers and Granny, both of whom lost children to the disease. When confronted with the fact of his son's disease, Sam must endure not only the idea that he has not adequately provided for his son's well-being. He also faces the self-satisfied comments made by Devers and Granny about their failures to combat the disease as well. Both characters certainly resent Sam's supposed arrogance in thinking he can succeed where they have failed, but he does, thanks to the whiteness of the milk he fights for and wins. We see an embedded metaphor here and truly recognize Sam as a character who represents cream rising to the top.

Unlike Fassbinder, Renoir creates films based on sources that fully embrace American white supremacy without any sense of guilt because those myths embody the deeper values of American entrepreneurship and collective benevolence which hide the harsher edges of invisible whiteness. While Renoir seems to have created his films with a view toward a quasi-internalization of some American precepts, he perhaps inadvertently failed to see the inherent links between those values and the unconscious patronage linked to invisible whiteness. To argue that he embraced invisible whiteness is to overlook the unique perspective provided by his films as an outsider to *American* white supremacy.

Studying Renoir's American films as generic hybrids provides a better understanding of how he manages to give us a representation of invisible whiteness that perhaps reveals unconscious racism but do not promote radical racist attitudes. As Jean-Loup Bourget points out in his article "*Woman on the Beach*: Renoir's Dark Lady," the film *Woman on the Beach* (1947) is a generic hybrid in the "best of senses." The film capitalizes on the then very popular film noir films being produced in Hollywood while ignoring other vital aspects of noir, notably, the femme fatale who drags the protagonist to his doom.[23]

The same can be said in many ways about *The Southerner* made two years before. Renoir's films of this period are deeply invested in testing the limits of the American genre system as well as the complicity between classical Hollywood narrative and the privileging of invisible whiteness. As mentioned at the beginning of this chapter, though Renoir was not critiqued specifically for his ambiguous representation of invisible whiteness, black spectator and filmmaker Charles Burnett was able to see some subtle mitigation of America and whiteness in *The Southerner*. The fact that the film studies professor suggested that the film failed to represent American culture accurately may have much to do with the film's refusal to illustrate classic conventions that Burnett was in the process of defining.

It would be impossible to grasp the importance of Renoir's Hollywood years without the benefit of Elizabeth Vitanza's work "Interconnected Sties of Struggle: Re-contextualizing Renoir in America" in *A Companion to Jean Renoir*, cited earlier. Vitanza overviews the critical reception of Renoir's work and characterizes it in terms of three distinct categories: (1) the prewar and postwar criticism that largely dismisses Renoir's Hollywood work as hopelessly compromised by the Hollywood production methods at odds with his own intentions for his film, as is echoed in the work of Viry-Babel, Christopher Faulkner, and even to a large extent André Bazin; (2) the postwar rehabilitation of Renoir in the critiques of the *Cahiérs du cinéma*; and (3) the contemporary recuperative critique of Renoir in Hollywood pioneered after Renoir's death and spearheaded by Alexandre Sesonske. Vitanza's critical framework puts into context the many critiques of Renoir's work, bringing clarity to what might otherwise seem to be a random sampling of critical receptions.

Vitanza's overview includes the observation that Renoir himself bought into the idea that his work in Hollywood was inferior, which makes critical reevaluation more difficult. She concludes by arguing that given numerous strong readings of the American-made films, "[f]aulting the studio system and dismissing Renoir as a failure in Hollywood is no longer a valid or sufficient critical option."[24] Her argument is crucial for grounding an examination of *The Southerner* as a film that both stretches and effectively challenges the divide between classical Hollywood narrative and art cinema. Clarifying this divide is vital to understanding the film's contribution to granting the invisibility of whiteness in the Hollywood industry as well. In part, Renoir's ability to assert his own conditions in the making of these films, in defiance of Hollywood studio demands, is crucial.

Renoir won his battle with producer Darryl Zanuck in the filming of *Swamp Water* in that he was able to use American source material. By also being granted the right to shoot on location in Georgia, he moved closer to his European techniques. Even so, *Swamp Water* was by and large controlled by the narrative and genre strictures of the studio producers and assistants. In contrast, *The Southerner*, due to the fact that its producers David L. Loew and Roger Hakim were independent, provides more material for analyzing Renoir's grasp of the America's agrarian myth, the American Dream, and their ideological underpinnings. His outsider's take on those myths is shaped in *The Southerner*.

As stressed by Viry-Babel, speaking from the group of critics who see Renoir's American filmmaking as compromised by Hollywood production methods, no matter what Renoir's ultimate intentions, the system of production in Hollywood is an ideological apparatus that does not allow for the production of anything *but* an American image, as previously mentioned.[25] The *positive* implication of this negative critique is that no matter what Renoir might have given us on the screen, even with the significant independence of the producers of *The Southerner*, the legacy of his images could be read only through an American lens.

As pointed out by Lutz Bacher, the genre of *The Southerner* becomes somewhat unrecognizable due to Renoir's need to balance Hollywood production methods with his own vision of the film that he wanted to make as well as with the sources from which he was working.[26] In the final analysis, the hybrid nature of his Hollywood films and, in particular, *The Southerner* creates a rich ground for analyzing the ways in which American white supremacy controls narrative and generic structures in the Hollywood apparatus, but it equally attests to Renoir's clever negotiation of that controlling ideological structure. This argues for a reevaluation of his American filmmaking that Vitanza prescribes. As Renoir states throughout his chapter on *Swamp Water*, even though he had vowed to adhere to Hollywood filmmaking policies, he found them very much in contradistinction to his own methods. As he states, "A bit Hollywood film is dished up like a melon, in separate slices. This is at the opposite pole from my belief in unity. It is a process of dividing the work and collecting important names."[27]

The real challenge to appreciating Renoir's Hollywood period is to recognize that he was not only making films about America, he was making films about American filmmaking. This latter aspect of his American-made films makes them invaluable for understanding the complicity between Hollywood and invisible whiteness. Understanding the self-reflexivity of his American career requires looking more closely at the varying critical interpretations of Renoir's career over the long term. Christopher Faulkner focuses his analysis on the reasons why *The Southerner* is generally taken by critics to be Renoir's best American-made film. Faulkner's fundamental position is that it is the best precisely because it is so generically American. In the process of his analysis, he traces out the various dichotomies—such as country versus town; farm versus factory; wife versus whore—that invariably control the genres of the American pastoral or New Deal farm films of the 1930s. Faulkner goes so far as to argue that almost all of classical Hollywood cinema of the 1930s and early 1940s were dependent on this genre. He suggests that Renoir is "fed by the great generic river that is the American cinema."[28]

Faulkner's critique echoes the work by Robin Wood, cited earlier, and Sam Rohdie, both of whom assert that certain codes and conventions belong inextricably to the genres honed in Hollywood studios.[29] Renoir's reading of the American South is thus, like Fassbinder's, guided not purely and simply by his response to real Southerners but also by his response to the codes of other films of these genres. Filmmakers such as Fassbinder and Renoir are prone to questioning the genres, structures, and cinematic language of the films that influence them. Since they are at times working actively against audience expectations in their explorations, they risk being misunderstood in their intentions.

In the case of *The Southerner*, Renoir uses some of these codes and "abuses others," thus creating a film that is less concerned with naturalism and the real lives of Southern whites but more concerned with the poetic resonance of certain aspects of the agrarian myth. André Bazin suggests that the film is not very believable and especially so if you are not an American able to distinguish the boundaries between reality and fantasy that are represented in the film. He concludes his critique by claiming that the film's images are perhaps intended to as more dreamlike than dramatic: "que les images que *L'Homme du Sud* nous laisse en mémoire ont une intensité bien plus onirique que dramatique."[30] It is largely as a result of this dreamlike quality that Agee and Corkin read the film as a form of unconscious patronage and an unfortunate attempt to perpetuate the agrarian myth with all of its ugly undertones.

Nonetheless, the film's value is testimony to what Renoir learned about invisible whiteness during his study of American cinematic narratives and genres. The lessons he learned may be seen to have affected his own sense of his role and responsibility as a filmmaker. While Christopher Faulkner contends that Renoir is not actively questioning the "contradictions and tension inherent in his codified debts to genre and ideology," he does admit that Renoir himself seems to have experienced a major ideological shift from stressing historical processes to relying on natural processes.[31] Despite whatever other critiques of the Hollywood films Faulkner offers, he does rightly suggest that this ideological shift was pivotal in Renoir's move from his prewar European films to his postwar films, such as *The River*, *The Golden Coach*, and *The French Cancan*.

JEAN RENOIR IN HOLLYWOOD

If Renoir seems to have skimmed over the ugly undertones of invisible whiteness in *The Southerner*, it was not because he had not been exposed to humanity's ugliness. As has been traced in Renoir's letters, as well as in the works of Celia Bertin, Faulkner, Alexander Sesonske, and others, Renoir went to Hollywood in 1941 in order to flee occupied France and the possible trap of having to collaborate with the Vichy regime.[32] One of his main champions in the United States, Robert Flaherty, helped him to find work and to establish a circle of friends that included Charles Laughton, Dudley Nichols, William Faulkner, and others. Indeed, William Faulkner was extremely instrumental in helping Renoir to find a certain authenticity for his dialogue in *The Southerner*. Their working relationship was built out of mutual respect, and both men cherished their time spent together.[33]

Renoir began film work in Hollywood with a contract at Zanuck's 20th Century Fox-Film Corporation, and it was under Zanuck's production prowess that *Swamp Water* was made. As a testing ground, the film was Renoir's first lesson in just how different Hollywood studio production was from the working conditions he had experienced in France. As Vitanza has pointed out, a thorough study of Renoir in the American context is better judged on the basis both of the films he made and the projects he proposed that were rejected by studios. *Swamp Water* is nonetheless remarkable in that it indicates Renoir's almost immediate desire to work with American source material rather than being contracted to making films about French contexts that were reduced to stereotypes of French culture suitable for American audiences. To Zanuck's suggestion that he film French subjects, Renoir remarked, "I shuddered at the idea of directing sequences with moustached policemen and gentlemen in velvet jackets and imperial beards parading against a bogus-Montmartre, bogus café background."[34] He showed himself to be completely unwilling to be boxed in by studio decisions.

Swamp Water was indeed very foreign material for Renoir. He was nonetheless determined to engage in the project since, as he observed upon his arrival in America, the country was not "one America but as many Americas as there are racial groups."[35] *Swamp Water* is a story of a man, Tom Keefer (Walter Brennan), wrongfully accused of murder who, rather than face the punishment that his small-minded neighbors are prepared to hand out to him, escapes to the swamps of Okefenokee, Georgia. He spends years there fending for himself in the untamed backwoods of the swamps. Tom is eventually proven innocent and returns to civilization with the help of a younger man, Ben (Dana Andrews), who has discovered him in the swamps and befriends him. The community which has rejected him over many years can be described as the Mob at the Gates, in Reich's term. Nonetheless, when Tom returns, he is reunited with his young daughter, Julie (Anne Baxter), who is now a young roughly 20 year old woman though she was just a child when Tom escaped. In recognition of his newfound respect from the community, his daughter is also newly appreciated and is transformed from a downtrodden quasi-servant to a young woman in her own right. Her romantic relationship with Ben is as redemptive as her own father's return to the fold of the community.

As mentioned earlier, Ben Dooley has argued that the film might be considered as a racial allegory. He calls attention to the multiple uses of untamed, dark, and savage animals. In particular, snakes serve as representations of the racial "Other" that challenge the social order of the American South. Though Alexander Sesonske does not specifically address the question of racial allegory, his article "Jean Renoir in Georgia: *Swamp Water*" suggests that Renoir was peculiarly drawn to the southern swamplands of Georgia and that his doubts about continuing in Hollywood were somewhat quelled by the chance to work on the *Swamp Water* script. According to Sesonske, this was inspired by Renoir's visit to Georgia and his fascination with the place. Fritz Lang had also expressed interest in directing the script, and he may also have seen potential for a racial allegory in the script material. As argued previously, Dooley's point holds weight since Lang's earlier films, such as *Fury* (1936) and *You Only Live Once* (1937), can be read as racial allegories.[36]

Perhaps more important, *Swamp Water* echoes Renoir's long fascination with water, particularly rivers, as being both life-giving and deadly forces.[37] Water in some shape or form figures into all three of the films Renoir made based on American source material and serves as an integral part of the agrarian myth. Water is the thematic that is also a key to understanding how Renoir's personal trademarks find their way into the otherwise conflicted Hollywood working environment. The use of water in the landscape of *The Southerner* resonates with uses of water in *Swamp Water* and *Woman on the Beach*, and noting the relationships helps in contextualizing Renoir's extant films and his education about filmmaking during the Hollywood years.

THE AGRARIAN MYTH AND WHITE SUPREMACY IN AMERICA

Renoir insisted on maintaining many of his personal themes and filmmaking techniques while learning about American filmmaking methods and dictates. His real opportunity to blend the two was greatly facilitated in the making of *The Southerner*. In his article "David L. Loew, Jean Renoir's 'French Method' and *The Southerner*" cited earlier, Bacher traces the working relationship forged between Renoir and his independent producer, a relationship of trust and relative financial freedom. This generous relationship ultimately allowed Renoir to make use of his "French method" in making the film that both he and others generally regarded as his best American-made film. Renoir was allowed to assemble his own production team and was able to film partially on location. Wartime conditions that restricted transportation made it impossible for him to film in Texas, as he originally wished, though he was able to film a good portion of the scenes on location in California. Interior shots and shots involving the Tucker home were the only ones shot in studio locations.

Despite some ups and downs, funding for the film was ensured throughout, and Loew proved to be a hands-off producer despite some initial negative reactions to rushes of the film on the part of Charles Einfeld, vice president of Advertising and Publicity at Warner Brothers and a friend of Loew's who claimed that the film was a "piece of shit." When members of the production company vehemently defended Renoir and reacted angrily to Einfeld's remark, Loew became insulted by the way those production people were treating his friend. Sparks flew at the December 19 viewing and threatened to compromise the film.[38] Aside from this conflictual encounter, Renoir enjoyed relative production freedom and was able to develop both his source material and his camera work according to his own dictates and was even able to avoid the overly determinate classical Hollywood narrative structures.

Renoir ended up producing what Kevin Hagopian has referred to as a "Renoir story": "a will o' the wisp, a fragile even vague thing that sufficed mostly as a place to create memorable, melancholic characters who commented ironically on the human condition."[39] Renoir himself in an oft-cited quote stated that what attracted him to the source material was its nonlinear construction. "What attracted me in the story was precisely the fact that there really was no story, nothing but a series of strong impressions—the vast landscape, the simple aspiration of the hero, the heat and the hunger."[40] For Renoir, the material represented a chance to make a film that could vindicate his thus far somewhat negative experience of Hollywood methods of filmmaking.

Under such conditions, a perfect balance of quasi–art cinema techniques and Hollywood production methods, Renoir forged a film that, while dismissed by some and lumped together into an unsuccessful Hollywood career, still succeeded in remaining dear to his heart. At the center of his depiction of a Southern farming family is a representation of the agrarian myth in its noblest form. The irony of this representation is its dependence on an assumption of white supremacy, invisible whiteness, and its glorification of a world that many claim is the fabrication of a false paradise.[41] Those who critique the film are ultimately questioning whether

Renoir captures the appropriate balance between French perspective and American mythologies, and positions on that point change over time.

For example, Stanley Corkin posits in his article "Jean Renoir's *The Southerner* and the Agrarian Myth" that *The Southerner* answers the general intention of the Hollywood industry in that it does nothing to challenge the American audience's desire for escapism. *The Southerner* indeed exploits the details of a nostalgic past in which heroic farmers grappled with the natural elements and conquered them. After setting up a precise reading of the episodic structure of the film and its purpose in exhibiting the "religious responsibility to work the land," Corkin observes two crucial elements. First, the film is almost entirely in deep focus attributing to its realism.[42] Second, he points out that Renoir's "filming style defines the film's emphasis, the Tucker's labor to reap their heavenly reward." Corkin asserts that in making this religious element so central to the film's intent, Renoir has departed from most historical accounts of the hardships of the kinds of people whom the Tuckers are intended to represent. He quotes Leonard Doob's more historical study of a Southern community as saying that "the vast majority feel that religion has not played a role in their lives."[43]

Both Leonard Doob and John Hayes undertook to study in greater depth the role of religion in Southern communities of both blacks and whites. It should be noted that though religion may not have played a great role in the lives of poor whites in the South, the churches as segregated institutions that help to maintain white supremacist doctrines were vital to perpetuating racist resentments in the South. Hayes maintains that the fact that black communities in the South were assured their own churches solidified their sense of community.[44]

In defense of Corkin's argument, Sam Tucker in Sessions's novel does not seem particularly religious and even refers primarily to the gods rather than to a Christian God when his thoughts do go that way.[45] In contrast to Renoir's Sam Tucker, there is very little religious sentiment in the novel. In the novel, Sam describes Sundays as a day for being lazy and spending time down by the river or playing penny-ante poker with the Negroes and the Mexicans down the road. The very long and detailed description of Sundays contains no mention of going to church.[46] The one time Sam suggests that he is going to give a blessing for the food he has finally managed to put on the table, everyone in the family is heartily surprised with Granny remarking that she that that God was "a stranger" in this house.[47]

Renoir paints a more Christian and devout Sam Tucker, but he also explicitly states that his goal was to represent the newly acquired spirituality of the Tucker family, as mentioned previously, and this is in keeping with Sam's remarks to himself that he needs to ensure that something bigger than the truth was needed for him if he was going to save his family.[48] Corkin's primary critique is not the same as Agee's, but it bears a close resemblance. Corkin is more concerned with historical accuracy and claims that misrepresentation of such historical factors makes the film problematic. Agee was deeply disturbed that Renoir's depiction of Southerners was "unbearably wrong." He claimed that "the basic understanding of the basic and emotional and mental—or merely human—attitudes were wrong, to the point of unintentional insult."[49] Agee, as a Southerner himself, was almost personally insulted whereas Corkin takes a more distanced approach and is far more concerned with how the film helps to perpetuate an overly idealistic image of agrarian life.

Corkin observes that historical fact is not necessarily in tandem with the aims of Hollywood and that "audiences entering the theater do not do so in the interest of having their beliefs challenged." He then claims that Renoir's *The Southerner* is in keeping with the intentions with Hollywood tradition in that it offers its "vision as a broad one of the region and its inhabitants."[50] Corkin concludes his article by stating that "Renoir's film, when considered within the range or elements which presented the agrarian myth, effectively helped form the blinders which have created such a myopic view of the region's needs and actualities."[51]

As argued throughout this chapter, Renoir's Hollywood career has received mixed responses, and for many different reasons. There is indeed an "unconscious patronage" to be read in the film, and re-reviewing *The Southerner* shows that Renoir did not exactly render whiteness visible or challenge supremacist doctrine. The film does document Renoir's delicate balance between realism and dream states inspired the risk he took in allowing his French methods to confront the Hollywood studio methods of production that he so despised. Renoir produced a hybrid film that is instructive in understanding just how at odds representations of American white supremacy were in the Hollywood script and genre he inherited and the French filmmaking techniques with which he sought to represent them. *The Southerner* is perhaps not a corrective to the harshness and poverty of Southern agrarian life; it is nonetheless an intriguing view of Hollywood filmmaking from an outsider's perspective.

In *Whity* and *The Southerner*, Fassbinder and Renoir produced films that were readable in terms of their generic borrowings but were subjected to critical scrutiny due to their hybrid natures and their need to be read against the grain to be appreciated for the exploratory films they proved to be.

Finally, despite Renoir's negative experience in Hollywood, he gathered around him very good friends and colleagues. The inspirations of those colleagues were no doubt important in leading Renoir to make his masterpiece, *The River* (1950), just five years after the appearance of *The Southerner*. Two of those influences bear mentioning. Robert Flaherty, who was a close associate of Renoir's very early in Hollywood, had made a documentary *The Land* (1942), and Pare Lorentz had made a documentary *The River* (1938). Both films were made for the United States Department of Agriculture and were considered some of the most aesthetically powerful American documentaries. Both treat issues similar to those that Renoir picked up in *The Southerner* and seem "strangely linked to Renoir's film," according to Charles Silver, film curator at the Museum of Modern Art.[52]

Lorentz depicts the river in a film made in order to garner support for the Tennessee Valley Authority's dam-building project and depicts the ravages of the river as an incredibly lyrical temporal evolution of the dangers of not intervening to protect poor workers from the river's flow over time. Since as Braudy has mentioned and has been previously discussed, one shift in Renoir's attention to rivers and waters when making *The River* was to stress even more the symbolic nature of the river as a flow of time. When one considers the opening shots of *The Southerner*, the viewer is indeed presented with an almanac shot, indicating a preface of the film that will precisely look at the river as part of the necessary flow in the seasonal changes over the course of a year. By treating this particular American source material, Renoir was perhaps additionally beginning to link up the lessons he learned in making this film with his future directions, even though those future directions would take him to return to his own uncompromised filmmaking techniques.

Notes

1. Elizabeth Vitanza's pivotal article, "Interconnected Sites of Struggle: Resituating Renoir's Career in Hollywood," in Alastair Philips and Ginette Vincendeau, eds., *A Companion to Jean Renoir* (Wiley-Blackwell, 2013), 514–532, provides the best framework for reconsidering Renoir's Hollywood career. Much of the work on the reconstruction of Renoir's Hollywood career is dependent on William Harry Gilcher's unpublished dissertation thesis, "Jean Renoir in America: A Critical Analysis of His Major Films from *Swamp Water* to *The River*," Ph.D., University of Iowa, January 1979. https://www.researchgate.net/publication/

35598581_Jean_Renoir_in_America_microform_a_critical_of_his_major_films_from_Swamp_water_to_The_river.

2. Charles Burnett, Quoted in *Wednesday's Editor's Picks*. July 31, 2011, by http://altScreen.com/07/31/2011wednesday-editors-pick-the-southerner-1945.

3. *Agee on Film: Essays and Reviews by James Agee* (New York: Perigree, 1958). 167–168.

4. *Agee on Film*, 167.

5. Laura McMahon, "Imitation, Seriality, Cinema: Early Fassbinder and Godard," in Brigitte Peucker, ed., *A Companion to Rainer Werner Fassbinder* (Hoboken, New Jersey: Wiley-Blackwell, 2012). 79–100, 97. McMahon suggests that Fassbinder eventually turned from this self-reflexive approach to a more emotionally oriented Hollywood form of filmmaking. My reading is slightly different. Fassbinder was on his way to deconstructing Hollywood from the inside out. He was beginning to create a new cinematic language for Hollywood productions.

6. Jean Renoir, *My Life and My Films*, trans. Norman Denny (New York: Da Capo Press, 1974), 238.

7. Michael Finger, "Banned in Memphis: The Dark Days of Lloyd T. Binford Known from Coast to Coast as the Toughest Censor in America," May 8, 2008. https://www.memphisflyer.com/memphis/banned-in-memphis/Content?oid=1144204. "Binfordized" was the term applied to any films banned by Binford in Memphis.

8. Ralph Tutt, "Realism and Artifice in Jean Renoir's *The Southerner*," *Postscript* 2 (1989): 36–55. 53. He is responding to Braudy's claim that *The Southerner* was one of Renoir's seminal films illustrating his technique of "creating nature," Leo Braudy, *Jean Renoir: The World of His Films* (New York: Doubleday, 1972). 41.

9. Roger Viry-Babel, "Jean Renoir à Hollywood ou la recherche américaine d'une image française," https://www.erudit.org/en/journals/cine/1990-v1-n1-2-cine1499404/1000992ar.pdf.

10. Ben Dooley, "Swamp Water: Renoir's American Outsider Film," September 24, 2007. https://ayearinthedark.wordpress.com/tag/renoir/. Though the parallel I draw between Renoir and Fritz Lang in this regard references *You Only Live Once* (1937), Dooley makes the comparison to Lang's *Fury* (1936), following suggestions from Lotte H. Eisner's *Fritz Lang* (Boston: Da Capo, 1988), 146. That both films can be used to consider Lang's construction of racial allegories in his early years in Hollywood attests to the strength of the position.

11. Richard Dyer, *White* (London: Routledge, 1997); Robert Reich, *Tales of a New America: The Anxious Liberal's Guide to the Future* (New York: Random House, 1987); Jane Tompkins, *West of Everything: The Inner Life of Westerns* (Oxford: Oxford University Press, 1993).

12. The term "Southern" to define the genres most appropriate for examining the structure of the film *The Southerner* is used extensively by Vitanza, "Interconnected Sites of Struggle."

13. Dyer, *White*, 9.

14. Dyer, *White*, 122. Dyer's argument in *White* is reiterated in his essay "Into the Light: The Whiteness of the South in *The Birth of a Nation*," in R. H. King and Helen Taylor, eds., *Dixie Debacles: Perspectives on Southern Culture* (London: Pluto Press, 1996), 165–176.

15. Jane Tompkins, *West of Everything: The Inner Life of Westerns* (Oxford: Oxford University Press, 1993), 3.

16. Reich, *Tales of a New America*, 4.

17. James Baldwin, *The Fire Next Time* (New York: Vintage, 1993/1963), 101.

18. Jean Renoir, *My Life and My Films*, trans.Norman Denny, (New York: Da Capo Press), 1974, 234.

19. Bruce J. Reynolds, "Black Farmers in America, 1865–2000: The Pursuit of Independent Farming and the Role of Cooperatives," Rural Business Cooperative Service, Report 194, sponsored by the United States Department of Agriculture, 2002. 1–28. On p. 2 of that report, Reynolds quotes Pete Daniel, *The Shadow of Slavery: Peonage in the South, 1901–1969* (New York: Oxford University Press, 1972).

20. George Perry Sessions, *Hold Autumn in Your Hand* (Albuquerque: University of New Mexico Press, 1975/1941), 34.

21. *Jean Renoir: The World of His Films* (London: Robson Books, 1977). 24–64. 36. See in particular Chap. 2, "The Necessities of Nature, 1977.

22. Sessions, *Hold Autumn in Your Hand*, 11–12.

23. Jean-Loup Bourget, "*The Woman on the Beach*: Renoir's Dark Lady," in Philips and Vincendeau, eds., *A Companion to Jean Renoir*, 544–554. 552.

24. Vitanza, "Interconnected Sites of Struggle," 518.

25. Viry-Babel, "Jean Renoir à Hollywood ou la recherche américaine d'une image française."

26. Lutz Bacher, "David L. Loew, Renoir's 'French Method' and *The Southerner*," *Film History* 21, no. 3 (2009): 229–256.

27. Renoir, *My Life and My Films*, 203.

28. Christopher Faulkner, *The Social Cinema of Jean Renoir* (Princeton, NJ: Princeton University Press, 1986). The chapter on the Hollywood films is from 123–161. 146.

29. Sam Rohdie. "Totems and Movies" in Bill Nichols, ed., *Movies and Methods, vol. 1*(Berkeley: University of California Press, 1976), 469–480.

30. Roughly translated, "The film leaves us with a dreamlike memory rather than a dramatic reality." André Bazin, *Jean Renoir* (Paris: Editions Ivrea, 2005/1971), 87. This is similar to Tutt's suggestion cited earlier that the film is more like a "Hollywood dream in the guise of reality." Tutt, "Realism and Artifice in Jean Renoir's *The Southerner*," 53.

31. Faulkner, *The Social Cinema of Jean Renoir*, 162.

32. Celia Bertin rightly notes that other factors came into play with Renoir's final decision to leave France, both personal and political. The failure of his film *Les règles du jeu* was one such factor, along with marital difficulties. Bertin, *Jean Renoir: A Life in Pictures,* trans. Mireille and Leonard Mueller (Baltimore: Johns Hopkins University Press, 1991), 166. Also vital for biographical research into Renoir's life in is Dido Renoir and Alexandre Sesonske's *Lettres d'Amérique.* Ed. Alexander Sesonske (Paris: Presses de la Renaissance, 1984).

33. Bertin, *Jean Renoir: A Life in Pictures,* 222.

34. Renoir, *My Life and My Films,* 193.

35. Renoir, *My Life and My Films,* 187.

36. Alexander Sesonske, "Jean Renoir in Georgia: *Swamp Water,*" *Georgia Review* 36, no. 1 (Spring 1982): 24–66. 27.

37. This theme has been explored by many, notably Frank Curot, *L'eau et la terre dans les films de Jean Renoir* (Paris. Caen: Lettres modernes Minard), and Braudy, *Jean Renoir: The World of His Films.* Braudy specifies that this theme culminates in Renoir's film *The River* (1951), where rivers and waters become more than just symbols of accepting the processes of nature but also representations of "time in its inexorable flow." 146.

38. Bacher, "David L. Loew, Renoir's 'French Method' and *The Southerner,*" 250.

39. Kevin Hagopian, "Film Notes: *The Southerner,*" New York State Writers Institute (Albany: State University of New York, Albany). https://www.albany.eduwriters-inst/webpages4/filmnotes/fns03n10.html.

40. Renoir, *My Life and My Films,* 234.

41. Ronald Bergan, *Jean Renoir: Projections of Paradise* (New York: Overlook Press, 1995).

42. Stanley Corkin, "Jean Renoir's *The Southerner* and the Agrarian Myth," *Southern Studies: An Interdisciplinary Journal of the South* 26, no. 1 (1987): 52–62.

43. Leonard Doob, "Poor Whites: A Frustrated Class," in John Dollard, *Caste and Class in a Southern Town* (New Haven, CT: Yale University Press, 1937), 460. Doob is quoted in Stanley Corkin's "Jean Renoir's *The Southerner* and the Agrarian Myth," 57.

44. John Hayes, "Hard Hard Religion: The Invisible Institution of the New South," *Journal of Southern Religion* 10 (2007): 1–24. 2. http://jsr.fsu.edu/issues/vol10/Hayes.htm.

45. Sessions, *Hold Autumn in Your Hand,* 153.

46. Sessions, *Hold Autumn in Your Hand,* 172–177.

47. Sessions, *Hold Autumn in Your Hand,* 48.

48. Sessions, *Hold Autumn in Your Hand,* 36.

49. *Agee on Film I,* 168.

50. Corkin, "Jean Renoir's *The Southerner* and the Agrarian Myth," 52.

51. Corkin, "Jean Renoir's *The Southerner* and the Agrarian Myth," 62.

52. Charles Silver, "Jean Renoir's *The Southerner,*" *Inside Out,* August 2, 2011. https://www.moma.org/explore/inside_out/2011/08/02/jean-renoirs-the-southerner/.

CHAPTER 8

Invisible Whiteness mise en abyme: *J'irai cracher sur vos tombes*

In spite of the book's naïveté, *Vian cared enough about his subject to force one into a confrontation with a certain kind of anguish. The book's power comes from the fact that he forces you to see this anguish from the undisguised viewpoint of his foreign, alienated own.*
—*James Baldwin, on* I Shall Spit on Your Graves

Sad individuals, critics par la bande ... when will you dare to speak of a book without authenticating your views by hiding behind appeals to the author's intention?
—*Boris Vian[1]*

Unlike Renoir, Michel Gast never worked in Hollywood, and he created his 1959 film, *J'irai cracher sur vos tombes,* on the basis of his spectatorship of American films. His perceptions of visible and invisible whiteness, like Fassbinder's, are gained primarily through his impressions of the cinematic language of American films. The film focuses on a black, Joe Grant, who passes for white in order to seek revenge for his brother's brutal lynching. James Baldwin opens the second section of *The Devil Finds Work* with a scathing review of the film despite his high praise for the author of its source material, Boris Vian. Extensive critical attention has been given to the novel, but the film has routinely been overlooked. Douglas Field's "Even Better than the Real Thing: Boris Vian, Vernon Sullivan and Film Noir" is one article that engages with a comparative analysis of the two.[2]

© The Author(s) 2018
A. M. Craven, *Visible and Invisible Whiteness,*
https://doi.org/10.1007/978-3-319-76777-2_8

The film nonetheless deserves greater reconsideration as it illustrates how Hollywood narrative strategies and genre conventions often work against a clear appraisal of invisible whiteness. This is particularly the case when a white actor is cast as the black man passing for white.[3] It is indeed difficult to speak about the film without relying heavily on its source material, the novel *J'irai cracher sur vos tombes* (I shall Spit on your Graves) written in 1947 by Boris Vian under the pseudonym of a fictitious Negro American, Vernon Sullivan.

In the film, Joe Grant, the light-skinned Negro protagonist, has very distinct motives for passing. He wants to exact revenge for the death of his darker little brother who was lynched due to his romantic intrigue with a white woman.[4] Field's comparative analysis focuses on the film's participation in a film noir aesthetic, which also serves as a consideration in the analysis here. In this chapter I consider how film noir as a genre or phenomenon impacts on the debates concerning invisible and visible whiteness as well as on classical Hollywood narrative. How does Gast's film reveal, perhaps unconsciously, the simultaneous confrontation and embrace of Hollywood offered by the early film noirs? What issues of cinematic adaptation technique are raised when analyzing Gast's film?

The necessary symbiosis between novel and film suggests a lot about filmic adaptation versus literary translation. That symbiosis equally allows for deeper scrutiny of how Hollywood–style genres might intrude into the purity of a cinematic adaptation. The controversy surrounding Vian's novel indeed ultimately concerned questions of literary translation in that Vian first produced a French "translation" purportedly written by the fictional black writer Vernon Sullivan. When critics began to suspect that Vernon Sullivan did not actually exist, Vian produced the English "original" for publication.[5]

In the film, in addition to passing for white, Grant plots his revenge while hiding in small-town America as well as behind a fictional narrative about having been educated in Europe. Grant seeks to seduce the town and its inhabitants with his singing as well as his other musical charms. Having seduced them all, he then plans to choose his victims. Those victims are eventually identified as young women born of a supremacist family … a "good family," according to the dictates of small-town America. Their unquestioned embrace of white supremacy is constantly evoked in both the novel and the film but is particularly pertinent when the younger sister remarks while dancing with Lee Anderson that she "just hate[s] the colored race."[6]

In the novel, Lee's violent double murder of the women brings about his doubled death, first as a result of being cornered and shot down by the police. Despite the fact that he is already dead (or passing for dead, it's not clear from the film or the text), he is nonetheless lynched by the townspeople simply "because he was "un nègre.""[7] By contrast, film protagonist Joe Grant's demise comes when he and the woman he wanted to kill out of revenge admit to their love for each other, their acceptance of their racial difference. Their attempt to escape the ravages of American racism ends in failure as they are shot down trying to cross the Canadian border to freedom.

The novel's double death of Lee Anderson is one of the several plot details that has suggested the film's power to represent the authenticity and rage of the American black man, as commented on by James Baldwin. Vian's ability to hear the American black man's rage in the jazz music with which he was so familiar gave him access to creative ways of expressing that anger from an outsider's perspective.[8] Lee Anderson's rage is nonetheless equally matched by the self-righteous though irrational emotions of the townspeople. Just as Lee is bent on revenge against racial discrimination, the townspeople are not satisfied with Anderson's "first" death. Though this death is justified due to his murderous crimes, it cannot answer to their rage against blacks, as interpreted by Vian's decision to create a second death purely racist in nature.

The ritualistic lynching with which the novel ends shows that the novel wants to stress the violence of white rage against the black man in America. Lee was first killed because he committed murder. He was "killed" again because he was a Negro. The film transforms this ending in a way more in keeping with American-style endings dictated by classical Hollywood narrative though it is by no means a happy ending.

Baldwin also speaks about a "double remove liberating both fantasy and hope" when he specifies that the novel takes place in America and concerns a black man who passes for white. He claims that the book, which was condemned as pornographic, is ultimately not about sexual fantasy but rather about the "rage and pain" of black Americans.[9] Baldwin asserts that Boris Vian could hear the rage and pain of the African Americans in the music of the black musicians with whom Vian befriended in post-war Paris. Rashida K. Braggs develops this connection between the music of black American expatriates and Baldwin's appreciation of the novel in her book *Jazz Disaporas: Race Music and Migration in Post-World War II Paris*.[10] Braggs suggests that Vian draws on the blues to write his way into an African American experience.

The concept of doubling is clearly a vital structural component of the novel and is also crucial in any analysis of the film. In an interview about the filming, Gast suggests that his motivations sprang from his own distaste for American racist tendencies.[11] He nonetheless insists that the film was also intended as a tribute to Vian's novel. This is a case of considering cinematic adaptation as a kind of doubling, but Gast does not manage to incorporate Vian's active play on double entendre fully in his film version.

For example, Vian claimed that the novel was eventually published in France rather than the United States because it was considered unacceptable in America. Hence, the preface to the 1947 novel, penned by Vian in his own name, is in itself a doubled fiction about the victimization of black Americans. The publishing industry in the United States, controlled by whites is condemned in this preface as yet another form of suppression of black American creative freedom. As Vian points out, "Sullivan did not hesitate about leaving his manuscript in France, all the more so as his American publishers had just shown him the timidity of any attempt to publication in his country."[12]

Vian becomes a white man passing for black, and his revenge is to publish an "American" novel with a French press. All forms of doubling that appear in the film or the novel therefore transform into a situation so convoluted that one is finally left with a mise en abyme. Gast's film itself tests the limits of how cinematic adaptation affects questions of visible and invisible whiteness expressed in its source material. The film also serves as a paradigmatic test case for considering whether film noir in Hollywood was a successful confrontation with the invisible whiteness of classical Hollywood narrative or not.

Depending on which approach one takes to the existence and history of film noir, doubling is a prime concept in film noir theory. James Naremore's *More than Night: Film Noir in Its Contexts* is a central text for the gaining access to the broad theories surrounding the phenomenon. Film noir was for the most part introduced into Hollywood by the exiled German directors Fritz Lang, Otto Preminger, and Billy Wilder and might be reasonably viewed as their distanced critique of the American mythologies that informed Hollywood filmmaking.

As Lutz Koepnick points out, films of the 1940s, inspired by noir techniques imported to some extent by the German exiles, began to be increasingly occupied with "repetition, stasis and ambiguity." Koepnick further argues that "[i]n face of the continuing battles on and off-screen many Hollywood films of the 1940s abandoned the teleological master plot.

They gave voice to a plurality of narratives and perspectives that no longer allowed one to think of history as a linear dynamic of development."[13] As such, it is a genre or phenomenon in the evolution of classical Hollywood narrative, which begins as a form of confrontation only to be normalized as the genre develops and becomes domesticated by the studio system.

If we consider *J'irai cracher sur vos tombes* in the context of the film noir phenomenon, we see that Gast attempted to "double down" on the structuring of Vian's novel. Taking Gast's intention to offer a critique of racism in American into a deeper analysis of the film can offer valuable insight into how the *structure* of cinematic adaptations instruct us on whiteness and its functions in American or American-style films. Unlike *The Southerner*, which was an American-style film made in America by a European director, Gast's film is an American-style film made by a European from across the Atlantic.

Both Vian and Gast looked through a doubled lens of American cinematic production that had already been long saturated by mythologies. For Bernard Tadié, this mythologizing of American culture is a question of language as well as themes or narratives. Though he speaks primarily of the *série noire*, Tadié notes that "*[n]oir* fiction embodies the myth of a pure, indigenous and autonomous American language."[14] In the case of Vian and Gast, the mythologies are also linked to the particular species of white supremacy that they both rely on in their critiques of American racism. They nonetheless experience it through fiction and Hollywood studio production.

By 1959 when Gast's film was made, film noir was a phenomenon that many have argued had reached its apotheosis two years before with Orson Welles's 1957 *Touch of Evil*. Though the question of film noir's chronology as well as its continuing influence is an endless subject of debate, Paul Schrader, in an oft-cited phrase, referred to *Touch of Evil* as the "epitaph of noir."[15] Film noir had by no means disappeared by 1959, but it had evolved considerably and had, as in the case of *Touch of Evil*, been domesticated by Hollywood studios. Gast's film is based on a novel written during the high point of the European fascination with European postwar *Americana*. Film noir and the *série noire* were also beginning to take center stage. By contrast, Gast makes his film during the giddy new wake of the French nouvelle vague. Though Field suggests, following the lead of Naremore, that film noir is still a vibrant phenomenon at the advent of the nouvelle vague, it is worthwhile to take this important time gap into account.

Despite the rich themes concerning visible and invisible whiteness in Vian's novel itself, the very timing of Gast's film contributes to the argument that filmmaking techniques of representing whiteness are completely intertwined with a chronology of new film movements and their subsequent appropriations by Hollywood. Eric Lott and Manthia Diawara have both convincingly argued that film noir is ultimately more about the moral depravity of white America than it is an allegory for darkness as a racial dimension of the films' narratives. As Lott suggests, that "noir may have pioneered Hollywood's merciless exposure of white pathology but by relying on race to convey that pathology it in effect erected a *cordon sanitaire* around the circle of corruption it sought to penetrate ... Black film [film noir] is the refuge of whites."[16] Lott claims throughout his article that the same marginalization of blacks exists in early film noir as in other mainstream Hollywood films.

As a result, one must clarify that whiteness is still very invisible in the mainstream cinema of 1947 with the advent of noir films. By 1959, however, when Gast makes his film, whiteness has been rendered more visible precisely because the Civil Rights movement is beginning to be anticipated and the Hays Code in America is unraveling in terms of its control of gratuitous white supremacist themes. Vian's novel and its sequel, *Les morts ont tous la meme peau* (1948), tested the limits of cultural translation.[17] Gast's film speaks to a different set of issues ten years later.

Gast's film illustrates that cinematic adaptation functions very differently from the intricacies of cultural translation in which Vian engaged when writing these two novels under the pseudonym of a black American writer. This has ultimately to do with the difference between seeing what happens within a *screen* space as opposed to within the narrative space of a film. There is also a crucial role played by a person's skin color in a visual representation as opposed to a racial identity determined in nonvisible or "essential" ways. In this respect, the nuance Vian could bring to the first-person narrative of his convoluted passing narrative was a challenge for filmmakers in 1959. This is the case despite the fact that the film was made at a time when, as André Bazin had proclaimed, the filmmaker could now be considered as the equal to the novelist. The camera was being transformed into the *camera stylo*, capable of nuance on the same level as that of the written text.[18]

As indicated by Baldwin's critique of Gast's film, Gast's American-style film on the basis of Vian's novel about American racism was not common fare in 1959. Because of the notoriety of Vian's novel, the film drew a sizable audience but has since been largely dismissed as a B movie made by an inexperienced director. The film was most certainly not appreciated by Vian, who, as common currency would have it, passed away at the Parisian premiere of the film. Vian's dying words, according to multiple sources, were "these people are supposed to be American ... my ass." The story of Vian's demise is told in many ways. Baldwin refers to the story of Vian's death as possibly "apocryphal," but he believes it.[19]

Gast claims that Vian was only able to see the opening credits of the film, and most critics consistently confirm this version of the story.[20] The anecdote still lingers due to the contention that the film in no way does justice to the complex levels of the literary text. In reducing these levels to one continuous narrative, fashioned on the basis of classical Hollywood narrative, the screen space of Gast's film must carry the weight of his critique of American racism. This requires that it rely on visual codes and clichés linked to racially inflected ideologies.

Baldwin plays on this when he describes the two opening scenes of the film. The first scene is of a black boy sitting on a bale of cotton in a dockyard. The boy is playing a harmonica. He meets up with his lighter-skinned brother, Joe Grant, who warns him against getting involved with a white girl. As Baldwin puts it, "Harmonica says that he will be. The brothers separate and we next see Harmonica in the cool of the evening (not yet in the heat of the night) unconcernedly walking along a deserted country road. Headlights flash behind him; white men leap out of their cars, the boy turns to face them; and the next time we see him, he is hanging from a tree."[21] This comment anticipates Baldwin's critique of *In the Heat of the Night* that follows shortly after but also intimates the clichéd nature of this opening sequence in Gast's film.

Gast's earnest intent in making the film is nonetheless articulated in an interview conducted just after a public showing of his film on June 16, 2004, in France. Gast claims in the interview that he wanted his film to be seen again in 2004, given, in his view, its relevance to contemporary problems of racism. He remarks that he was happy to have found a sympathetic audience among Algerian spectators. For Gast, this was a partial redemption of the film, which is indeed a point well taken. Despite the vast differences between the racism of Franco-Algerian racial tensions in the year leading up to the Parisian *banlieues* riots (2005) and American racism in the late 1950s, Gast's film resonated with these spectators.[22]

It must be noted, however, that the primary critiques of both the novel and the film in Anglo-American criticism rest on the idea that Vian and by extension Gast have failed in their confrontations with American racism. Critics claim that both the film and the novel are imbued with essentialist articulations of racial identities. Braggs argues that the image of black Americans is too primitive, suggesting that Vian has missed the point of black American protest against white supremacy. This critique is also echoed in varying ways by Stephanie Brown and Rebecca Brita Ruquist.[23] Field's critique does draw attention to the race essentialism debate though it does not focus on it as a primary thesis. Nonetheless, each of these authors avows, according to slightly different perspectives, that Vian, in impersonating a black American, is telling a story of racial abuse that he has no right or ability to tell. According to this critique, Gast would be faulted as well.

Ralph Schoolcraft countered these arguments by suggesting that the goal of Vian/Sullivan is ultimately more about an attack on the academy of French literature and its perceptions of black Americans. Schoolcraft's argument is that Vian also wants to unmask the deeply embedded racial prejudices of his critics. Schoolcraft points out the many puns on passing from black to white and vice versa that are incorporated into Vian's text. Namely, the fictive author Vernon Sullivan is named after various black and white musicians on the Paris jazz scene, the black Vernon Story as well as the white Paul Vernon and Joe Sullivan. Schoolcraft diplomatically suggests that these authors are perhaps insufficiently acquainted with Vian's work to catch the nuance and intention of his critique.

Whether Schoolcraft's point concerning the validity of these critical perspectives is well-taken or not, he does point the analysis of the novel in a very different direction. He notes that Vian's real target is the Gallimard *série blanche* and that Vian as a result is working "au noir" (without recognition, though literally without pay) to produce a competitive *roman noir* for a Parisian editor whose offices are situated on the rue Blanche.[24] In this one paragraph, Schoolcraft shows the extent to which Vian's genius consists in writing a regrettably questionable novel that gave way to a film equally of questionable value. He argues that Vian has nonetheless exceeded himself in terms of parody.

Schoolcraft's argument notwithstanding, the claims by Braggs, Brown, and Ruquist that the novel is a gratuitous use of American racial tensions for whatever ulterior motives cannot be brushed aside. This makes Gast's position even more tenuous since his film has no concern with probing French psychic reactions to race in America as are evidenced in the novel. The mythical America that Tadié has indicated as crucial in the case of the novel is common to many of the *série noire* novels written by British or European authors. It could be argued that Vian's foray into this mythical America in *J'irai cracher sur vos tombes* ultimately launches a social critique due to its self-reflexive or multilayered structure. Since most of the *série noire* novels that rely on the same tactics, such as those of James Hadley Chase, are not bent on serious critique of either European or American culture, the Vian novel becomes singled out. The same self-reflection and parody cannot be found in Gast's film, which does not mitigate his original intentions in making the film.

Indeed, parody is the key to understanding the social critique of the *série noire*. Gilles Deleuze's "Philosophie de la *Série Noire*" (1966) speaks of the importance of parody in the *série noire* when he says that "the very beautiful works of *La Série noire* are the ones in which the real finds itself parodied and this parody guides us in directions towards the real that we could not have found on our own."[25] In keeping with the *série noire* tradition, Vian's novel mounts a parody of the French unconscious patronage with respect to American racism. Gast's film, on the contrary, is a dramatic thriller totally devoid of humor.

Braggs and Rubquist definitely can fault Vian's mise en abyme of whiteness and blackness in terms of his ability to mount an effective protest against American racism, and it is definitely not my purpose to question those arguments. Rather it is to suggest that all of the various assumptions about whiteness and blackness that can be discerned in Vian's choice to use American mythologies to critique French culture exhibit how a Frenchman's perception of American racism is affected. Those impressions are *not* caused by actual racial relations in the United States at the time but rather by the mythical America on which the novels of the *série noire* were based. Whether those novels and films reflected correctly or incorrectly a true critique of American white supremacy is therefore a question that must be addressed.

In following Vian's source novel and trading its parody for the semblance of a Hollywood-style film noir, Gast inadvertently proves that Hollywood films reinforce Negro stereotypes though genre, casting, and narrative lines. Further, by making his film at a time when the film noir "genre" was becoming increasingly domesticated and co-opted by Hollywood, it was difficult for Gast to incorporate the added complication of film noir as an indirect critique of classical Hollywood narrative techniques practiced by studios from the 1930s to the mid-1940s.

What therefore passes in writing as a kind of mise en abyme is much more difficult to achieve in a French film attempting to pass as an American film. In Gast's case, the encoding of images relies heavily not only on the aesthetics of a Hollywood film but equally on the recently emerged nouvelle vague aesthetics. Baldwin has little sympathy for Gast's confusion concerning the cinematic path he should follow and claims in his review of the film that it has "no viewpoint whatsoever except that from the window of the Stock Exchange."[26] Baldwin's disdain is understandable, and one cannot claim that it is a stellar or influential film. It has long been overlooked for plausible though perhaps unfair reasons.

Baldwin's critique nonetheless falls short since Baldwin asserts that "Vian *himself* points out, somewhat savagely, that *I Shall Spit on your Graves* is not a very good novel: he was enraged (and enlightened) by the vogue it had in France."[27] Most accounts of Vian's motivation in writing the novel is that it was done for financial gain. Motivations aside, the crucial concern is the impact of both film and novel on reader and spectator perceptions. The reception of these cultural products is a key to understanding how they rely on encoded notions of visible and invisible whiteness. In the case of the film, Gast's directorial choices worked against him due to his inability to read the encoding of racially inflected tropes in the Hollywood films he was imitating. One is led to consider what might have been different had the film been made by someone more in control of their aesthetic choices and cinematic apparatus.

Since neither Vian nor Gast had ever been to America or experienced the racial tensions of that country firsthand, both were left with a need to create on the basis of American cultural products and French perceptions of American white supremacy. Whereas Gast's source is Vian and his perceptions of classical Hollywood narrative, Vian's source is the recent publications of *série noire* novels, such as those of James Hadley Chase.

As mentioned earlier, Gast's stated purpose was to expose the ugliness of American racism. But with some notable exceptions, the reception history of Gast's film suggests that it failed as a meaningful protest film against American racism. Its lack of authenticity in this regard nonetheless recommends it as a film that faithfully though blindly mimics those American films which represent invisible whiteness by default. Whether approved or condemned, these concepts of white supremacy therefore can be shown to be embedded in the aesthetic of classical Hollywood narrative and are ever more glaringly visible when seen through the eyes of a young and impressionable French filmmaker.

Whose Story Is It and What Color Are They?: Subject Position and Race on Screen Space

In considering the shortcomings of Gast's film, one must focus on the differences in representations of subject positioning in the film and the novel. Reader or spectator identification with the protagonists Lee Anderson (Vian) and Joe Grant (Gast) can be a key to understanding how Gast's film partially fulfills noir genre expectations and fails to do so with respect to others. Schoolcraft argues that readers of Vian's novel would no doubt be led to identify with the narrator Lee Anderson as a white man who seeks revenge for the heinous crimes against his little brother and stresses that the use of interior monologue is essential for this identification to take place. He argues that the novel progresses from a trusting relationship between the protagonist and the reader to a sense of revolt at the grotesque caricatures of most of the white characters.[28]

Vian uses interior monologue to confound the reader's attempts to find a subject position with which to identify in the novel. Schoolcraft points out that the temporal beginning of the novel is after Lee has taken his place as a bookseller in a small bookstore in Buckton, which is to say sometime after the crime against his brother has been committed. Hence, the reader is not aware of the fact that Lee is passing for white. The reader's identification with the protagonist is indeed stymied by the reader's delayed realization that the protagonist is not white but simply passing for white.

Lee's interior monologue controls the reader's ability to find a subject with whom he or she can identify. This crucial dimension of the novel fails to be successfully adapted by Gast, and this accounts for the flatness of the film in terms of an effective racial critique. Though interior monologue can be represented visually, Gast does not do so. He also establishes in the opening of the film, before the credits even roll, that Joe Grant is passing for white.

This is significant since the two opening sequences, described earlier through Baldwin's critique of their clichéd nature, occur before the film itself begins. This may have been a way for Gast to follow the lead of the novel and use the lynching as a preface to the subsequent relocation of Grant and the film's proper narrative beginning. Yet, if we are to believe Gast's comment in his interview about the film, which was that Vian saw no more than the opening credits of the film, this implies that Vian did see those opening sequences that Baldwin so condemns as stereotypical depictions of black Americans and their lives.

In terms of the novel, the critiques of both Brown and Schoolcraft clearly establish that one's right to speak about American white supremacy and its link to racism is always questionable when linked to a white author supposedly representing a black victim's voice. Though they are concerned with very different perspectives, they each raise issues that are pertinent to my analysis of Gast's film. Schoolcraft suggests that it is the interior monologue of Vian's novel which legitimates the idea that this is an authentic narrative by an American Negro. At the very least it is a justifiable project since it creates a semblance of the American Negro's voice concerning victimization in ways that might be understood from broader perspectives.

Brown asserts that Vian's qualifications of the French "translation" of an American story written by a Negro again bring into question the authentic voice of the African American and how it is compromised by a white French writer. A crucial consideration here is that Vian has already anticipated the reactions of readers and critics to a victimized American Negro author. He is therefore ready to reveal their prejudices once they discover they have been duped. Like him, they have been educated by the cultural products of a mythological America and, in the case of the cinema, the mythic America. Baldwin nonetheless notes an authenticity to Vian's attempts to raise the specter of the black American's suffering and rage, which Gast's film is unsuccessful in doing.

The choices Gast makes in his film raise the question of subject position and spectator identification in other ways. Like Vian, Gast is a white French man who desires to make a critique against American racism but has to do so not only through the lens of his source material but equally through the lens of the classical Hollywood narrative film. These parameters inevitably inform his ideas about how to structure an American-style film made in France. How to represent the subject position of the protagonist visually is therefore crucial for Gast. Gast must strike a delicate balance between he relationship of the screen space and the space of the narrative to be conveyed. Since the actor Christian Marquand is a white man, the screen space will always register him as such. The narrative space of the film will always register him as a black man passing for white.

In a parallel fashion, what has been suggested by Brown in terms of translation can be applied equally to the theory of filmic adaptation. Cinema language is susceptible to the same dangers that Brown claims are present for literary translation in that it is hard to avoid falling into stereotypical representations of racial difference, certainly in the pre–Civil Rights period. Bogle's study of black actors, actresses, and the stock characters they were confined to in early to midcentury Hollywood echoes Baldwin's own critiques of characters like Stepin Fetchit. Of Stepin Fetchit and other characters like him, Baldwin says, "[I]t seemed to me that they lied about the world I knew, and debased it, and I certainly did not know anybody like them."[29] The same could easily be said about the character of Joe Grant played by white French actor Christian Marquand.

Issues of black American stereotypes aside, the primary critique against the film has most often been that it fails to capture the true essence and complex structure of Vian's novel. As Brain MacFarlane points out, comments on the success or failure of cinematic adaptations range from those of "novels being 'betrayed' by boorish filmmakers to those who regard the practice of comparing film and novel as a waste of time." As Dudley Andrew points out, there are many modes of adaptation, such as "borrowing, intersection and fidelity of transformation"; Andrew likens the process of adaptation to "appropriation of meaning from a prior text."[30]

All adaptation categories named by Andrew are legitimate forms of appropriating meaning from their source materials, and Gast's film is most appropriately seen as a borrowing from Vian's novel. Andrew additionally argues that in borrowing, a filmmaker "hoped to win an audience by the prestige of its borrowed title or subject."[31] Andrew claims that this is one of the central purposes of borrowing in adaptation. Even though the film was made ten years later, Gast no doubt benefited from the notoriety of the novel. Sales of the novel skyrocketed once there was the scandalous real-life strangling of a woman in Montparnasse by her boyfriend. As many versions concur, the corpse of the woman was found with a copy of Vian's novel in the room where she was strangled in a fashion mimicking the strangling of the two white women in the book.[32]

One issue that has plagued Gast's film is that it borrows from a novel that was banned in France. In addition, the novel was already considered substandard by its own author and ultimately drew its prestige from its paratext, that is, the creation of a fictitious author, the black American Vernon Sullivan, and the scandals surrounding its publication. The subtext of criticism thus seems to be more about Gast's capitalizing on the sensationalism surrounding the novel and less about his lack of faithfulness to his source in his cinematic adaptation. And yet, in the case of Gast's film, the two are intertwined in that by adapting the straightforward narrative without incorporating the puns, parodies, and layers of Vian's structure, he essentially creates a dangerous and misleading caricature of black American rage, one that Baldwin for one could simply not accept.

Another crucial issue to consider is that borrowing and fragmentation were trending in the nouvelle vague. Though Gast was not part of that nouvelle vague core of filmmakers, he made his film at the beginning of this vital French cinematic movement. Baldwin argues, as mentioned previously, that Gast had "no viewpoint other than that from the window of the Stock Exchange."[33] Gast is essentially caught in the crosshairs of a genre that has become somewhat formulaic and studio-controlled in Hollywood by 1959 and the newer forays into reappropriations of Hollywood films that characterizes much of the nouvelle vague style. It may indeed be possible to imitate the American-style film, but does that guarantee that one can get at the heart of the black American problem? Hollywood filmmaking had made little headway in confronting invisible whiteness in ways that were valuable to black spectators, with few notable exceptions. For example, Ralph Ellison argued in his 1949 article "The Shadow and the Act" that Clarence Brown's film *Intruder in the Dust* (1949) was the "only film that could be shown in Harlem without arousing unintended laughter."[34] A mere ten years later, it is difficult to imagine that a French filmmaker who has never been to America can launch a worthy critique of the black American problem through his study of late 1940s and early 1950s American films.

Gast's stated desire nonetheless was to critique American racism. His choice to flirt with some film noir techniques while passing over others is telling. Though Lott rightly argues that film noir was a refuge for whites, the phenomenon of noir does contribute to unlocking the social rigidity of classical Hollywood narrative and provides structural grounds for an eventual loosening of the hold of invisible whiteness on the classic narrative style. It does this not through its attention to racial issues but rather through its representation of gender and familial relations, which are routinely represented as dysfunctional. Film noir in its inception indeed targeted social dysfunction albeit in a world where the privilege of whiteness was taken for granted.

Film noir could therefore potentially have been used as a means of structuring a probe into dysfunctional *race* relations in America. This seems to have been Gast's intent, though his film lacks certain conventions of noir that might have made his critique more successful. One of the differences in Gast's film as opposed to the novel is its ending when Joe Grant and Lisbeth, the white woman he intended to murder, accept that they are indeed in love with each other and try to escape to the Canadian border together. The novel ends with the grisly and sexually charged murder of the two women who were targeted by Lee Anderson. Shortly after, his double death by shooting and by lynching brings the novel to its tragic end, although, in a certain sense, one could argue that even the "tragedy" of the novel's ending is a cruel parody intended to mortify its readers.

Gast's narrative resolution is totally devoid of parody in keeping with the major contrast between the novel and the film. Gast had his own share of protesters against his film but, as a French filmmaker, he obviously had no need to be concerned with the strictures of the Hays Code. Nonetheless, his narrative resolution is totally resonant with the miscegenation-themed films that were allowed post-1957 and totally at odds with the ending of Vian's novel. The ending is also reminiscent of one of Lang's first American-made film noir films, *You Only Live Once* (1937). A comparison of their closing imagery attests to an allusion, whether conscious or not, to Lang's film (Figs. 8.1 and 8.2).

Since Baldwin claims that *You Only Live Once* was a film where Lang had finally grasped the essence of the American-style film, the fact that Gast so radically transforms the ending of his film to one that is more in keeping with the kind of Hollywood take typical of Lang's filmmaking is significant. The ending also emphasizes what Field has stressed in his article on Vian, Sullivan, and film noir: that much of the movement of film noir involves crossing borders or going to the dark side. The fact that the couple metaphorically crosses the borders of Jim Crow America and attempts to cross national borders between that America and a country where their biracial relationship would go unnoticed is in keeping with

Fig. 8.1 *J'irai cracher sur vos tombes.* CTI SIPRO. Attempted Escape from Racial Prejudice Across the Border. 1:42:18

Fig. 8.2 *You Only Live Once.* Walter Wanger, United Artists. Unjustly Accused Heads for the Border. 1:42:56

Field's remarks to this effect. He notes, following Lott's lead, that much of film noir is indeed about crossing moral borders metaphorically, and this ending is a literal interpretation of that aspect of noir film. Whether Gast intended an explicit reference to Lang, the trope is present in the endings of both films.[35]

Indeed, in "American Film Noir: the History of an Idea," James Naremore offers one of the most nuanced analyses of the film noir "phenomenon" and resists the impulse to reduce it to a formulaic genre. He rightly prefers to speak of it as an eternally debatable paradox of cinema history, sitting somewhere in between surrealism, existentialism, pulp fiction, and geographically located somewhere between America, France, and Germany. One of his more important observations is that "if one could ask the original French commentators what *film noir* represented, they might agree that for all its romanticisms, it was a challenge to Hollywood conventions: it used unorthodox narration."[36] He adds that other qualities of film noir might be its resistance to sentiment and censorship, its revelry in the social fantastic, its treatment of the social ambiguity of human motives, and its tendency to view commodity culture as a wasteland.

Naremore expands on these ideas in his book *More Than Night: Film Noir in Its Contexts* in ways that are significant to the chronology of Vian's novel and Gast's film. He argues that as the concept of the *auteur* takes hold with the nouvelle vague critics, it is more plausible to view film noir as "a collective style operating within and against the Hollywood system: and the *auteur* was an individual stylist who achieved freedom over the studio through existential choice." Naremore asserts that the "French began to lose interest in *noir* at about the same time their own art cinema became internationally successful." He notes that "clearly an art cinema based on transformation of 'the worst material was about to appear.'" Naremore equates the death of Vian in the theater where he watched the premiere of Gast's *J'irai cracher sur vos tombes* with the death of the first phase of film noir.[37]

Gast's film does use noir techniques and though it was not in and of itself the death knell of film noir, his film is made at a time when transformations in the phenomenon of noir were being felt. As Naremore remarks, art cinema was reasserting its hold over Hollywood's complacent genres. Ultimately, Gast's film fails to adapt the mise en abyme of Vian's narrative techniques, but it might have had a greater chance of doing so had Gast appealed to the one aspect of film noir technique to which he does not. The use of unorthodox narrative techniques in the form of flashbacks and first-person voice-over are absent in Gast's film. To have appealed to these techniques might have moved him closer to a more faithful adaptation of Vian's book but, more important, toward a more effective criticism of the problems of black America. Adapting Vian's mise en abyme in cinematic language was a challenge that was difficult to meet.

In the case of the novel, there are two subject positions to be considered, that of Vernon Sullivan and that of the protagonist Lee Anderson. Despite close parallels between these two subject positions, there are nonetheless important differences. First, Sullivan is ostensibly a black American who chose to leave the United States in order to express his rage concerning racist conditions in Jim Crow America. We are introduced to him in Vian's preface to *J'irai cracher sur vos tombes* as a man who self-identifies as more black than white despite the fact that he has managed to cross the line. He contrasts himself to Negroes who are complacent with respect to their relations to whites. In his preface, Vian claims that Sullivan has nothing but disdain for those "good Negroes."[38]

Anderson, in contrast, is a man whose desire for revenge is fully contained by his concern for the violence perpetrated against his brother. As mentioned earlier, though Lee invents an elaborate story about his upbringing and education in Europe, he himself informs the reader that none of this is true and that his actual experience in Europe was abject servitude to a man who is described in notably negative terms.[39] In the case of the film, the only subject position to be taken is the parallel to that of Lee Anderson. Joe Grant, the vengeful black man passing for white, is the only source of audience identification available in the film. Vernon Sullivan is not part of the filmic representation of a subject position in Gast's film. Gast does not take into account paratextual characters, such as the supposed author of the primary narrative.

The Subject Position in Film Noir: Innovations in Hollywood Filmmaking and Innovations in Narrative Technique

In an article titled "Homosexuality and Film Noir," Dyer offers a useful definition of film noir. Dyer's thesis in this article concerns film noir with respect to representations of homosexuality in the cinema, but the definitions he provides help in analyzing Gast's adherence to an American style.[40] Gast's film is paradoxically rooted in a structure built to question Hollywood conventions while he simultaneously seeks to replicate the Hollywood narrative and aesthetic style. Dyer describes the structure of film noir as a labyrinth in which mysteries are often not solved and in which heterosexual couples are not able to succeed in the end. This is decidedly the case with respect to Joe Grant and Lisbeth Sanders. They are killed just as they are about to reach the Canadian border, where they would presumably have been able to live in peace as a biracial couple, since no one would have been privy to the real information concerning Joe's racial identity.

Dyer stresses that the voice-over and flashback or dream techniques that define film noir are instructive since they allow for more reflection on the moral fiber and especially the reliability of the protagonist's participation in the narrative displayed in the screen space of a film. Indeed, one option open to Gast that he failed to pursue was a labyrinthine use of flashback, dream sequence, and voice-over narration in order to capture the presence of Vernon Sullivan in some small way in the course of the film.

As mentioned previously, the strongest move toward a potential mise en abyme is in the opening sequence, which Baldwin criticized in his review of the film as being too stereotypical. The sequence establishes facts that are not included in the active narration of the novel. Just after this opening sequence, when Joe takes his brother down from the tree where he has been lynched, the film's credits begin to roll. This sequence thus reads as a preface to the rest of the film. For the rest of the film sound is limited to dialogue, a jazz soundtrack, and an endless repetition of the song the young brother was playing on his harmonica just before he was lynched. No voice-over is ever used in the film.

Mary Anne Doane in her article "The Voice in the Cinema" suggests voice-over is a vital innovation for film noir. Doane suggests that film noir as a phenomenon is indeed a function of postwar social transitions but, more importantly, she argues that film noir's prominent use of voice-over is an innovative questioning of how the transition to sound should be incorporated into filmmaking in creative ways. Though sound film comes into existence in the late 1920s, Doane argues that it profoundly affected postwar Hollywood in that questions about how sound should be used becomes a dominant concern. Doane cites the importance of the screen space, the *diegetic* space, and the audio space of movie theaters in order to advance her main thesis: that the real contribution of film noir was its success in enlarging the space of the narrative through its development of voice-over narrative.[41]

By creating a space in which the protagonist may tell his story either authentically or not, the subject position of film protagonists becomes complex and deepened. Though not all film noir films rely on voice-over narration, this innovation is crucial for many of the early noir films, such as Billy Wilder's *Double Indemnity*. It is precisely noir's voice-over narration that provides ongoing commentary on the moral dimensions figured in the films' narratives. In like manner, Vian's novel provides the reader with a constant commentary/justification of the protagonist. The reader is left to decide about the protagonist's psychopathology or justified rage against white supremacy based on the inner monologue that controls the text.

In the film, this inner monologue is replaced by dialogue and by a jazz sound track, which means that the film falls short of one of the primary aesthetic features of early film noir filmmaking. The voice-over monologue is the privileged narrative of a protagonist who has been abused by the system. The intensification of the protagonist's confession or self-justification is dependent on a viewer's simultaneous exposure to a series of events that unfold within the narrative versus a narrative controlled by the protagonist himself. Not only is much of film noir dependent on this technique; Vian's novel is utterly enriched and deepened by the creation of the protagonist's internal dialogue with the reader.

The protagonist of Gast's film is a black man passing for white, played by a white French actor, and therefore many questions about confession and *justification* are put into play. Again, we have a doubling down or mise en abyme in terms of how spectators in 1959 France or America might or might not have identified with the protagonist. At the time, the Civil Rights movement is gearing up in America, and the October 17, 1961, Parisian massacre of Algerians is only three years away in France. The irony is that with respect to the screen, the suggestion is that only the French white actor is in a position to save his brother, the young black man, from the injustice of American white supremacy at the beginning of the film. Though Gast wished to make a film about the injustices of American racism, it must be noted in retrospect that an insidious form of racism in France coexisted at the time of his making this film.

Though Baldwin does not speak directly to the salvation of the young black brother of the protagonist Joe Grant, he does raise this issue of America's white supremacist tendencies as curable only by Europe to a metaphoric level. He claims that the film represents the European dream of America "which, after all, is how we *got* America: a dream full of envy, guilt, condescension, and terror, a dream which began as an adventure in real estate."[42] Baldwin equally claims that Europe's look at America through this film ultimately fails, despite its intentions to understand the grim truths of American white supremacy. He follows his remarks on Gast's *J'irai cracher sur vos tombes* with a transition into a discussion of D. W. Griffith's *Birth of a Nation*. Though seemingly illogical as a transition, Baldwin's point is driven home: Only America can save itself from itself. Baldwin suggests that Europe cannot learn from America's supremacist mythologies but must tend to its own.

NOTES

1. This quote is taken from Boris Vian, *Les morts ont tous la même peau* (Paris: Editions Scorpion et Christian Bourgois, 1973/1947), postface. The original quote from Vian has been truncated, and I have translated it liberally. The free translation of the quote serves the purposes of this chapter. The original quotation reads as follows: "Tristes individus, critique par la bande, Presque tous aussi idiots que Claude Morgan ... Quand oserez-vous parler d'un livre sans vous entourer de références sur l'auteur..." (149).

2. Doug Field, "Even Better than the Real Thing: Boris Vian, Vernon Sullivan and Film Noir," *African American Review* 45, no. 1/2 (Spring/Summer 2012): 157–166. James Baldwin, *The Devil Finds Work* (New York: Laurel, 1976), 45–52. I am dependent on Field's analysis of the film due to his more in-depth critique of its film noir elements, since my argument hopes to expand on the ways in which film noir has been co-opted by Hollywood in 1959 and thus perhaps inadequately understood by Gast.

3. Donald Bogle's *Toms, Coons, Mulattoes, Mammies and Bucks* offers valuable insight into the difficulties of black actors and actresses but also into the practice of casting white actors as blacks passing for white. Despite the slow progress of blacks in the Hollywood industry, such a practice was detrimental to actresses such as Fredi Washington, a light-skinned actress who played Peola in John M. Stahl's 1934 *Imitation of Life*. As Bogle points out, "[T]he spectacular looks that had opened the door for an important film role ultimately closed that door in her face" (New York: Bantam, 1974), 85.

4. The name of the protagonist in the novel is Lee Anderson. I primarily distinguish between discussion of the novel and the film by using the different names of the protagonists in the two.

5. Most articles on the Vian controversy trace the issues concerning the Vian-Sullivan hoax in terms of this issue of translation, though particularly in-depth articles are Ralph Schoolcraft, "Boris Vian: bon chic, mauvais genres," *Europe* 967–968 (Novembre–Décembre 2009): 61–71, and Stephanie Brown, "Black Comme Moi: Boris Vian and the African American Voice in Translation," *Mosaic* 36, no. 1 (March 2003): 51–67. The positions taken by these two authors are contrasting, but their accounts of the hoax are consistent with each other.

6. Boris Vian, *I Shall Spit on Your Graves*, trans. Boris Vian and Milton Rosenthal (Los Angeles: Tam Tam Books, 1998), 98. The translation was originally published in 1948 by Vendôme Press. Boris Vian, *J'irai cracher sur vos tombes* (Paris: Editions Scorpion and Christian Bourgois, 1973/1947). When I have use of a direct quote, it will be taken from the English version of the novel.

7. Vian, *J'irai cracher*, 210. In the English version, this phrase "un nègre" is translated as "a n***ger." 177.

8. As with James Baldwin, Rashida K. Braggs in "Hearing the Rage in *J'irai cracher sur vos tombes*," *Nottingham French Studies* 43, no. 1 (Spring 2004): 100–107, suggests that the desire for revenge can be heard through the jazz music and the musical references throughout the text.

9. For a detailed account of the pornography trials against Vian's novel, cf. Ralph Schoolcraft, "Hard Boiled French Style: Boris Vian Disguised as Vernon Sullivan (Authorship and Pseudonymy)," *South Central Review* 27, no. 1 (Spring and Summer 2010): 21–38.

10. Rashida K. Braggs, *Jazz Disaporas: Race Music and Migration in Post-World War II Paris* (Berkeley: University of California Press, 2016).
11. A video version of Gast's interview with Alain Riou, "Sexe, Jazz et Violence," is available on the DVD version of the film. C.T.I. Gaumont Tristar, Tristar home video (2006).
12. Vian, *I Shall Spit on Your Graves*, xi.
13. For the expanded and updated edition of Naremore's text (Berkeley: University of California Press, 2008/1998). Another text dealing more explicitly with relations between film noir and German origins is Lutz Koepnick, *The Dark Mirror: German Cinema Between Hitler and Hollywood* (Berkeley: University of California Press, 2002), 165.
14. Bernard Tadié, "Enoncer L'Amérique: Les langues fantômes du polar," *Revue Française d'Etudes Américaines* 80, no. 1, 1999, 56–58. 57.
15. Orson Welles's fifty-two-page memo to Universal Studios when they took him off postproduction for *Touch of Evil* is a case in point. Essentially, Welles accuses the studios of desecrating his film. *Touch of Evil* is ultimately an active challenge to film noir techniques. Universal's changes are a text-book case in rendering the film more relatable to audience expectations from a genre that had well-defined norms by 1957. The memo was written on December 5, 1957, to Edward I. Muhl, vice president in charge of Production at Universal Studios, and is widely available. One available copy of the memo is also commented upon by Lawrence French, "Orson Welles Memo on *Touch of Evil*." http://wellesnet.com/touch_memo1.htm. Paul Schrader's comment on the film as the epitaph of noir appears in his 1972 "Notes on *Film Noir*," in Leo Braudy and Marshall Cohen, *Film Theory and Criticism*, 7th ed. (New York: Oxford University Press, 2009), 581–591. 589.
16. Eric Lott, "The Whiteness of Film Noir," *American Literary History* 9, no. 3 (1997): 542–566. 545. This article came to my attention as result of reading Field's article "Even Better than the Real Thing." Manthia Diawara's "Noir by Noirs: Towards a New Realism in Black Cinema," *African American Review* 27, no. 4 (Winter 1994): 525–537, highlights the racial stereotypes of blacks in film noir and, in particular, analyzes the film adaptation of Chester Himes's film *A Rage in Harlem* (Dir. Bill Duke. Forest Whitaker, Robin Givens, Palace Productions, 1991). Though the subject is outside the scope of this chapter, I maintain that Himes's work is impossible to adapt cinematographically and hence the shortcomings of this film.
17. Brown's "Black Comme Moi," is important for considering how cultural translation functions in Vian's works published under the Vernon Sullivan pseudonym. Brown takes exception to the idea that a French white man should feel entitled to speak in the voice of an American black man. Her position is countered by Schoolcraft's suggestion that Vian is not exclu-

sively concerned with racial identities but rather with verbal puns on the difference between white and black on a broader scale. Ralph Schoolcraft, "Vian, Sullivan: bon chic, mauvais genres", *Europe*, 967–968, Novembre–Décembre 2009, 61–71, 63. The most important for my purposes is that all of this gets lost in the cinematic "translation" of the text.

18. André Bazin's "The Evolution of the Language of Cinema" is in excerpt form in Braudy and Cohen, *Film Theory and Criticism*, 41–53. 53. The coining of the term "camera stylo" must be attributed to Alexandre Astruc, "Du stylo à la caméra et de la caméra au stylo," *L'Ecran française*, March 30, 1949.

19. Baldwin, *The Devil Finds Work*, 45. James Campbell, in *Exiled in Paris: Richard Wright, James Baldwin, Samuel Beckett, and Others on the Left Bank* (Berkeley: University of California Press, 2003), suggests that "a black American author" actually snuck into the theater to watch the premiere. He claims that "the 'invisibility' of the novelist in the Salle du Petit Marbeuf was due to the fact that the screen version of the story, directed by Michel Gast, was one he disapproved of but was powerless to prevent." 238.

20. Video version of Gast's interview with Alain Riou, "Sexe, Jazz et Violence." It is in this DVD interview that Gast claims Vian died before the film actually began. His earnest intent in making the film is much clearer in an interview conducted just after a public showing of his film on June 16, 2004, in France. Gast claims in the interview that he wanted his film to be seen, given, in his view, its relevance to contemporary problems concerning American racial tensions. Michel Gast Biographie et entretien, *J'irai cracher sur vos tombes* de Michel Gast, http://www.r7afr.st, webzine sur le cinéma indépendant.

21. Baldwin, *The Devil Finds Work*, 49.

22. "Biographie Michel Gast. Questions à Michel Gast." webzine sur le cinéma indépendant. www.r7a.fr.st.

23. Braggs, "Hearing the Rage in *J'irai cracher sur vos tombes*," 104; Brown, "Black Comme Moi"; Field, "Even Better than the Real Thing"; Rebecca Brita Rubquist, "Paris, Race and Universalism in the Black Atlantic: Léopold Senghor, Simone de Beauvoir, Boris Vian, Richard Wright" (PhD diss., Yale University, 2004).

24. Schoolcraft, "Boris Vian," 62–63.

25. My translation. Gilles Deleuze, *L' île deserte et autres textes: testes et entretiens, 1953–1974.* Ed. David Lapoujade (Paris : Editions de la minuit, 2002), 114–119. 119.

26. Baldwin, *The Devil Finds Work*, 48.

27. Baldwin, *The Devil Finds Work*, 45.

28. Schoolcraft, "Boris Vian," 66.

29. Bogle, *Toms, Coons, Mulattoes, Mammies and Bucks*, 23. Baldwin, *The Devil Finds Work*.

30. Brian MacFarlane, "Backgrounds," 381–389. 381. Dudley Andrews, "Adaptation," 372–380. 373–374. Both are excerpted Leo Braudy and Cohen, *Film Theory and Criticism*.

31. Andrews, "Adaptation," 374.
32. Most critiques of the novel mention the real-life drama of the strangling that took place after sales of the novel began to take off. The initial jump in sales is attributed by many, notably, James Campbell, to the charges of pornography brought against Vian by Daniel Parker. Campbell's rendition of the strangling episode can be found in Campbell, *Exiled in Paris*, 82. Campbell also draws parallels between Richard Wright's *Native Son* and *J'irai cracher sur vos tombes* and suggests that the Wright novel most probably influenced Vian's own novel. 17.
33. Baldwin, *The Devil Finds Work* (New York: Laurel, 1976), 48.
34. Ralph Ellison, "The Shadow and the Act," *The Reporter*, December 6, 1949. www.unz.org. 17–20. 19.
35. Field, "Even Better than the Real Thing," 165.
36. James Naremore, "American Film Noir: The History of an Idea," *Film Quarterly* 48, no. 2 (Winter 1995–1996): 12–28. 24.
37. James Naremore, *More Than Night: Film Noir in Its Contexts.* (Berkeley: University of California Press, 2008), 26–28.
38. Vian, *J'irai cracher sur vos tombes*, 9.
39. Vian, *J'irai cracher sur vos tombes*, 141.
40. Richard Dyer, "Homosexuality and Film Noir," *Jump Cut: a Review of Contemporary Media* 16 (1977): 18–21.
41. Mary Ann Doane, "The Voice in the Cinema: The Articulation of Body and Space," in Braudy and Cohen, *Film Theory and Criticism*, 318–331.
42. Baldwin, *The Devil Finds Work*, 53.

CHAPTER 9

Rachid Bouchareb's *Two Men in Town* and His American Trilogy: Cultural Transpositions

*He saw it as clearly as though it were only inches from him—that face
he knew so well, the face in America he had tried to escape.*
—*William Gardner Smith*, The Stone Face

*[He pivots] on the geometry of destruction and self-destruction. This is
a delicate tightrope stretched taut and high, above unimaginable
chasms, coming close to the truth of many black lives: many have fallen
but many have not.*
—*James Baldwin*, The Devil Finds Work

Freud's concept of the uncanny outlines the many ways in which resemblances can be disturbing. In the quotation from Smith, his black protagonist, Simeon, recognizes that the face of a white policeman beating Algerian protesters in the Algerian massacre of October 17, 1961, was a ghostly mirror image of the abusive policemen he had encountered in America and from whom he thought he had escaped by coming to Europe.[1] Similarly Baldwin praised Vian for his ability to portray the black American's rage from Vian's "strange alien own" perspective.[2] He nonetheless condemned Gast for his controversial appropriation of Vian's text in his film adaptation. Baldwin implies throughout *The Devil Finds Work* that Hollywood productions, because of their reliance on a seamless narrative surface, are most often unable to question the insidious invisible white mythologies that lie beneath those surfaces. His overall claim is that

© The Author(s) 2018
A. M. Craven, *Visible and Invisible Whiteness*,
https://doi.org/10.1007/978-3-319-76777-2_9

Hollywood productions actively incorporate and reify those myths. His readings of films throughout *The Devil Finds Work* are exercises in reading against the grain of those surface narratives.

This is relevant to Baldwin's critique of Gast's film, which was made in France and, in Gast's view, with honest intention. Gast indeed desired to make an honest American-style film based on Vian's novel which could effectively critique racial tensions in the United States, as was discussed in Chap. 8. Gast's "American" film has nonetheless been judged by many to resemble a decidedly mythical America in disturbing ways. Whether his aim to critique American racism was successful or not, his ultimate message inadvertently reproduced a violent America fueled by the power of invisible whiteness based on a myth born and bred in Hollywood.

As has been noted by Naremore, following Bazin's lead, film noir is rooted in the aesthetic base of surrealism and existentialism of the early modern period in France in particular.[3] French surrealism in turn, in groups headed by André Breton, is deeply invested in using Freud's notion of the uncanny as an aesthetic base. In *Compulsive Beauty*, Art historian Hal Foster argues that the Freudian uncanny is indeed the most plausible unifier of the myriad of surrealist works that have long presented problems for categorization.[4] Walter Benjamin's concept of the aura draws from the surrealists' dependence on the uncanny, and in his infamous essay, "The Work of Art in the Age of Mechanical Reproduction" (1936), Benjamin applies this concept to film art. Disturbing resemblances reproduced in cinema, Freud's return of the repressed, are important to Benjamin's purposes in this essay.

Franco-Algerian director Rachid Bouchareb employs yet another technique in his study of resemblances, though it is a technique ultimately drawn from these theoretical bases. Following Benjamin's lead, Foster, in *The Return of the Real*, emphasizes the importance of the aura as an experience of transposing common responses in human relationships of the sensation of looking at that which then looks at us in turn, resulting in a kind of uncomfortable recognition.[5] An example of this, again from Smith, is when he is looking at a photograph in the Paris *Herald Tribune*: "He studied the white faces. Yes, he knew them, recognized them: the faces of the stone souls ... As he looked at the photograph, the old terror and hatred swept over him again."[6]

In Bouchareb's early films, he transposes his Franco-Algerian–authored films, such as *Little Senegal* (2001), onto partial American settings. In others, such as *Hors-la-loi* (*The Outlaws*, 2010), he borrows liberally from an American-style gangster genre in order to portray the Franco-Algerian conflict from an Algerian perspective. Effectively, Bouchareb's films transpose differing articulations of white supremacy in order to draw links between the mythologies of American culture and the racial hatred and violence of Bouchareb's own national culture.

Bouchareb speaks from the perspective of a Franco-Algerian filmmaker, and his films have long been entrenched in a politics of memory. From the poignant journey of an elder black Senegalese slave museum guide to America in search of the descendants of his enslaved ancestors, to the filmic narrative of the Franco-Algerian war from the perspective of the Algerian gaze, Bouchareb creates innovative and challenging angles from which to view painful events and practices that have been informed by racial hatred and imbalance.

Bouchareb equally grafts the hurtful racial messages of one national culture onto the paralleled sufferings of other national cultures, suggesting that understanding one's own identity in the face of such suffering can be enhanced by looking at the memories and experiences of the "Other." The memories that are mirrored in each culture are much easier to repress from within the context of one's own culture and thus, Bouchareb's primary tactic is to lead the viewer to recognize his or her desire to repress memories by casting them in an alternative national light. As Cécile Mury emphasizes in her review of *Two Men in Town*, the film offers a "reflexion douce et déseseperée sur la fatalité sociale" (a soft and desperate reflection on social fatalities).[7]

Bouchareb's trademark projection of national commemorations onto other cultures has evolved throughout his works and has deepened, displaying how memory shapes the identity of his protagonists but also reveals the comparative resistance of such forged identities to the varied hegemonic structures they confront. In his American trilogy, *Just Like a Woman* (2012), *Two Men in Town* (also known as *Enemy's Way*, 2014), and *Belleville Cop* (announced for 2018), Bouchareb makes intentional and systematic use of Hollywood genres and American settings in order to explore Arab-American cultural confrontations. American geographic settings and cinematic landscapes dominate in the first two films, and the third is set to be filmed in the Belleville section of Paris as well as in Miami. *Two Men in Town* is particularly pertinent to issues of invisible and visible whiteness.

Though Bouchareb scrupulously adheres to the dictates of the American thriller genre, *Two Men in Town* is in no way a typical Hollywood thriller. It is, rather, a quasi-psychological inquiry into the hopes and fears of a black ex-convict. Its rhythm and its pacing, like Fassbinder's *Whity*, disrupt spectator expectations about the generic structure being employed and thus render the privilege of whiteness more visible. The film is a remake of French filmmaker José Giovanni's *Deux hommes dans la ville* (*Two Men in Town*, 1973), which is set in France. Though there are some shared generic and narrative elements for the two films, Bouchareb departs from his source material in many ways.

By being set in America, Bouchareb's film reflects on American white supremacy as a thematic concern. It also exhibits just how the aesthetics used by Bouchareb in this film reinforce the idea that not only is the content but also the form of American filmmaking ultimately controlled by the privileging of whiteness. In his choice to cast Forest Whitaker as William Garnett, an ex-convict trying to go straight, Bouchareb facilitates an unsettling resemblance between white supremacist mythologies and the Franco-Algerian sensibilities that inform his work. These sensibilities serve as a uniting thread for the American trilogy as well.

In essence, *Two Men in Town* becomes a palimpsest for American racial issues. Through an appeal to Jean-Louis Baudry's concept of the cinematic apparatus, one can explore how this palimpsest might appeal differently to French and American viewers. Bouchareb's trademark focus on memory and commemoration also reveals much about the surface of this film and its deeper meanings. The film is hailed by Barbara Théate as philosophically reflective with a contemplative rhythm—"rythme contemplative"—despite its adherence to a formulaic genre.[8]

The film does indeed allow the astute spectator to go beneath the Hollywood narrative that has been put in place and to appreciate Bouchareb's deconstruction of invisible whiteness upon which that surface narrative relies. François-Guillaume Lorrain quotes Bouchareb as saying that he has long been intrigued by America as the land of immigration as well as fascinated by Americans' pride in their country. Lorrain adds that it has been rare for French directors to make successful films in the United States but suggests that we should consider Bouchareb, in making this film, to be one of those successful directors, along with Jean Renoir in his film *The Southerner*.[9]

Bouchareb claims in an interview that the purpose of the American trilogy was to examine Arab-American relations as well as to experiment with different genres that inform Hollywood films.[10] In the first of the films, *Just Like a Woman* (2012, with Sienna Miller and Golshifteh Farahani) Bouchareb uses the road movie genre. The film features an American woman and an Arabic woman as they forge new lives after extricating themselves from destructive relationships. By contrast, *Two Men in Town* is a film in the noir or thriller vein in terms of genre. It also participates very strongly in aspects of the Western or Southern genres, which have been analyzed in earlier chapters on Fassbinder, Renoir, and Raoul Walsh. In an interview with Patrick Simonin, Bouchareb specifies that one of his reasons for filming in the desert at the border between the United States and Mexico was to change the settings of a purely generic noir film and take the confrontations between the various characters outside the city. He wants to stress the violence of the desert and show that the confrontations are still very much the same, despite the alternative settings.[11]

Both *Just Like a Woman* and *Two Men in Town* are set and filmed entirely in America. The third of the trilogy, which adheres to the comic buddy movie genre, *Belleville Cop*, is in production at present and is being filmed in the Belleville section of Paris and in Miami. Through the use of American casting, the English language, and landscapes that are reminiscent of Hollywood films, the three create a commentary on racial violence, supremacist ideologies specific to Arab-American relations. They equally function as palimpsests for Hollywood's silent reliance on invisible whiteness in terms of generic and narrative structure. In an interview with Mathias Greuling, Bouchreb argues that political cinema in America and political European cinema are dependent on extremely different methods and have completely different goals. One of his primary complaints in this videotaped interview was that American methods insist on haste to finalize production and are generally less direct in their address of political issues. He mentions that in America, he was constantly trying to get people to slow down and take the time necessary to get things right.[12]

The American trilogy films hold up a mirror for each of the national cultures concerned. That is, American racial tensions are used in the trilogy as a mirror of the tensions between Franco-French and Franco-Algerian cultures. Confrontations between individuals and cultures are continuous themes with most if not all of Bouchareb's work. The American trilogy in particular provides perspective on how Hollywood filmmaking relies on the simmering nature of American white supremacy to shape conflict and confrontation in many of its genres. The trilogy also shows how Bouchareb uses American commonplaces in order to create resonance between racially charged American contexts and the contexts of his own Franco-Algerian culture. Stuart Jeffries suggests that "some critics find Bouchareb's moralizing unconvincing. For me, the performances and the meditative approach to incendiary material subvert these criticisms."[13]

Two Men in Town follows the progress of a young black American, William Garnett (Forest Whitaker), upon his release from prison. Though the spectator is informed about his violent criminal past only through the allusions made by other characters, it is clear that he is actively attempting to put that past behind him. In prison, he has converted to Islam, and he is resolved to avoid any connections with his past. He is overseen by his parole officer, Emily Smith (Brenda Blethyn), but is also dogged by Sheriff Bill Agati (Harvey Keitel), whose deputy was killed by Garnett years before. The sheriff still holds a grudge against Garnett, and much of the dramatic tension of the film revolves around the respective roles played by these two figures of white authority Bill Agati and Emily Smith. As *Libération* critic Bruno Icher puts it, Agati is a caricature of the morally rigid white sheriff.[14] The sheriff has long been a prominent figure of power and respect in his community, and thus his long-standing tenacious grudge against Garnett is depicted as out of character and even irrational.

From a strictly diegetic point of view, the film is indeed about an ex-convict converted to Islam. The effects of this conversion on Garnett's life are therefore of central narrative concern. From the perspective of the *screen* space of the film, the spectator witnesses a black American trying to reintegrate into a white world. Pierre Eisenreich argues that the uniqueness of Bouchareb's film derives from his choice to integrate the conversion to Islam into the narrative, thus creating a distance between formal puritanical repressions associated with American racial themes and the conflicts for an ex-convict newly convicted to Islam.[15]

By placing the black man between a nurturing parole officer who believes redemption is possible and a vengeful law enforcement officer who believes Garnett will never be able to go straight, the film inevitably poses the question of American ideologies that assume the supremacy of the white race, whether that superiority is gained through pity or attack. The protagonist can be saved or destroyed, but it will always be at the mercy of the white characters whom he must confront. The nature-nurture battle Smith and Agati are fighting over Garnett places him inevitably as a pawn in the game. Both Smith and Agati are continually referenced as experienced, as having seen all of this before. The stakes of Garnett's future are predicated on their infinite understanding of the ex-convict and his possibilities for a second chance in a racial culture where the odds are stacked against him. As Cécile Mury suggests, the film shows Garnett's struggle against the phantoms of the past, the cruelty of the present and his inner demons.[16]

Couched inside this larger ideological spectrum are the personal efforts of the newly freed Garnett. He has spent eighteen years in prison and, when he emerges, he seeks total freedom and a sense of security by buying a motorcycle, getting a job, and beginning a relationship with a Hispanic bank teller, Teresa (Dolores Hernandez). His trajectory is laid out incredibly quickly in the film, suggesting that he has had years to think about what it means to live the American Dream, and he intends to live it right away. His ability to regain his place so quickly seemed artificial to many critics.

This is one of the reasons that the film met with critical opposition. In his review "La voie de l'ennemi: Rachid Bouchareb au peril des mythes américains," Thomas Sotinel outlines Bouchareb's transposition of Giovanni's French film. Sotinel suggests in his title that Bouchareb's hybridic film noir is trapped by the American myths and landscapes to which Bouchareb appeals. Sotinel argues that these particular elements of American culture are difficult to master by a foreigner ultimately unfamiliar with Hollywood cinematic norms. Sotinel claims that Bouchareb's film finally falls short of its potential. His point is well-taken for various reasons. Most importantly, the quick pacing of Garnett's return to society is a small but vital component of those cinematic norms and the mythologies which support them, notably that of the Triumphant Individual.[17] In a classic Hollywood narrative, a Triumphant Individual has about 87 minutes to fall into disgrace and then rise again to prominence. As mentioned earlier, part of Bouchareb's tactic is to use the genre of the thriller in order to scrutinize the genre. Therefore, certain narrative aspects of the film seem calculated to play on how the genre works in Hollywood filmmaking versus how it, and its rythyms, can be deconstructed.

Garnett's dream of the perfect life dissolves just as quickly as does the hope created by his release from prison in the time scheme of the film. He is continually harassed both by Sheriff Agati as well as by his own ex-partner in crime (Luis Guzman), who tries to lure him back into his questionable criminal existence. In Bouchareb's typical fashion of circular filmmaking evidenced in *Little Senegal*, *Two Men on Town* begins with a sequence where we see Garnett killing a man out in a vast Western-like landscape and ends with him killing his ex-partner in a similar landscape after the partner has aggressed Garnett's new girlfriend. The film ends with Garnett walking into the sunset, having repeated similar crimes to those for which he was originally punished.

This circular technique also characterizes other Bouchareb films, notably *Little Senegal*, and is maintained in the ending of *Two Men in Town*. There is no strong resolution, which is more characteristic of European art cinema than classic Hollywood narrative.[18] The viewer does not know whether Garnett will endure the same fate for killing a known criminal as he did for killing a sheriff's deputy. One of the central questions of the film reemerges here: Did he kill again because he was unable to control his personal rage, or did he kill again because he has realized that the system is set against him and that he has to fight back? By leaving this question unanswered at the end of the film, Bouchareb distances himself from the American genre he has chosen to dissect as well as from the conclusions of his source material, Giovanni's *Two Men in Town*. Since Giovanni's film is ultimately a critique of the death penalty in France, its ending is tragic but unambiguous.

Sotinel's critique also suggests that the cinematic landscapes used by Bouchareb, while stunning, are perhaps not used to their full potential. As he says, "les grands espaces sont un piège pour les cinéastes venant d'ailleurs, quel que soit le caliber" (the great American landscapes are a trap for film-makers coming from elsewhere, no matter what their caliber-my translation).[19] Nonetheless, with Yves Cape as cameraman for the Bouchareb film, the shots of these desert landscapes, particularly in the opening and closing scenes, have a majesty that can also be seen in the excellent camera work of Michael Balhaus in Fassbinder's *Whity* (Figs. 9.1, 9.2, and 9.3).

The film captures the importance of American-style landscapes or what Bouchareb referred to as "the violence of the desert."[20] Though both *Whity* and *Two Men in Town* are made by European directors, they perfectly capture the fated nature of the Western genre and its noble though tragic protagonist. Despite the fact that Bouchareb seems to have had directorial control over these productions, he still distances himself from methods of filmmaking in Hollywood versus filmmaking in Europe. His

Fig. 9.1 *Two Men in Town*. Artists and Co., Tessalit Productions. Bleak but Majestic American Western Landscape 1:45:52

Fig. 9.2 *Two Men in Town*. Artists and Co., Tessalit Productions. Bleak but Majestic American Western Landscapes 1:47:32

Fig. 9.3 *Whity*. KirchMedia. Landscape Ending in the Desert. 1:31:58

settings are American, and his methods are European, similar to what can be found in Renoir's films made in Hollywood.

Responses to the film by American critics are nonetheless geared toward what one should expect from a Hollywood thriller and therefore are largely negative. The Berlin Film Review by Jay Weissberg published in

Variety makes mention of a "classic Western overlay" and points to the excellent casting of the film. However, the review intimates that the film is overly predictable, not faithful to its source material, and has huge gaps in logic in terms of the plot. Weissberg remarks that "stateside biz is unlikely to deliver solid returns." The idea that it will not be popular at the box office is in keeping with Elsaesser's differentiation between art house cinema and Hollywood expectations for American genre films. Bouchareb's attempt to use as well as scrutinize Hollywood genres was most often passed over by American critics.[21] While it's clear that the film was not intended as Hollywood entertainment, its hybrid nature makes it valuable for understanding the structure of a Hollywood thriller and the racial undercurrents under examination here.

One American critic, A. O. Scott, reviews the film " and again praises the acting of the ensemble. He notes the importance of the desert landscapes and though he faults the "clumsy" narrative, he reserves judgment on the film by claiming that Bouchareb "is a methodical, thoughtful director."[22] What most reviews of the film overlook, some enthusiastically or sarcastically, others with trepidation, is what Bouchareb's language reveals about his technique and about his insistence on personal and collective memory within the diegetic space of the film.

Considering *Two Men in Town* through the lens of Baudry's concept of the cinematic apparatus, one can show how the film functions to create the mirror effects so crucial to Bouchareb's filmmaking. As noted earlier, Baudry likens the cinematic apparatus to Freud's understanding of the structure of psychic life. Whether consciously or not, Bouchareb managed to tap into underlying ideologies of the thriller genre and applied them to both American white supremacist issues and to Franco-Algerian racial issues. He creates a facsimile of a Baudry-like apparatus. The film is designed to mirror the fears and desires of an ethnic American and a Franco-Algerian response to white supremacist authority. Unlike the Giovanni original in which religion plays no role though redemption of an ex-criminal does, Bouchareb has centralized Garnett's conversion to Islam, which adds another dimension to the film.

Baudry's concept of the apparatus is developed in his article "The Apparatus: Meta-psychological Approaches to the Impression of Reality in the Cinema" and is reliant on certain basic Freudian concepts. According to Baudry, Freud states in *The Interpretation of Dreams* that "psychical life is the function of an apparatus to which we attribute spatial extension". Freud claims that it resembles a "microscope or a telescope."[23] While Freud does not mention applying these concepts to cinema,

Baudry himself argues that these Freudian ideas can indeed be used to understand the cinematic apparatus. Baudry's concept of the apparatus is exemplified in Bouchareb's insistence on representations of personal reflection or the "psychical life" of his protagonist, William Garnett. Other characters in the film are represented in much more flattened characterizations which thereby emphasizes the intensity of Garnett's inner life as visualized by Bouchareb. Bouchareb's film language reveals much about his trademark technique of intense focus on a "microscopic" viewing of certain character's internal dilemmas. Bouchareb's equal insistence on the vast Western-style landscapes to which Garnett escapes when feeling threatened by the social realities that he confronts provides the viewer with both microscopic and "telescopic" visions of Garnett's fears and desires, in accordance with Freud's uses of these terms and Baudry's application of them to cinematic language. Critics such as Weissberg, mentioned above, found such techniques to be tedious as is evidenced in his review of the film. It must nonetheless be noted that Bouchareb's technique is linked to the art house tradition rather than an appeal to the box office more characteristic to classical Hollywood narrative. Weissberg reads the film only through the Hollywood lens suggested by Bouchareb's use of the Western genre.

Baudry adds the cinematic apparatus to Freud's analogy and explores its means of evoking conscious and unconscious spectator response. Bouchareb relies on the idea that the American-style landscapes will play on audience expectations. As noted in Chap. 6, Jane Tompkins in *West of Everything: The Inner Life of Westerns* refers to the Western genre as one that has been interiorized by young male Americans, and Rainer Werner Fassbinder speaks at length about his psychic absorption of Hollywood films. Baudry also develops further on Bertram D. Lewin's concept of the dream screen, which Lewis claims is built on the model of Plato's cave allegory.[24]

Baudry inaugurates a significant turn toward the merger of semiotic and psychological theory in film theory. His primary argument is that like cinema, dream is a projection that evokes at once the analytic function as well as the analytic use of the defense mechanism. This defense mechanism consists in referring and attributing to the exterior affects and representations that the subject refuses to acknowledge as his or her own. According to Baudry, this dream screen echoes the cinematic since it parallels the idea of images that, once projected, come back to the subject as a reality constructed and perceived from the outside. This move is called for, again according to Baudry, because:

> Instead of considering cinema as an ideological apparatus, as it has rather stupidly been called, the impact of which would be entirely determined by the *content* of the film … it is necessary to consider it from the viewpoint of the apparatus that it constitutes, an apparatus which in totality includes the subject. And first of all, the subject of the unconscious (my italics).

In this passage, Baudry is essentially actively calling for the need to read films on the basis of what happens on the screen as opposed to relying on an ability to extract the main narrative points or content on the basis of what is happening on the screen. Baudry further asserts that cinema is capable of creating an "impression of reality" through (1) characteristics of an image and (2) depth of field, off screen space, single shot sequence, montage, and so on. He insists that what has been generally ignored is that that "impression of reality" is dependent on subject effect or the effects on the unconscious. His conclusion is that this subject effect must be analyzed in order to determine the film's raison d'être. In other words, cinematic apparatus equals means of production and Freud's model of psychical life. Even if we block some of it out, we have to live that moment of "impression of reality" in order for the film to have an impact. [25]

Written in 1975, Baudry's work calls for stronger analysis of the effects of the cinema on the spectator and on the unconscious of the spectator in which perhaps the ingrained racism of many spectators resides. Similarly, critics such as Laura Mulvey and Manthia Diawara are part of a wave of critics in the mid-1970s who launched the question of race and gender in terms of spectator response.[26] This trend, though already well documented in works such as Anna Everett's *Returning the Gaze*, has expanded over the years with scholars such as Jacqueline Stewart and others taking up research in this area.[27] Though Baldwin's book is not typically characterized in this way, it is not a stretch to see Baldwin's *The Devil Finds Work* as an extension of this *theoretical* move toward a study of psychic effects of the cinema on audiences who self-identify in racial or gendered ways. Also, at the root of Bouchareb's transpositions of cultural confrontations between Franco-Arab cultures and American cinematic landscapes, one can note that the shift in emphasis argued by Baudry might well implicate the filmmaker as well. The unconscious as well as the conscious intellectual positions of the filmmaker drive this transposition.

In short, Bouchareb's cinema is in large part structured to enhance the notion of representation as projection viewed from the outside. He and his spectators, as well as his protagonists, are viewing traces of past events or violent events of a racially inflected nature. Through his technique of transposition, spectators are privy to a mirror of their own prejudices or repressed desires. Shifts in settings, such as in the American trilogy or *London River* (2009), provide an oblique angle or mirror for Bouchareb's own passionate concern for the psychological legacy of French colonialism. As he states:

> As a Frenchman of Algerian descent, I am torn between two philosophies, i.e. in *London River* the fated acceptance of the Muslim character in the film and the philosophy of intolerance and emotional turmoil embodied by the Christian character. I always tell the same story. [That is] the drama of difference and the insistence that we are not so very different from each other.[28]

Since most of Bouchareb's films feature a collective or individual violence, his statement does not suggest that intellectual acknowledgment of its truth (that we are not so very different) is enough to deter further acts of religious or racial violence. Rather, his films use techniques that insist on the mirror projected for the unconscious of the subject. He therefore equally insists that the topics he treats cannot be handled effectively on a conscious or intellectual level alone.

This technique could have some bearing on why American critical responses to *Two Men in Town* were largely negative whereas French critical responses were much more nuanced and ultimately positive. Much of the American critique is prompted by the fact that the film does not manage to live up to the standards of the genre it invokes in terms of rhythm or timing but ironically also because the plot feels manipulative and overdetermined. French critics, in contrast, readily indicate that the film is different from the usual Hollywood treatments of the themes in question because it is made by a thoughtful deliberative filmmaker.[29] The divide between art cinema and Hollywood studio production can definitely be felt in these diverse assessments of the film.

When considering Bouchareb's approach in *Two Men in Town*, much of what has constructed the mirror to the American unconscious has already been evoked. The Western landscapes, the iconic long shots of Garnett as he rides his newly bought motorcycle across those vast landscapes are key elements. He experiences moments of sheer joy and a sense of liberation that play on the spectator's sympathy for the newly released prisoner. Spectators are encouraged to believe that Garnett might well succeed in overcoming his past and his inner demons. There is a microscope into his contemplations and a telescope on the landscape long associated with freedom. These scope perspectives work in tandem throughout the film.

Nonetheless, one critique that emerges in reactions to the film on the American side is that it moves too slowly in terms of the subscribed timing demanded of a thriller and it moves too fast with respect to the verdict on whether Garnett can succeed or not.

From a narrative perspective, Garnett has been in prison for eighteen years and his desire to succeed is fervent. His idea of what he can do to succeed is based on the myths embodied in American films that portray the realization of the American Dream or even in an episode of a television series. He has, after all, spent eighteen years with no experience of the world outside but perhaps with some experience of how it is portrayed on TV. As earlier recounted, upon his release, he proceeds as quickly as he can to realize this dream. He finds a job, he finds a girl. He even finds a home. As quickly as his life comes together, it falls apart. While this might be considered a fault on Bouchareb's part, it could be argued that Bouchareb is exploring the Hollywood rhythm of the American Dream and its real-ization as well as the artificiality of such a dream. No doubt Garnett spent his eighteen years in prison scheming and planning on how different his life would be once he was free again.

That none of this plays out leaves spectators in the position of asking themselves why Garnett cannot succeed on an even playing field. As men-tioned earlier, from the point of view of the film's screen space, Garnett is a black American trying to reenter a white world lorded over by a long-established white sheriff who is clearly at a social advantage, given his prominent position in a supremacist environment. This already introduces tragic dimensions to the film. For Bouchareb, this dimension needs to be framed, and he does so in an early episode. While Garnett is living in a home that has been set up for parolees, he finds that his hour of prayer as a new Muslim is being disrupted by the noisy television of his neighbor across the hallway. In this scene we see the first shift from a man who believes in his calm and tranquil acceptance of a new religion to a man overtaken by rage. He destroys the neighbor's television, and it is only thanks to the interception of Smith, his parole officer, that he is not charged with destruction of property.

The rancor and violence of the neighbor as well as his obsession over his destroyed property is opposed to Garnett's spiritual aspirations. This epi-sode potentially masks what becomes increasingly pronounced in the rest of the film, which is that Garnett fights many forces, interior and exterior alike. Despite his conversion to Islam, Garnett spent his early years growing up as a black American and under circumstances to which the spectator of the film is not given access. The spectator nonetheless tends to identify unconsciously with Garnett's rage due to the crassness of his brash and aggressive adversary. Should the sounds of a no doubt substandard American TV show interfere with the fervent prayers of a newly converted Muslim? The entire tension between the parole officer who believes in redemption and the sheriff who believes that Garnett can and should not reintegrate into society is foregrounded in this episode of the film.

The episode introduces a microscopic view concerning life as it should be lived in America as well as Garnett's response to those norms. This episode is one of the few very interior or confined spaces of the film. It is also one of the first instances in the film where doubts about which demons are going to be more determinate in Garnett's life, the interior ones or the exterior ones, is presented. The viewer witnesses Garnett's first outburst of rage though still tends to give him the benefit of the doubt, given the crassness exhibited by his neighbor.

The film offers a more definitive scene a bit later that creates more doubt in the spectator's mind than any earlier ones. This is the scene where the parole officer decides to take Garnett to reunite with his long-estranged mother (Ellen Burstyn). The encounter between the white mother and her black child is not at all present in the original source material of the film, José Giovanni's *Two Men in Town*. As a result, it reveals more about Bouchareb's intent than many other scenes in the film. It also feels more intimate in that are a greater number of shot-reverse shots of close-ups of the mother and her son, which create the impression that the film's screen space is controlled by their bodies rather than by the mise-en-scène that frames their encounter. The parole officer, for reasons unexplained in the film, pushes Garnett to look deep back into his past and memories by nudging him to speak to his mother whom he has not seen in eighteen years. Their interaction indicates that they have not had any meaningful contact in much longer than that.

No explanation is given for why Garnett has a white mother, and yet the screen space of the film begs one to ask the question: Is she a biological mother, an adoptive mother, or perhaps a foster mother? The acting for this film was universally praised. Burstyn is excellent as she plays the part of a deeply aggrieved mother who informs her son that she just can't go back to that past where she was trying to raise him in a correct fashion. Her presence on the screen illustrates deep compassion, but her words belie that compassion as she says to Garnett "I just can't go back there. What do you want? Money?"

Arguably, this is the first time in the film that spectators begin to doubt their belief in Garnett. Up to this point, the spectator and Garnett have been played as pawns between the unforgiving sheriff and the overcompensating though tough parole officer. Even with the softening of their characters provided by Bouchareb (the sheriff acts humanely toward illegal immigrants crossing the border, and the parole officer has long, heartfelt talks with her aging father on the phone), the spectator is for the first time confronted with a character whose past associations with Garnett are not known and will not be revealed by the film. The primary dialogic message Garnett has for his mother that belongs to the narrative space of the film is "I made some mistakes." The screen space represents his intense and heartbreaking desire for affection and acceptance.

The spectator is deprived of the history and the memory of that divide between confession and desire. The need to judge the situation is dependent on the emotions projected on the screen. This is illustrative of Baudry's sense of the cinematic apparatus. What do spectators believe they are seeing, and how will that play out in their judgment about the ending scenes of the film? In keeping with Bouchareb's trademark narrative of circularity, the ending scene mimics the opening one. In the opening we watch from afar as Garnett murders a man, again with no history of how this has come about, whether it is justified or not, or if it is a sign of his inability to control his rage. In the ending long shot, the spectator sees Garnett avenging his girlfriend who has been attacked by one of his old partners in crime. After he completes what appears to be the murder of his partner, we witness his departure in a long shot as he walks off into the sunset.

Garnett is surely bound to be incarcerated, justly or unjustly, yet again. His very brief liberation is no doubt to be followed by another eighteen years in prison, and yet his girlfriend's beating by his partner and Garnett's swift retribution suggests to spectators that they wish he could be recognized for the compassion and justice of his rage. *Two Men in Town* does not rely on American source material and therefore does not rely on following the traces of American white supremacy in the source material. Rather, Bouchareb has transposed his source material onto an American landscape and has enhanced the presence of a Hollywood generic structure. While Giovanni's film reads as a courtroom drama defense of an errant but nonetheless charming criminal charged primarily with theft until the final moments, Bouchareb's film ends with a black man who has committed a second murder in a white world. The stakes are different, and in the case of Bouchareb's film, racial dimensions play a definitive role. Indeed, Bouchareb has strayed from his source material but, in doing so, he has created a reflective space for how race is represented in the treatment of societal retribution for violent crimes.

THE CINEMATIC GAZE IN BOUCHAREB'S WORK

Bouchareb's work relies not only on experimentation with American genres but also on the pressing issue of how Franco-Algerians work to find their place in mainstream society. Bouchareb uses American genres, as in *Two Men in Town*, in order to question issues of belonging in French culture and how those anxieties about belonging can be allegorized through an examination of American culture as opposed to French culture. In *Black Paris: The African Writer's Landscape*, Benetta Jules-Rosette introduces the concept of Parisianism, which is identifiable when "the cultural exile becomes an immigrant." Parisianism as a genre groups together "narratives of longing and belonging."[30] Its goal is to define and reflect on "the identity discourse of a new generation."[31]

In Jules-Rosette's analysis of works that might be attributed to this genre, she highlights the ultimate questions posed by the emergence of the genre in 1959 that are resonant with Bouchareb's work in his American trilogy: "Should the writer be an activist, a witness, or an engaged artist? The narrative structure of Parisianism pushes the writer towards witnessing the world by assuming an ethnographic and journalistic gaze on their social environments."[32] The claim that Bouchareb's pacing is too slow and distanced in terms of its observation of Garnett's plight is similar to the ethnographic gaze described by Jules-Rosette. One difference is that Bouchareb's gaze is not focused on America itself but rather on the genres he temporarily inhabits and their cinematic language, which reinforces the American mythologies created by Hollywood as early as D. W. Griffith's *Birth of a Nation*. The Parisianist genre grew out of seminal work by artists who wanted to belong to a landscape that they encountered as foreigners. Bouchareb passionately engages with the American landscape in *Two Men in Town* in a similar manner, though whether wanting belong or not is a more complex question in his case.

His use of creative cinematic techniques that mimic narratives of longing and belonging dominate. The key to Parisianism that Bouchareb again transposes to an American context is the belief that lived experience must be transformed through aesthetic distance but full analysis of shared visions must come through awareness of an unvarying dependence on the tripartite gaze structure that characterizes Parisianism and that settles finally into the silences of the environmental gaze. The tripartite gaze evoked in the Parisianist genre is composed of (1) the gaze of virtual long-ing, (2) the gaze of loss, and (3) the environmental gaze.[33]

One could argue that the forgone conclusion that Garnett will once again be incarcerated is what fills the space of the film's last shot in the film and is what therefore qualifies that shot as a form of environmental gaze. The viewer no longer shares Garnett's gaze; Garnett rather becomes an object on which the camera gazes in silence. This is similar to Courtney's observation about the black characters in *Birth of a Nation* when referring to the image of a black man's eye "peeping out from a political gathering." As she claims, "Unlike the classic white male *voyeur*, this black peeper exposed is represented not as the source of the film's vision but as one of its objects."[34] The silence of the environmental gaze is thus one that works to put on display the justices or injustices of particular cultures. Those cultures can then be read as mirrors onto other cultures.

In Bouchareb's case, he portrays a black man, Garnett, whose chances for redemption have been destroyed. Garnett will once again be swal-lowed up by the justice of white America. He will be denied the chance to assimilate into or normalize within that world. The question that has been driving the debate throughout the film concerns whether he is to blame or whether it is rather the system against which he has fought his entire life that is to blame. The last shot is silent on this issue.

It's as if Bouchareb suggests that whatever actions the court takes, the answer to that question will never truly be answered. He additionally appeals to the viewer to look beyond the assumptions, often racist or supremacist, of certain cinema genres, particularly those that dominate in Hollywood filmmaking. One might claim that he is condemning only Hollywood, but in analyzing his techniques and concern with transpositions of racial ten-sions from one culture to another, it is more accurately arguable that he is putting a cinematic mirror up to his own culture as well. Parisianism as a genre groups together "narratives of longing and belonging."

Unlike the silent ending to Bouchareb's film, Giovanni's film ends with justice having been carried out against the character on whom Garnett is modeled (Gino Strabliggi played by Alain Delon). Gino is guillotined, and then a final voice-over commentary by the character upon whom Bouchareb's social worker is modeled (Germain Cazeneuve played by Jean Gabin) closes the film. The voice-over monologue spoken by Germain Cazeneuve throughout the film and, in particular, after the execution of Gino, serves as a running commentary on the pathos with which the viewer experiences Gino's tragic end. Cazeneuve never argues explicitly for the justice or injustice of Gino's execution from a legal point of view, but the fact that he had a caring, intimate and almost paternal relationship with Gino places the issue of his death on a different and more emotional plane.

As in Bouchareb's film, there is nonetheless a circular nature to the voice-over. The film begins with Cazeneuve speaking in voice-over about the theatrical aspect of the law. He creates a hiatus by ending this opening monologue with the words "and behind all that"; the hiatus comes full circle in the closing monologue when Cazeneuve says "and behind all of that there is the machine that kills." Gino is not reduced to an object; he becomes more like a lost friend, whom the social worker both mourns and redeems through his harsh judgment of execution by guillotine. Bouchareb's ending does not allow for this particular kind of sentiment.

As previously mentioned, Bouchareb's *Two Men in Town* was largely though not universally dismissed by American critics. It was mostly but not entirely embraced by French critics. One American critic encourages audiences to go and see the film despite its very limited release. Bilge Ebiri insists that the film's real intentions have been misunderstood and thus overlooked.[35] *Two Men in Town* is a case in point for the argument that films that have been overlooked, misunderstood, forgotten, or banned are perhaps the ones most in need of analysis.

NOTES

1. William Gardner Smith, *The Stone Face* (New York: Cardinal Pocket Books, 1964), 174.
2. James Baldwin, *The Devil Finds Work* (New York: Laurel, 1976), 48.
3. James Naremore, *More than Night: Film Noir in Its Contexts* (Berkeley: University of California Press, 2008/1998), 17. The English translation of André Bazin's "Six Characters in Search of an Author" in *Cahiérs du Cinéma*, ed. Jim Haller, trans. Liz Heron (Cambridge, MA: Harvard University Press, 1985), 37.
4. Hal Foster, *Compulsive Beauty* (Cambridge, MA: MIT Press, 1993), 19.
5. Hal Foster, *The Return of the Real.* (Cambridge Massachusetts: MIT Press, 1996), 267.
6. Smith, *The Stone Face*, 115.
7. Cécile Mury, "La voie de l'ennemi," *Télérama*, May 7, 2014. http://www.telerama.fr/cinema/films/l-voie-de-l-ennemi,491116,critique.php.
8. Barbara Théate, *La journal du dimanche*. This excerpt of Théate's comments from *La journal de dimanche* is excerpted in the *AlloCiné Critiques-Presse*. http://www.allocine.fr/film/fichefilm-203583/critiques/presses/.
9. François-Guillaume Lorrain, "Bouchareb trouve sa 'voix,'" *Le Point*, May 1 2014, http://www.lepoint.fr/cinema/bouchareb-trouve-sa-voix-01-05-2014-1819887_35.php.

10. Steve Pond, "Rachid Bouchareb Kicks Off Arab-American Trilogy with Sienna Miller Road Movie," August 12, 2011. https://www.reuters.com/article/idUS337528928620110812.
11. "Rachid Bouchareb: 'La voie de l'ennemi'" entretien avec, Patrick Simonin, April 30, 2014. *TV5 monde.* https://youtu.be/xH1cOxElCyk.
12. "Rachid Bouchareb Interview: *Two Men in Town. La voie de l'ennemi,*" YouTube, February 8, 2014. Copyright Mathias Grueling.
13. Stuart Jeffries, "Rachid Bouchareb: My Film about 7/7 Bombings," *The Guardian,* July 6, 2010.
14. Bruno Icher, "Two Men in Town," *Libération,* May 6, 2014. Icher uses the sheriff as a prime example in demonstrating Bouchareb's reappropriation of the generic codes of an American thriller.
15. Pierre Eisenreich, "*La voie de l'ennemi* : un cri dans le desert," *Positif,* May 14, 2014.
16. Cécile Mury, "Contre les fantômes du passé, la cruauté du présent, mais aussi ses démons intérieures". "La voie de l'ennemi."
17. Thomas Sotinel, "*La voie de l'ennemi*: Rachid Bouchareb au péril des mythes américain," *Le monde,* May 6, 2014. The term "the Triumphant Individual" is given to one of Robert Reich's four Morality Tales in *Tales of a New America: the Anxious Liberal's Guide to the Future* (New York: Times Books, 1987). I single out Sotinel's review here because even though there are many other critiques that simply dismiss the film, he is careful in his analysis of the film's shortcomings without totally misunderstanding the intent of the transposition attempted by Bouchareb.
18. Ambiguity or the "open-ended resolution" is one of the characteristics often cited as an element of art cinema. Elftheria Thanouli, in "'Art Cinema' Narration: Breaking down a Wayward Paradigm," *Scope* 14 (2009): 1–14, offers a concise overview of these various elements.
19. Sotinel, "La voie de l'ennemi."
20. "Rachid Bouchareb Interview."
21. Jay Weissberg, "Berlin Review: *Two Men in Town,*" *Variety Magazine,* February 7, 2014. http://variety.com/2014/film/festivals/berlin-film-review-two-men-in-town-1201091531/.
22. A. O. Scott, "In *Two Men in Town* a Parolee Is Hounded by a Cop," *New York Times,* March 5, 2014.
23. Jean-Louis Baudry, "The Apparatus: Meta-psychological Approaches to the Impression of Reality in the Cinema," in Leo Braudy and Marshall Cohen, eds., *Film Theory and Criticism,* 7th ed., (New York: Oxford University Press, 2009), 171–188.
24. Bertram D. Lewin, "Sleep, the Mouth and the Dream Screen," *Psychoanalytic Quarterly* 15, no. 4 (1946): 419–434.
25. Baudry, "The Apparatus," 184–185.

26. Laura Mulvey's groundbreaking article "Visual Pleasure and Narrative Cinema" is printed in Braudy and Cohen, eds., *Film Theory and Criticism*, 711–722. A reissue of her book *Visual and Other Pleasures* (New York: Palgrave Macmillan, 2009), where in an introduction she reassesses the effects of that article, is also crucial ... Manthia Diawara's "Black Spectatorship and Resistance: Problems of Identification and Resistance," *Screen* 29, no. 4 (1988): 66–79, is also a seminal text for race-related theories of spectatorship.

27. Anna Everett, *Returning the Gaze: A Genealogy of Black Film Criticism, 1909–1949* (Durham, NC: Duke University, 2001). Jacqueline Stewart, "Negroes Laughing at Themselves?: Black Spectatorship and the Performance of Urban Modernity," *Critical Inquiry* 29, no. 4 (2003): 630–677.

28. Quoted in Jeffries, "Rachid Bouchareb."

29. Two representative reviews from both sides of the Atlantic are François-Guillaume Lorrain's "Bouchareb trouve sa voix," *Le Point*, May 1, 2014, and Deborah Young's "Two Men in Town: Berlin Review," *Hollywood Reporter*, February 2, 2014. Lorrain essentially sees the film as Bouchareb's successful confrontation with America's controversial immigration policies and American pride whereas Young sees it as an example of old-fashioned storytelling.

30. Benetta Jules-Rosette, *Black Paris: The African Writer's Landscape* (Urbana: University of Chicago Press), 2000, 9–10.

31. Jules-Rosette, *Black Paris*, 185.

32. Jules-Rosette, *Black Paris*, 186.

33. Jules-Rosette, *Black Paris*, 157–158.

34. Susan B. Courtney, *Hollywood Fantasies of Miscegenation: Spectacular Narrative of Gender and Race, 1903–1967* (Princeton, NJ: Princeton University Press, 2005), 88.

35. Bilge Ebiri is a Turkish American journalist. His review "Two Men in Town Has a Raging Heart," March 7, 2015, can be read at http://www.vulture.com/2015/03/two-men-in-town-movie-review.html.

CHAPTER 10

Conclusion: Cinema, Our Dark Mirror

In Hollywood, it is no longer necessary to censor a writer, it is easier to
buy him.
—*Ossie Davis*

All cinema and, in particular, Hollywood cinema creates plausible realities, relying on tested narratives and genres. To use a phrase employed both by A. O. Scott and Matt Zoller Seitz in their reviews of Nate Parker's *Birth of a Nation* (2016), Hollywood films also function according to characteristic beats.[1] Plausible realities are in many cases propped up by easily glossed over ideologies such as the myth of American white supremacy, a claim explored throughout the chapters of this book. Mythological metanarratives often come back to haunt us when we pause to study the deeper fabric or cinematic excess of those films' compositions.

The film theories explored in this book—those of Bordwell, Dyer, Thompson, and others—argue that understanding cinema language requires giving more than passing attention to the narratives and genres of these complex texts. As Stanley Corkin points out in his analysis of Renoir's *The Southerner*, this is not something Hollywood spectators can be expected to do. Nonetheless, the cinematic excess, the sensibilities of the spectators, the means of production, and the cultural backgrounds of the directors and producers … all of these factors play a role in determining how films affect our perceptions of our world. Quite often, cinema becomes the mirror that

© The Author(s) 2018
A. M. Craven, *Visible and Invisible Whiteness*,
https://doi.org/10.1007/978-3-319-76777-2_10

allows us to see the darkest side of ourselves. At other times, that mirror is mere smoked glass, obscuring the realities that lie behind the narratives and genres employed.

As this book contends, films can either reaffirm or challenge the ideological underpinnings of classical Hollywood narrative. American white supremacy perpetuates the Hollywood industry and can render the most somber truths visible. Or these truths can be hidden under the invisible cloak of the dream screen and the happy ending. Racist sentiment is one of the more crucial themes that calls for increased responsibility in the creation of visual images, narrative structures, and genre-controlled works. Though Hollywood and even independent cinema have long been white male-dominated, there is always the hope that progress can be made and that films can be produced which effectively challenge the mythologies that allow for film language, film theory, and film criticism to prop up invisible whiteness or unconscious patronage.[2]

This book brings attention to the misinterpretations and miscalculations that have occurred in the voyage toward a potentially more progressive film language. An assessment of the contemporary cinematic scene indeed requires an inquiry into the past and into the forgotten trials and tribulations of filmmaking related to visible and invisible whiteness. Many notable filmmakers have recently distinguished themselves as worthy of the formidable challenges presented by the American racist ideologies embedded in filmmaking technique by D. W. Griffith's 1915 film *Birth of a Nation*; they include Ava Duvernay, Lee Daniels, Barry Jenkins, Raoul Peck, Jordan Peele, and Justin Simien to name only a very few. Nonetheless, in contemporary "real-life" America, white supremacy is alive, well, and horrifyingly vibrant.

Quentin Tarantino's questionable *Django Unchained* (2012) and Steve McQueen's *12 Years a Slave* (2013) have drawn criticisms and elaborate praise respectively. Films concerned with visible and invisible whiteness and made in the past five or six years are subjects for yet another book-length study. The objective of my research has been to revive the forgotten past of Hollywood, art cinema, and independent cinema forms that have affected American, European, and émigré directors and from which such a future study might benefit. Even though the misunderstood past of American cinema has not yet been fully uncovered, it can be further excavated from the film criticism of James Agee, James Baldwin, and others. This past indeed compels further exploration.

The films for specific examination in this brief conclusion are high-lighted due to their direct confrontations with D. W. Griffith's legacy and their insistence on challenging the legacy of invisible whiteness. The question of perspective is a key factor. Who owns legacies of white supremacist or racist struggles and who has the right to transform them into cinematic language? DJ Spooky's (a.k.a. Paul D. Miller, 1947–) *Rebirth of a Nation* (2007) challenges the legacy of D. W. Griffith's propagandistic and revisionist film directly through an examination of how the mise en scène and Griffith's other filmic techniques control spectator response. Miller probes deeply into Griffith's technique and provides in periodic voice-over an argument about how the film enraptures its spectators and lulls them into a reaffirmation of American white supremacy. As has been discussed in this book, Anna Everett's *Return of the Gaze* scrupulously traces the critical press surrounding this film and its reception. Susan B. Courtney among others has offered in-depth analyses of how Griffith revolutionizes cinematic language to give voice to a privileging of whiteness.

Miller's film remarkably echoes the perspectives of these numerous scholars of the film into an incredibly succinct visualization of this privileging, and he does so through cinematic language. Through his music and his elaborate overlaid diagrams of precise aspects of the screen space of *Birth of a Nation*, Miller shows how Griffith orchestrates an apologetics for invisible whiteness. DJ Spooky's techniques are restrained but analytically sharp. They radically alter the spectator's appreciation of Griffith's film. More precisely, Spooky renders the invisible whiteness of the film painfully visible.

Ironically, Miller's techniques unintentionally illuminate and dissect the missteps made by Nate Parker in his film *Birth of a Nation* (2016), which is simultaneously well intentioned, ambitious, heartfelt, and vengeful in ways that hearken back to the very techniques Griffith used in mounting his 1915 attack on the affront to Southern state sovereignty. This is not to be interpreted as a negative critique of Parker's film but rather as a case in point about how difficult it is to escape Griffith's influence in terms of film language. As emphasized in Chaps. 2 and 3, though one may be unable to endorse Griffith's content, even Baldwin admits that his cinematic technique is unprecedented.

Mixed reactions to Parker's film indicate that he too used film language in the name of precise ideological goals. Contrary to Seitz's assessment of a film that he claims does not go far enough in terms of the fiery storytelling techniques à la Mel Gibson, Parker exercises a modicum of restraint in order to balance his revenge-based storyline with certain pedagogical goals. Griffith uses the slave narrative as a means of revalorizing white supremacist ends, whereas Parker uses his film to advocate for a reeducation about Griffith's goals and beliefs in terms of content. Reactions to Parker's film on the part of distributors, critics, and spectators is key to understanding why it met with such success prior to distribution and why it was not well received at the box office.

Parker's film is indeed compromised, based on an analysis of its narrative and generic structure, but it content has specific and justifiable purpose. The fate of the film has been and is nonetheless bound to be continually compromised in terms of a third obstacle: contextual concerns about the filmmaker himself. However, it *is* one of the most direct assaults on Griffith's *Birth of a Nation*, as Melvyn Stokes implies and as Seitz makes explicit, in that it goes by the exact title of Griffith's film. While it is by no means a remake of Griffith's film, Stokes has suggested that though even Griffith considered the possibility of remakes himself, such a thing never happened. Until 2016, *Birth of a Nation* was never used as a title for another film.

The direct confrontation with Griffith's title generated interest in the film before it was even released and, as Seitz points out in his review of the film, necessitates that anyone searching on Google for Griffith's film will land on references to Nate Parker's film as well. This is one of the savvy strategies for delivering "a blow to white supremacy in this country and abroad," as Parker suggests in his comments about his goals for making this film.[3] Parker suggests that the nation that has been given birth to in his film is one that is not only about white righteousness against black violence but also about black righteousness against white violence. Both films are concerned with building legacies.

Contextual considerations about Parker's own violent tendencies nonetheless mar the ultimate message and reception of the film in that Parker was accused of sexual violence 17 years before the film was made. As suggested by A. O. Scott in his review of the film, it demands a "Must-See/Won't See" dichotomy due to the personal accusations of rape charged against Parker. Parker was acquitted of these charges. It is not my purpose to retry him here, but, clearly, the supposedly flawed personal life of an artist often becomes part and parcel of the spectator's response to the artist's work. There are innumerable reactions to the details of Parker's case, which are similar to those directed against artists such as Woody Allen and Roman Polanski.

Parker's case did not become public until after he had garnered praise at the Sundance Film Festival and had also landed one of the most lucrative distribution deals in the history of independent cinema.[4] The case nonetheless impacted box office returns. As late as December 11, 2017, Spike Lee insisted, along with *Birth of a Nation* star Armie Hammer, that Parker was the victim of a double-cross by a rival production studio.[5] Though they do not want to name names, they speak with conviction and plausibly suggest that Hollywood infighting might possibly be responsible for taking an overly ambitious young black director down. Again, there is no proof to this assertion, but it does play nicely into the details of the racial politics of the Hollywood industry. In fairness, the ambiguities of Parker's case have been difficult for many to dismiss.

The book *The Birth of a Nation: The Makings of a Movement*, edited by Parker and which accompanies the making of the film, clarifies that not only was Spike Lee an important support for Nate Parker but that Parker's film was also intended as a project steeped in passion. Parker wanted to revisit the character of Nat Turner and use that podium as a way of rectifying what he claims was a gaping hole in his own education about distinguished black men and women in American history and about slavery in America. That his well-intentioned efforts might have been stymied by Hollywood infighting is indeed regrettable. That his past came back to haunt him at this point in his career is equally regrettable. Though most reviews of the film necessarily address the issue of these allegations, perhaps the most measured review is authored by Kareem Abdul-Jabbar.[6] Abdul-Jabbar rightly begins his review by alluding to the earlier controversy concerning Nat Turner's story, that is, the very negative responses to William Styron's novel, *The Confessions of Nat Turner* (1967) by black writers at the time of the novel's publication.

Abdul-Jabbar uses this earlier controversy in order to stress the general perils for anyone attempting to tell Nat Turner's story and compares Parker's fate to that of William Styron's novel *The Confessions of Nat Turner*. Both Parker and Styron faced difficulties in separating their artistic intent from their personal contexts. In Parker's case, his past was linked to one specific alleged crime and this led to his film being maligned in the press and in cinema awards circuits. Styron was faulted for being a white writer recounting the fictional history of a black slave. Styron's novel was based on the short document penned by Thomas L. Gray in 1831 as well as 10 years of research into whatever other documents or archives he could access about Nat Turner. Styron won a Pulitzer Prize for this novel but was nonetheless blighted by negative critiques from the black community.

Thomas L. Gray's document was purportedly based on the confessions of Nat Turner as spoken to Gray, (Nat's hired attorney and by necessity a free white man) and is therefore not necessarily factual unless we accept that the white supremacist values of the time allowed for some license in reproducing the truth of a black man's actions. Though well researched and offering some contradiction to the testimony authored by Gray, Styron's novel was heavily attacked by black writers. Styron claims in his exchanges with James Baldwin and American actor Ossie Davis that his storyline was ultimately in contradiction to the details of Gray's account since his research led him to believe that Turner was indeed a hero. This idea does not emerge from Gray's accounts, and many readings of Styron's characterization of Turner claim that Styron turned the black insurrectionist into a psychopath due to the fact that one of his motivations was linked to his secret lust for a white woman.

At the time of publication there was avid interest in producing a film version of the novel to be directed by Norman Jewison, but the angry criticism with which Styron was met from blacks resulted in the failure of the film project. Black writers essentially claimed that Styron was co-opting part of their history and was attempting to provide them with the basis for a fictionalized version of a historical hero that they themselves should be responsible for creating.[7]

The only black writers of the time to support Styron's work, according to Abdul-Jabbar's review, were James Baldwin and Ralph Ellison.[8] Indeed, the radio broadcast of Styron's exchanges with Davis and Baldwin is one of the most powerful defenses of Styron as well as one of the most effective articulations about why black writers and artists might take exception to his novel.[9] Though Abdul-Jabbar does not cite this radio broadcast, his review discusses similar issues as were raised in the broadcast and questions whether seeing or refusing to see a movie constitutes a moral act. Baldwin's role as mediator was prompted by the fact that he supported Styron, who was a close friend of his, and he was also very close to Davis. His interventions aid in articulating the complexity and urgency of their debate about racial relations in America in 1968.

Abdul-Jabbar concludes his discussion on the personal context of the Parker's past by suggesting that he, as a responsible reviewer, did his "due diligence" and read as much as he could about Parker's trial. Abdul-Jabbar concluded that he would appeal to the idea that the man is innocent until proven guilty. Davis equally voices his respect for Styron and recognizes his right to make his own artistic choices and decisions. Abdul-Jabbar refrains from judging Parker in order to clear himself for making comments about the film itself. In fairness, he also provides bibliographic reference for authors such as Goldie Taylor, who do not accept Parker's innocence but who nonetheless recommend a viewing of the film due to its importance as a pedagogic device in teaching African American history.

Abdul-Jabbar's greatest praise for the film is focused on Nate Parker's performance, which provides clues about how and why other reviews of the film are not quite as nuanced as his. These reviews also step away from Parker's past and instead fault his film on the basis of his role as both actor and director, suggesting perhaps an overinvestment of ego into the film on Parker's part. Abdul-Jabbar is careful to discuss both the good qualities as well as the missteps of the film. His review remains even-handed. He does however caution that "black-washing" history is no more excusable than whitewashing it, intimating that Parker's film might well be read by some as participating in black-washing.

Abdul-Jabbar suggests that perhaps one of the greater missteps of Parker's film is its revisionist romanticized version of Nat Turner. Given the structure of Parker's film, which is to some extent trapped within the narrative and generic norms initiated by Griffith, the fact that Turner might have been romanticized by Parker is possible evidence of said black-washing. Abdul-Jabbar does not make this claim specifically, but it is the logical extension of his argument.

In contrast to Abdul-Jabbar, A. O. Scott and Matt Zoller Seitz take a distance from Abdul-Jabbar's more personalized review or at the very least insist on a certain distance, which they claim is necessary for their professions as film critics. Scott even speaks explicitly about what his job as a film critic prescribes for him in terms of discussing individual films. Both critics nevertheless equally accord praise to Parker for his admittedly laudable work. As a first-time director of a controversial story Parker deserves to be commended for transforming a difficult narrative into cinematic language. While praising the film where praise is due, Scott and Seitz nonetheless point out that it is ultimately a revenge narrative driven by Hollywood beats and thereby intimate that the motive for revenge rests on premises similar to those of D. W. Griffith's film.

As Susan B. Courtney decisively argues, Griffith's film is rooted in men's protection of *their* women against sexual violence and therefore one of the ultimate tropes of Griffith's film is rooted in a defense of white masculinities. According to Scott, the kinds of rage that one sees evidenced in

Griffith's film is also an important narrative motivator for Parker's film, namely that the violation of women is "the strongest, least arguable pretext for male violence. It's what makes killing the thing that man's go to do."[10] This suggests that escaping the cinematic language inherited from Griffith in the creation of unlikely heroes is perhaps more difficult than many directors imagine. Additionally, though both Scott and Seitz praise Parker's performance, Seitz suggests that his ultimate impression from seeing the film is that he is not watching a fire-and-brimstone story being told; rather Seitz suspects that he "is being sold a career."[11]

One might be tempted to accuse these critics of being unfair to a new director who is impassioned by the need to retell the story of an important though historically marginalized black figure. Parker's edited volume on the film, cited earlier, provides a necessary though somewhat self-congratulatory corrective to the discussion of missteps cited in all of these reviews. However, as all of these critics rightly conclude, there is much to love in this film. The conclusion here focuses on this film precisely because it provides a contemporary example of a film most comparable to the films examined in the preceding chapters, notably *White Dog*, *Two Men in Town*, and *Whity*. At the time of this writing, Parker's *Birth of a Nation* has been out for about two years. It is in itself a hybrid in that is makes use of Hollywood beats but was written, directed, and produced independently. Its long-term fate is still undetermined. If it does indeed become marginalized, then there are still many questions about why that might occur. This is in contrast to Steve McQueen's *12 Years a Slave*, which will guard its canonic significance by virtue of the fact that it has earned recognition through the industry's most influential system, the Oscar ceremonies. The film won awards for Best Picture, Best Actress (Lupito Nyong'o), and Best Adapted Screenplay (John Ridley), and was recognized by the Golden Globes as well.

Parker's film also raises the following question: To whom does the right to convey cinematic narratives critiquing American white supremacy belong? One of Ossie Davis's primary concerns about Styron's novel was not that he did not respect the right of the author to construct his own version of Nat Turner in his novel but rather that he feared for what kind of effect a cinematic adaptation of the novel, portraying a black but written by a white, might have on uneducated white and black Americans. Critiques of Parker's film and its missteps as well as the failure to produce a film version of Styron's novel allow for consideration of the extent to which the film language that has developed since the early twentieth century is still impeding greater expansion and experimentation with cinematic expression such as we see in DJ Spooky's *Rebirth of a Nation* or even James Agee's *Quiet One*.

As Davis rightly and eloquently suggests, though Styron, as a white man, had every right to tell the Nat Turner story, his well-intentioned novel, put to the screen, becomes a more public and less controllable entity. Comparison of these two alternative narratives of the same historical figure remind us that cinematic language is indeed about mythmaking as well as the artist's right to reinvent history and the effects of such mythmaking on spectator response. Similar points were made by Spike Lee when it was proposed that Norman Jewison be hired to make a film based on the autobiography of Malcolm X. Lee contended that only a black man should be allowed to write or direct a film based on this iconic figure.

As mentioned at the end of Chap. 9, it seems prudent to study films and/or actors and actresses who are forgotten and to study them in their singularity in order to explore if and how one might escape the invisible whiteness of cinema language as developed in classical Hollywood narrative. One must study these forgotten films and actors just as ardently as one studies the masterpieces recommended by critics, scholars, and film theorists alike. Bogle's groundbreaking work on a history of black actors and actresses is a case in point. Charles Burnett also makes this clear when he expressed his terrible disappointment in being told by his film professor that his favorite childhood film, Renoir's *The Southerner*, was proof that Europeans could not make films about America. Burnett was saddened that the details of Renoir's film, which had so deeply touched him so had been conveniently "dropped from" the curriculum. This is yet another argument for revisiting films that have been misinterpreted or forgotten. Margins do matter, particularly when the stakes are so high.

NOTES

1. A. O. Scott, "In Nate Parker's '*The Birth of a Nation*,' Must-See and Won't See Collide," *The New York Times* October 6, 2016; Matt Zoller Seitz, "*The Birth of a Nation* Review," Rogerebert.com, October 7, 2016, https://www.rogerebert.com/reviews/the-birth-of-a-nation-2016.

2. A crucial disclaimer must be mentioned here. There is absolutely no suggestion that because a director or indeed a novelist or artist is white and male he is destined to fall into traps of racist sentiments. Though proponents of the idea that racism is endemic to American society might argue otherwise, it seems that such a claim is difficult to sustain. A study of Stuart

Heisler's films or Clarence Brown's *Intruder in the Dust* (1949) (in which I intend to engage) would be important test cases for this debate.

3. This remark by Parker is quoted in Seitz's review, "*The Birth of a Nation* Review."

4. Details of fundraising and financial distribution issues can be found in the book edited by Nate Parker, *The Birth of a Nation: The Making of a Movement* (New York: 37 Ink/Atria, a division of Simon and Schuster, 2016). Kindle Edition.

5. Kevin Jugernauth, "Spike Lee Says Nate Parker Was the Victim of a 'Dope-Fiend-Double-Cross,'" December 11, 2017. https://theplaylist.net/spike-lee-nate-parker-double-cross-20171211/.

6. "Kareem Abdul-Jabbar Reviews 'Birth of a Nation' … and Nate Parker: Important and Flawed," *Hollywood Reporter*, September 9, 2016. https://www.hollywoodreporter.com/news/nate-parjrs-troubled-past-importance-birth-a-nation-926112. Accessed September 12, 2016.

7. John Henrik Clarke, *William Styron's Confessions of Nat Turner: Ten Black Writers Respond* (Boston: Beacon Press, 1968). It must be noted that in Nate Parker's *The Birth of a Nation: The Making of a Movement*, this response on the part of black writers in 1968 is listed as recommended reading whereas Styron's novel is not.

8. This too is the subject for another study. The controversy is summed up, for example, in Will Haygood, "A Novel Friendship," *Washington Post*, November 3, 2006.

9. *James Baldwin Speaks! The Confessions of Nat Turner with William Styron and Ossie Davis*, May 28, 1968. www.youtube.com, posted by Matthew Siegfried, from Vaultroadio.org, Pacifica Radio. Accessed January 12, 2018.

10. Scott, "In Nate Parker's '*The Birth of a Nation*,' Must-See and Won't See Collide," 4.

11. Seitz, "*The Birth of a Nation* Review," 3.

Index[1]

[1] Note: Page numbers followed by 'n' refer to notes.

© The Author(s) 2018
A. M. Craven, *Visible and Invisible Whiteness*,
https://doi.org/10.1007/978-3-319-76777-2

Printed by Printforce, the Netherlands